S0-CIF-405

45 YEARS OF HUNTING AND FISHING HISTORY
FROM THE PAGES OF MINNESOTA OUTDOOR NEWS

PUBLISHED BY OUTDOOR NEWS, INC.
PLYMOUTH, MINNESOTA
2014

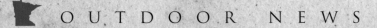

O U T D O O R   N E W S

45 Years of Hunting and Fishing History
From the Pages of Minnesota Outdoor News

Published in the United States of America by
Outdoor News, Inc.
9850 51st Ave. N, Suite 130
Plymouth, MN 55442
(763) 546-4251
(763) 398-3467 fax
www.outdoornews.com

First edition 2014

Copyright © 2014 by Outdoor News, Inc.
All rights reserved. No part of this book may be reproduced in any manner without the express written consent of the publisher, except in the case of brief excerpts in critical reviews and articles. Scanning, uploading, and distribution of this book via the Internet or any other means without the permission of the publisher is illegal and punishable by law.

Library of Congress Control Number: 2014913014
ISBN Number: (hard cover) 978-0-9649257-2-4
ISBN Number: (soft cover) 978-0-9649257-4-8
Published August 2014

Publisher: Glenn A. Meyer
Text by Joe Albert and Rob Drieslein
Layout and design by Ron Nelson
Printed in the U.S.A. by Corporate Graphics, Mankato, Minn.

Hard cover retail price: $29.95
Soft cover retail price: $21.95

OUTDOOR NEWS
PREFACE:

Like many of you, I've been reading Outdoor News since the introductory issue with Loral I Delaney on the cover in 1967. As publisher, I enjoy access to all of Outdoor News' past editions, which staff frequently peruse for researching contemporary news stories and features. Browsing through our archives is fascinating and addictive, because they contain a gold mine of Minnesota hunting and fishing history. Famous outdoorsmen like Les Kouba and Jimmy Robinson graced its pages for decades, and tomorrow's legends offer their insights to Outdoor News readers today.

With this book, we wanted to create a snapshot of the top headlines, photos, and stories from each year of this newspaper's history. It's the greatest hits from the Outdoor News' archives. More importantly, this book offers you an opportunity to share in the trip back through the memory lanes leading to hunting shacks and muskie haunts across Minnesota.

Outdoor News began in Minnesota in 1967 when a Star Tribune outdoors writer with an entrepreneurial streak decided to launch his own newspaper. Always willing to offer an opinion, and never afraid of criticism, Jim Peterson's columns and headlines kept readers intrigued for the first 20 years of Outdoor News.

Peterson regularly attended meetings of the Fur, Fin and Feather club in Minneapolis until he passed away in 2003. The membership heartily applauded every week when Jim held aloft his cane during introductions and declared, "Jim Peterson, still raising cane!"

During a special FF&F honorary event for Jim, Outdoor News Editor Rob Drieslein gave a toast and promised that long after Jim moved on to a better place, Outdoor News would still be raising cane. He liked that, and I believe the sentiment reflects the continuing role of Outdoor News as it approaches its sixth decade in publishing. We hope our newspaper informs, entertains, and occasionally challenges readers on matters of hunting, fishing, and natural resources management and policy in our great state.

Since purchasing Outdoor News from Jim in 1988, I've enjoyed every minute of exploring the issues and headlines that make for such a remarkably robust outdoors scene here in Minnesota. I've watched my own children, and now grandchildren, thriving in the hunting and fishing lifestyle this newspaper celebrates every week. I've befriended so many fine, high-quality people within the state's outdoor industry. And I've participated hands-on in the outdoor sports we all cherish. You can trust that the people behind this book and your weekly Outdoor News, live the outdoors the same as you and me.

To create this book, we opened the archives of Outdoor News and reprinted some of the famous photos and headlines that have graced its pages. Looking back at the final product brings back a rush of memories, smiles, and emotions for me every time I open it. I hope these 192 pages stir the same feelings and remembrances for you, too.

Delivering on a weekly deadline for more than 25 years has been sometimes challenging, often exhilarating, and constantly gratifying. It wouldn't be possible without all the fine employees who've devoted portions of their professional lives to making Outdoor News the best weekly sportsmen's publication in the nation. Thank you to all of our readers and advertisers for 45 years of support. We'll see you afield or on the dock.

Glenn A. Meyer
Publisher

◢ OUTDOOR NEWS

HIGHLIGHTS AND HISTORY
45 YEARS OF HUNTING AND FISHING HISTORY
FROM THE PAGES OF MINNESOTA OUTDOOR NEWS

THE 1960S

Jim Peterson launches Outdoor News, and in his pull-no-punches style, takes on issues like gun-control and DNR Fisheries management. Oddities like a white ruffed grouse and the "Eskimobile" highlight the news section while readers enjoyed the good old days of duck and ring-necked pheasant hunting.

THE 1970S

Tough winters resulted in the closure of the deer season in 1971, but other facets of the outdoor experience – notably growing numbers of big muskies and a state record walleye – improved for readers. Ice shanties ruled Lake Mille Lacs and new federal environmental rules went into effect.

THE 1980S

State sportsmen began spreading their political wings with the launch of the Minnesota Sportfishing Congress and Pheasants Forever. Wild turkey hunting gained steam in Minnesota, and white-tailed deer numbers began to expand. Also, lifelong Minnesotan Glenn Meyer purchases the newspaper from Peterson.

THE 1990S

The decade that saw tribal treaty rights cases unfold across the region also brought forth a big political victory during the 1998 election. Marking the milestone, Outdoor News launches its annual Man of the Year Award. Sportsmen also pushed back against anti-hunters across the country while moose populations plunged in the northwest portion of Minnesota.

THE 2000S

A new millenium brings the digital age into sportsmen's wallets and boats with the beginning of electronic licensing. The great wolf debate raged through much of the decade while cougar sightings increased. Meanwhile the state saw record deer kills and victories at the State Capitol, especially with the passage of the Legacy Act in 2008.

THE 2010S

With the loss of many legendary stalwarts who carried the torch for conservation, younger generations tackle modern challenges facing sportsmen and women, such as increased pressure on grassland habitat. Photos from the first modern wolf and sandhill crane hunts highlight the weekly news sections.

INTRODUCTION:

Outdoor sports occur in a natural cycle with the four seasons. When the days lengthen in March and April, outdoorsmen and women start thinking turkey hunting or walleye fishing. When the first chill wind blows across the Dakota prairies, the cackle of a pheasant rings clearer, and hunters – human and canine alike – feel the urge to run some grasslands and roust a rooster. Perhaps those natural rhythms are one reason sportsmen have a propensity for reflecting on their past days afield and comparing them to today.

Those are the kind of memories that the Outdoor News staff hopes will stir within readers as they flip through this volume. To create "45 Years of Hunting and Fishing History from the Pages of Outdoor News," staff chose compelling pictures and headlines to highlight a given year for readers. We've devoted three to four pages for each year with a sampling of text to summarize key stories and events. We consider it the ultimate collection of Minnesota sporting days gone by.

Associate Editor Joe Albert devoted several months to finding important headlines and recasting them for readers. You may not see an entry from every month of every year, but trust that the staff tried to select the biggest events from a given 12-month period. You'll see state fish and game records, faces and profiles of key DNR employees, and recurring news themes like the state-tribal lawsuits of the 1990s. To provide some frame of reference, Albert also included an introduction for each year with key national and world events.

Editorial production supervisor Ron Nelson selected some of the best vintage photography from the newspaper and scanned those images for your reading pleasure. He organized and designed the book's entire contents into the format you're now holding. It's worth noting that both Nelson and Albert completed this book while never missing their weekly deadline for Minnesota Outdoor News!

Subscribers today who receive a newspaper that averages more than 40 pages per week might barely recognize the 8- and 12-page editions from the late 1960s and '70s. The headlines and page counts may be different, but the dedication and mission remain the same: bringing readers in-depth, up-to-date news and information that they can trust.

Take "45 Years of Hunting and Fishing History from the Pages of Minnesota Outdoor News" a few pages at a time or spend several hours reading the whole works front to back. Enjoy at your own pace and as the seasonal winds come calling. In between, I'll see you cruising the pheasant haunts.

Rob Drieslein
Managing Editor

Special Introductory Issue

(See Page 5 for Subscription Details; Page 7 for Extra Copies)

Jim Peterson's Outdoor News
The Sportsman's Weekly

HUNTING • FISHING • SHOOTING • DOGS • CA

Outdoor News, P.O. Box 27145, Golden Valley, Minn.

OUTDOOR NEWS
P.O. Box 27145
GOLDEN VALLEY, MINN. 55427

WELCOME!

State Buys 200,000 Cohos

Legendary Minnesota wildlife artist Les Kouba created the distinctive Outdoor News masthead and logo.

Will Build Hatchery for Salmon

Copyright 1967,
Jim Peterson's Outdoor News, Inc.

Minnesota will launch its first Coho salmon program this month, it was learned exclusively by Outdoor News.

Hjalmar Swenson, state supervisor of fisheries, told Outdoor News that the first shipment of 200,000 Coho salmon eggs will arrive from Oregon before Christmas.

The eggs will be hatched at the Lanesboro, Minn., fish hatchery and placed in rearing ponds there. Next fall, some of the young salmon will be placed in Greenwood Lake north of Grand Marais, Minn., in the northeastern tip of Minnesota as "large fingerlings," Swenson said. The rest will be reared to "yearling" size, about 12 inches long, and stocked in North Shore streams in the spring of 1969. They are expected to work their way down into Lake Superior and then return to the streams to spawn as adults.

Future plans include the construction of a new fish hatchery near Roosevelt Lake near Outing, Minn., for hatching and rearing Coho salmon and lake trout. Aquisition of land for the new hatchery has already been started.

"We were waiting to see how the Cohos did in Michigan before making a decision," Swenson said. "But we don't want Minnesotans to get 'carried away.' Lake Superior can't be compared to Lake Michigan as far as its potential for Coho salmon. Lake Superior is much colder and the Cohos of the same age are about one-third the size of those in Lake Michigan."

Swenson said between 300 and 400 Coho salmon were caught in the Minnesota side of Lake Superior this fall. These were "Michigan fish" which strayed to the west.

Coho salmon caught in the Duluth area averaged 4 to 8 pounds each, Ben Gustafson, area fisheries manager at French River, said. More than two dozen Cohos were caught off the

Continued on Page 8

Here's 'Secret' Fishing Method

By JIM PETERSON
Outdoor News Editor

Hottest news for cold weather fishermen:

A "secret" method of fishing and a new winter trout season in Minnesota are arriving about the same time—and they certainly go together, even if their appearance on the scene is a co-incidence.

The new fishing method may soon be a fish-household word, just as jigging is now. It is called "thrumming" and was a closely-guarded secret in Finland.

Yes, it was Ray Ostrom and Ron Weber, the two Minneapolis businessmen - sportsmen, who brought the secret back from Finland during one of their trips to the land of the Rapala, Finbore and reindeer.

The Finns take their fishing seriously—probably a lot more seriously than Americans do. I especially noticed that when I had the opportunity to fish with Lauri Rapala, the inventor of the largest-selling lure of all time, when he visited Ostrom and Weber aboard their houseboat on Lake of the Woods.

Anything the Finns do in the way of fishing they do with intense concentration and purpose.

They go fishing to catch fish. And thrumming is designed to produce more fish by concentrating the jigging action and at the same time making it easier for them to execute it.

Ostrom and Weber brought back their first thrumming rod two years ago, and I was fortunate — and honored — to be selected to test it. So, I have used the thrumming technique two winter seasons (it can be

Continued on Page 6

Photo for Outdoor News by Virginia Space

LORAL I. DELANEY works out three of her dogs in preparation for the forthcoming sportsmen's show circuit, including the Northwest Sports, Travel and Boat Show at the Minneapolis Auditorium March 29-April 7. Mrs. Delaney and husband Chuck, who combined to set a new world record man-wife trap shooting record in August, begin their new dog column in Outdoor News on Page 6.

Season's Greetings

From Jim Peterson's Outdoor News, Inc.

ON THE INSIDE

SOUTH DAKOTA

Walleye Fishing Best in 5 Years Near Oahe Dam

By F. N. (Denny) Cosgrove

PIERRE, S.D. — Walleye fishing is "the best in five years" in the Oahe Dam tailwaters, said bait dealer Carl Walters, and the fishing should continue hot through the middle of February.

Pierre's most famous fishing couple, Russ and Betty Green, who specialize in walleyes, caught 12 walleyes Dec. 2 and then got 18 the next morning. The fish averaged three pounds each, with the biggest six pounds.

They fished in the Farm Island and Antelope Creek areas, casting with Canadian jig flies from their boat.

Russ said he expects to break the Great Lakes of South Dakota season walleye record of 10½ pounds before the winter is over. Fishing pressure has been generally light, and there is no ice yet on the reservoir for northern pike fishermen.

Outdoor News Photo by Jim Peterson

MALLARD DUCKS, crowded into open water areas on Lake Harriet in Minneapolis for their annual winter handouts from well-meaning citizens, inspired Russell B. Smith to write his "Duck Hunters' Prayer Come True" on Page 5 of this issue of Outdoor News. Future issues of Outdoor News will contain more "Old Timers' Tales" and "Favorite Outdoor Stories."

PROMO ISSUE!
- - - - - - - -
PRINTED AND DISTRIBUTED FALL OF 1967

BILL HUNTLEY
17, 14 pound Cohos

We Are Here

This special pilot issue of Outdoor News marks the end of several weeks of preparations, but it is just the start of a new era in outdoor news coverage, features, editorials and columns for readers in the North Central states.

In an area loaded with sportsmen and bulging with opportunities for outdoor activities, we feel there is a definite need for a genuine outdoor newspaper, written and edited by sportsmen who are also experienced newspapermen. Anything less would be selling everybody short, reader and advertiser alike.

We are starting out as the biggest outdoors publication in the area and intend to grow. We intend to be the real "eyes, ears and voice" of the sportsmen who deserve the best—or as close to the best as is humanly possible.

This goes for the printing, too. After exploring several locations throughout the area, we selected the Post Publishing Co. in Robbinsdale. Not only does it have the rotary offset presses necessary for printing large numbers of papers but it also holds several national awards for excellence.

We hope to maintain the Post's tradition.

* * *

Left to Right Are:

We firmly believe we have the best staff of writers ever assembled for an outdoor paper, and we intend to add one or two more. In this issue we have:

KIT BERGH—nationally-known outdoor writer and author of "Minnesota Fish and Fishing," the best book on angling ever published in these parts. Kit also is a magazine writer, photographer and a budding novelist. He lives at 1121 Hallam Ave., Mahtomedi.

GARY BENNYHOFF—Member of the Outdoor Writers Association of America, Associated Great Lakes Outdoor Writers, and former outdoor editor for WCCO Radio in Minneapolis. He has done a lot of tourist and travel promotional work. He lives at 1453 19th Ave. NW, New Brighton.

JOHN HENRICKSSON—Long-time outdoor writer, editor and film script writer as well as tackle representative. John specializes in fishing and likes the Park Rapids, Minn., area best. He lives at 79 Neptune St., Mahtomedi.

CHUCK AND LORAL I. DELANEY—They're not only the best dog training couple in the world but also the best trap-shooting man and wife, holding the world record of 395 out of 400 targets set last August in the Grand American at Vandalia, Ohio. They begin their tours of sportsmen's shows around the country in mid-January. Loral I. will appear in the Northwest Sports, Travel and Boat Show March 29 - April 7 at the Minneapolis Auditorium. They own and operate Armstrong Ranch Kennels, Rt. 2, Anoka.

LACEY GEE — Our Iowa correspondent holds the odd-name championship. But there's nothing odd about his outdoor credentials. He is one of the country's best fly-tiers, operating his own shop, and is co-author of "Practical Flies and Their Construction," a top-notch book for both beginners or advanced fly-tiers. He has a weekly radio show and writes a weekly column in his home town. He hunts and fishes all over Iowa and Minnesota, plus jaunts to western and southern states as well as Canada. He lives in Independence, Iowa.

F. N. (DENNY) COSGROVE—Former editor of the Pierre, S.D., newspaper, he has done considerable promotional work for the Great Lakes of South Dakota and its still-growing recreational facilities. He lives in Pierre, S.D.

LES KOUBA—Noted wildlife artist and designer of the 1967-68 duck stamp, designed the "Logo," the front page display art for Outdoor News.

In addition, JIMMY ROBINSON, the venerable trap and skeet editor of Sports Afield magazine who lives in St. Louis Park, has promised to write a piece for Outdoor News when he gets back from Europe. He and wife Clara are now in Spain after touring England, France and Italy.

We are honored to have DR. HOWARD CONN, minister of Plymouth Congregational Church, Minneapolis, write a special message for our first issue.

RUSSELL B. SMITH—(A Duck Hunter's Prayer) is a retired Viking Council Boy Scout Executive. A native of Omaha, Nebraska, he now resides at 5357 Logan Avenue South in Minneapolis.

* * *

And As For Me...

When I left the Minneapolis Tribune this fall, I told myself that I would now find out whether business friendships are just that . . . period. After 24 years of working with and writing about people, I knew I had a lot of business friends.

However, anybody who believes that the business world is all cold, hard dealings and that down-to-earth friendships have gone the way of the town pump, the general store cracker barrel and the 50-cent haircut now has to face a real argument from me.

This is a down-to-earth business, and I have many down-to-earth people helping me.

Since we here are all so down-to-earth, we expect to have our noses rubbed in the dirt now and then. But with some nourishment we expect to grow, mature and bear fruit. Some of it may be corn, to be sure. We don't intend to throw the dirt around, because that would only dislodge the roots we have worked hard to establish. However, we will face any storm of iniquity and hail of outrageous fortune with all the strength we can muster.

Strength comes only from truth. Truth, to a real down-to-earth newspaperman, not only is the name of the game, it's the entire game.

-- JIM PETERSON

Muskie Group Starts Survey of State Lakes

Members of Muskies, Inc., will make a statewide survey of Minnesota lakes to determine which are desirable for stocking muskellunge, the club announced.

Club members from all parts of the state will submit lists of lakes in their own areas to the Muskies, Inc., main office at 1708 University Ave., St. Paul. The club then will submit the compiled lists to the Conservation Department for recommendation as to water suitability for muskie stocking.

Muskies, Inc., then will prepare its list of lakes it will stock with muskies in 1968 and tentative lists for following years.

This year the club stocked 100 foot-long yearling muskies in Sugar Lake near Annandale, Minn., about 50 miles northwest of Minneapolis. The muskies were reared by Darrell Trumbauer in his minnow ponds near Battle Lake, Minn. Chuck Meyer, field editor for Sportfishing Magazine, observed and photographed the planting for an article in the magazine's spring issue.

Any sportsman wanting to join Muskies, Inc., may contact president Gil Hamm at the above address. Regular memberships are $10 per year and junior memberships $2. The club meets on the second Tuesday of each month.

For centuries, the Swiss Constitution has provided that every male be issued a gun by the army reserve. Even though these guns are kept at home, Switzerland has virtually no armed crime.

Champions...
in the field

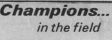

#877

Red Wing's
"Irish Setter"
SPORT BOOTS

Irish Setters are sport boot perfection . . . have been for a long, long time. They're crafted for the active man and the many challenges outdoors. Exclusive oil-tanned uppers repel moisture . . . stay soft and supple. Vibram lug soles or Traction-Tred cushion crepe soles put you in command of rough terrain. Try on a pair. See how great a sport boot can feel.

SIZES 6-16, AA-EEEE.

#823 Ladies

Write us for information and dealer name.

RED WING SHOE COMPANY
121 Main Street, Red Wing, Minnesota 55066

QUALITY LITTLE JOE PRODUCTS
TRADEMARK

LITTLE JOE JIGS

Little Joe quality jigs promote successful fishing. None are sold until proven to catch fish consistently in all fishing waters. The complete Little Joe line includes spinners, plugs, flys, and a complete line of fish stringers. Below are listed a few of the most famous fish getters.

CRAPPIE QUEEN

Try this one on pan fish. Most effective on Crappies, Bluegill, Bass, Perch and Trout. The Crappie Queen has a $\frac{1}{16}$ oz. weighted head, chenille body and life-like wings which gives it a slow sinking and planing action that fish can't resist.

BLUE TAIL FLY

This most famous fly of the Canadian Jig Fly family was first made in 1960 and is still tops. Try an assortment of Canadian Jig Flys in the many patterns available but don't pass up the Blue Tail Fly! Available from $\frac{1}{16}$ to 1 oz. in weight.

SCULLY

The weight of Scully is built into the body on the shank of the hook making it ride with the barb up precisely balanced with the spinner. The fluorescent body is overlayed with jungle cock hackle which makes it look very much like a live minnow in the water. Available in $\frac{1}{16}$, $\frac{1}{8}$, $\frac{1}{4}$ oz. weights and five patterns.

GET YOUR LIMIT IN JIG TIME

Write for this free article on how to fish Little Joe products. Written by a well known sports writer and fishing authority.

WRITE TO

MILLE LACS MANUFACTURING CO.
ISLE, MINNESOTA

FIRST FULL YEAR!

Jim Peterson's
Outdoor News
The Sportsman's Weekly

15¢

HUNTING • FISHING • SHOOTING • DOGS • CAMPING • BOATING • TIPS

VOL. I, NO. I · 11   Outdoor News, P.O. Box 27145, Golden Valley, Minn.   Phone 588-2066   Copyright 1968   January 5, 1968

 JANUARY

• Game specialists with the Conservation Department identified an animal shot during the deer season near Skibo in northeastern Minnesota as a wolverine.

• Controversy raged about what to do with 400 white-tailed deer stuck inside the 2,500-acre Arsenal munitions plant in New Brighton. Humane Society wants to tranquilize them and move them to a wildlife management area. The State argued killing them was the best option.

1968 — This marks Outdoor News' inaugural year. Who would have known the paper would become such a success? The headlines may be different, but the desire to make Minnesota a leader in fish and wildlife conservation lives on. What was the world like in 1968? Here's a sampling:

• *It was one of Minnesota's stormiest winters to date.*

• *The North Vietnamese launched the Tet Offensive, considered a turning point in the Vietnam War.*

• *Martin Luther King, Jr., was killed in Memphis, Tenn.*

Commercial fishermen near Duluth hauling in smelt by the ton along the north shore of Lake Superior.

Milford Nelson was charged by this timber wolf during the deer season. He had a heavy dose of buck scent on his boots and thinks that may have set the wolf off.

A snowmobiler with a net attempting to net and bag a red fox. The attempt is part of a study on how fox and coyotes cause depredation on pheasants in the Fergus Falls area.

ANIMAL SHOT NEAR DULUTH IS WOLVERINE

Examination of the skull and carcass has enabled the Minnesota Conservation Department to positively identify an animal shot near Skibo, Minnesota, as a wolverine.

MINNESOTA 2ND IN FISH LICENSES

A report from the U.S. Department of Interior shows that Minnesota was second only to California in the sales of fishing licenses in 1967.

12 Wild Turkeys Added to Flock

The Minnesota Game and Fish Division reports that 12 more wild turkeys have been released in the Whitewater Wildlife Management Area in southeast Minnesota.

SKULL FOUND

—Photo by Pine County Courier

BISON OCCIDENTALIS — Virgil Sjodahl, Sandstone, Minn., a highway department inspector, found this skull and complete set of 31-inch horns at a drainage ditch excavation project near Rock Creek, Minn. Prof. Leland Cooper of the University of Minnesota identified it as a Bison Occidentalis, an extinct species of bison, much larger than our present buffalo, which lived in Minnesota between 6,000 and 7,000 years ago.

HEAVIEST MINN. DEER ON RECORD

In 1926 Carl Lenander shot the largest deer in Minnesota history. The buck tipped the scales at 402 pounds.

Jerry Gutzkow, of Cambridge, shot this piebald ruffed grouse while hunting near Walbo.

Mike Smith shot this 10-point, 200-pound buck near Ray. He almost lost the deer when he went to get a knife, and when he got back a hunter was gutting it out.

WHERE THE ACTION IS!

Johnson REELS

"First on Famous Waters"

MODEL 710A
Closed-face
Spin-casting reel

Johnson reels set the standard for fishing reels around the world. The company was based in Mankato, Minn.

• Twelve wild turkeys were released at the Whitewater Wildlife Management Area in southeastern Minnesota.
• Outdoor News and the Normark Corp. co-sponsored a fishing contest for the "most outstanding catch" made on Normark equipment.

FEBRUARY

• Lake Superior was in danger of becoming the "world's largest cesspool," according to University of Minnesota scientist Dr. Charles Huver. Industrial pollution, including taconite tailings, was among his main concerns.
• Writer Gary Bennyhoff detailed a fox hunt on the plains north of Fergus Falls. The goal? Chase foxes with snowmobiles and use a net to catch them, at which point the animals can be killed or released.

MARCH

• Outdoor News founder Jim Peterson, lauded the Minnesota Game Protection League for its passage of a resolution against "harpooning."
• Wildlife officials reported a flock of 12 Merriam's wild turkeys released at the Whitewater Wildlife Management Area were thriving. The birds were transplanted to Minnesota from South Dakota's Black Hills.
• The state Conservation Department announced it would release 15 fishers into Itasca State Park in an attempt to cut down on a surplus population of porcupines.

APRIL

• Outdoor News editor and publisher Jim Peterson was awarded the Conservationist-Editorialist Award of the Year at the Northwest Boat, Sports and Travel Show.

MAY

• State Game and Fish Director Dick Wettersten advocated for an open hunting season for mourning doves.

Ostroms became a great resource for the outdoor recreation industry in the Twin Cities.

▼

GOLDEN VALLEY SPORTS CENTER

USED GUNS WANTED!

GENUINE "SOREL" CANADIAN

BOOTS
$12.66 Pair

For Hunters Trappers Ice Fishermen Snowmobilers Workers

Durable rubber boot with quality tanned leather upper. Heavy ½ inch replaceable wool felt liner, extends above boot. Built-in warmth for arctic climates. Sizes 6 thru 13.

Open Evenings and Sundays

PORTABLE FISH HOUSES....... $39.95 and u

GOLDEN VALLEY SPORTS CENTER

▲

Golden Valley Sports Center became a resource for hunters with a growing population in the Twin Cities west metro area.

He also floated the idea of seasons for moose and spruce grouse.
• Minnesota was second in the number of fishing licenses sold, behind only California.

JUNE

• The shooting of Sen. Robert Kennedy resulted in calls for stricter gun control regulations. Publisher Jim Peterson called sportsmen the whipping boys of "inept, panicky officials" who had failed to control criminals.
• In an Outdoor News poll, 51 percent of respondents opposed all gun registration. Twenty-four percent supported handgun registration only, and

OSTROM'S

Your Headquarters For:
JOHNSON MOTORS; LUND BOATS; BOMBARDIER SKI-DOOS;
Shooting, Handloading Equipment
All Types of Fishing Tackle!

YES! We Have THRUMMING RODS!

OSTROM'S

3540 East Lake St.
Phone 722-6601

BUD GRANT

TIME OUT – Bud Grant, coach of the Minnesota Vikings, took a break from his busy schedule to fish for bluegills at Lake Victoria near Alexandria.

AL LINDNER

STILL SWIMS!

AFTER CATCHING this 13-pound walleye on Gull Lake Al Lindner release it unharmed. to be fair game on Saturday's opener.

JIM PETERSON

AWARD – A state committee selected Outdoor News Editor Jim Peterson to receive the Conservationist-Editorial Award of the Year at the Northwest Sportshow.

25 percent supported registering all guns.

JULY

• Pheasant counts increased 35 percent from the previous year.

AUGUST

• Minnesota officials announced plans to hold the first split duck season in state history. It was Oct. 5-13, and Oct. 26-Nov. 12, which is a total of 27 days.

DECEMBER

• The state received 300,000 coho salmon eggs. The eggs went to the state hatchery in Lanesboro. Several groups also asked the state Conservation Department to make the salmon stocking program in Lake Superior more of a permanent program.

FIRST LAKE OF THE WEEK

LINWOOD LAKE

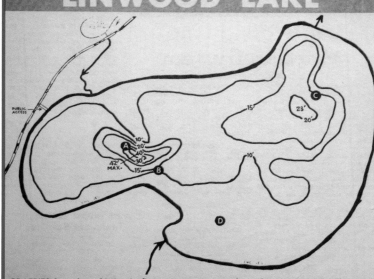

CRAPPIES have been hitting in five arm-lengths of water near the deepest part of the lake at point A on the above Conservation Department depth map, according to bait dealer John Vados. "Fishing has been terrific at Linwood all season and should continue for several weeks," he said. He added that some walleyes are being caught at point B, while point C on the east end of the lake is good for wall-eyes early in the winter season. The area around point D is best for northern pike in the winter and for panfish and bass in the spring of the year. Linwood Lake has an area of 559 acres and a maximum depth of 42 feet. It is in Anoka County northeast of Soderville. The public access is from County Highway 22. For late information, contact Vados Bait Shop in Fridley.

Each week Outdoor News will publish a lake map. Additional maps are available from the Bureau of Documents, Centennial Building, St. Paul, at $1 each.

▲ Linwood Lake became the first lake to grace the pages of Outdoor News. Since then, the map and profile each week has helped anglers fish waters otherwise unknown.

This photograph shows the first licensed snowmobile in Minnesota, a Model T refurbished in 1920 in Akeley.

Raymond Laska, of Finlayson shot this 105-pound timber wolf near Kroschel. The wolf was shot after it was found in a deer yard eating a fresh carcass, and charged Laska.

1969 — *The year began with the inauguration of Richard Nixon as the 37th president of the United States.*

• U.S. astronauts Neil Armstrong and Buzz Aldrin are the first humans to walk on the moon.

• More than 500,000 people gather in New York for the Woodstock festival, which featured artists such as Jimmy Hendrix, Janis Joplin, and The Who.

• Sen. Edward Kennedy pleaded guilty to leaving the scene of fatal car accident.

JANUARY

• A number of fishermen in their fish houses on Lake Mille Lacs were marooned after they either didn't hear about inclement weather, or didn't heed the warnings. The visibility was very low; most anglers waited for it to improve before heading to shore.

• There was 18 inches of snow on the ground in northeast Minnesota by the middle of December, which was tough on deer. When the snow is that deep, the deer concentrate and move into deer yards. It also makes it difficult for deer to move freely, and is tough on fawns.

• The Committee for Effective Crime Control was launched to fight gun registration and control.

• The Conservation Department announced it would launch an "all-out effort to save the state's deer herd from being decimated."

• A buck antelope broke its back after jumping from a bridge near Montevideo and landing on a railroad track. Staffers at the Lac qui Parle

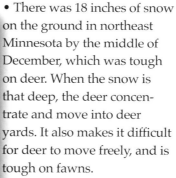

KILLER DOGS - Two farm dogs near Hinkley were killed after killing 40 deer, mostly does carrying twin fawns, (some shown in background). Officer Volkmann was required to kill dogs chasing deer.

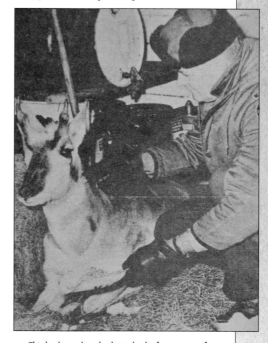

This buck antelope broke its back after jumping from a bridge near Montevideo.

An Eden Prairie hunter killed a white wolf that weighed 84 pounds. He shot it near Big Falls.

Lightning Kills Eight Ducks

—From the Melrose Beacon

MELROSE, Minn—A strange weather system crept into the area about the same time that the opening of the duck season on Saturday (Oct. 4).

As the warm air banged into a cold front that moved into the area from the west, there was a vicious thunder and lightning display that scared everyone in the duck swamps including the ducks.

It was reported by local hunters on Twin Lakes, near Grey Eagle, Minn., that during this display of static electricity two sharp bolts of lightning came crashing down just as a flight of mallard ducks were passing. Eight ducks fell to the water.

Drowning Toll at 20-Year High

Minnesota is experiencing its worst year of recreational drownings since 1949—and the year isn't over yet, Conservation Department officials noted grimly.

Robert Rygg, Assistant Commissioner of Conservation, said 147 persons have drowned so far this year in our lakes, streams and ponds "and it is virtually certain that more will drown before the end of the year."

605-Lb. Bear Shot by Iowan Near Baudette

—From the Baudette Region

BAUDETTE, Minn. — The bear shot Saturday (Sept. 27) by Ray Malcolm of Postville, Ia., was the heaviest black bear in many a year to be taken hereabouts, and just maybe it was the biggest ever.

70% DECLINE IN PHEASANTS

Minnesota's pheasant population is 70 per cent lower than last year, according to a report by the Conservation Department.

The count of adult breeding birds also is 90 to 95 per cent lower than 1960, considered a good hunting year.

Game Refuge cared for it.

FEBRUARY

• Columnist Fred Daugs wrote a column entitled: "It's time to have a trout stamp." At the time, such stamps didn't exist, and fishing licenses cost $2.25.

• Game and Fish Director Dick Wettersten called the winter "the worst in history." He predicted 60,000 to 100,000 deer may die, and said pheasants had been wiped out completely in some areas.

MARCH

• A bill introduced at the Legislature would have banned spearing of all gamefish. The bill failed to make it out of its first committee stop.

JUNE

• The state's pheasant population declined by 70 percent from the previous year. The number of breeding adult pheasants was down 90 to 95 percent from 1960, which was considered a good year for hunting pheasants.

JULY

• Minnesota was slated to hold an early teal-hunting season, even though DNR officials opposed it.

• Coho salmon fishing "exploded" in the Duluth area. As many as 200 boats were on the water each evening. Most boats were catching at least a fish or two, and some caught many more.

• An improper application of an algae treatment at Hall and Budd lakes near Fairmont wiped out two years worth of stocked walleyes and northern pike.

AUGUST

• A 110-pound paddlefish that a

Big Stone Lake angler Gerhardt Block, right of Ortonville, Minn., had a great day on the water catching four walleyes totalling 42 pounds. Officer Bud Breezee helped Gerhardt display the large catch.

Below, Gordy Meinke, poses with a brace of geese from Thief Lake, three of which are rare giant Canadas, and two are snows.

CHAMPIONS – Loral I. Delaney of Anoka, Minn., successfully defended her World Women's Trapshooting Championship in the Grand American Trapshoot at Vandalia, Ohio. She is shown with Paul Robey, Mpls., who won the Central Zone title at Sioux Falls, S.D. and competed in the "Grand" this week.

fishermen snagged in South Dakota broke that state's paddlefish record. It marked the third time in less than a month that the record fell.

• A proposal in Washington, D.C., would have resulted in the confiscation of handguns from people, unless they could demonstrate a reasonable need to own one.

• Everything is better with bacon. A recipe for walleyes: line each cup in a muffin pan with bacon. Roll up the walleye fillets and season with salt, pepper, and thyme. Insert the fillet into the pan. Fill the center, with any stuffing. Bake 30 minutes at 350 degrees.

• Loral I. Delaney, of Anoka, successfully de-

LONG SHOT – About once a year Outdoor News publishes a picture of its editor-publisher. (He's the one without the antlers). The South Dakota late season 9-pointer was shot at 400 yards.

OUTFOXES FOXES - Larry Traver, Faulkton, S.D., has bagged more than 1,000 foxes and several coyotes since Dec. 15. A commercial pilot, Traver uses a Champion 150 plane and does his own flying and shooting. His best day was 60 foxes on Jan. 19, while he had 55 on Jan. 25.

CANADIAN CAPER - Dr. Dennis Peterson of Milaca, Minn., (left) and Lloyd Thompson of Brainerd, Minn., show their limits of bluebill and mallards bagged near Boissevain, Manitoba, Canada.

Treatment for Algae Kills $30,000 Worth of Fish

Dick Wettersten, state director of game and fish, said Tuesday he was "shocked" to learn that $30,000 worth of fish in the re-stocking program in the Fairmont, Minn., chain of lakes had been killed by the improper application of copper sulphate to control algae.

The city of Fairmont applied the chemical to Hall and Budd Lakes last week and apparently killed thousands of stocked walleyes and northern pike. "Two years of fish stocking efforts appear to be wiped out," Wettersten said. He called a meeting with Fairmont officials.

Jim Peterson's
Outdoor News
The Sportsman's Weekly

15¢

Anglers Marooned on Mille Lacs

From the Mille Lacs Messenger

ISLE, Minn. — A number of fishermen who failed to see last Saturday and Sunday's storm coming up — or failed to heed the warning, were marooned in their fish houses over Sunday. In most cases fishermen simply waited out the storm until visibility improved.

In the Isle area, two Minneapolis men, Louis Nolden and Milton Best and Nolden's son Richard, were fishing in a portable house on Three Mile Reef on the east side. They fished on Saturday and when they prepared to come in Sunday morning visibility suddenly was reduced to zero. The three were forced to spend all day Sunday and Sunday night in their car.

Bluebills Jam Blackduck Lake

STILTMOBILE – Here is a strange vehicle used by deer hunters in Wisconsin. The Eskimobile is believed to have been manufactured by John Swansen of Almena, Wis., in the early 1920s. The vehicle was equipped with caterpillar-type tracks and double rear tires. This may be the pioneer model of the snowmobile. And, would you get a look at the size of that buck deer!

Sportsman's Kitchen

By GERRY PETERSON

MUFFIN PAN WALLEYE

If you've tried to roll up walleye fillets, you know that it is not too easy. Use your muffin pan to help you.

Line each cup with bacon, then roll up walleye fillets seasoned with salt, pepper, and thyme, and insert. You can then fill the center with any stuffing mixture you like. Bake ½ hour at 350 degrees.

Recipes for game and fish became a popular addition to Outdoor News. They have evolved over the years to a gourmet status.

fended her World Women's Trapshooting Championship in the Grand American Trapshoot. She broke 198 of 200 targets.

OCTOBER

• A man who lived north of Swatara shot an 88-pound wolf that measured 6 feet, 7 inches long. Farmers had lost more than 100 sheep and cattle in the area.

• A hunter killed a 605-pound bear near Baudette.

• A lightning strike killed eight ducks in the Melrose area.

• Publisher Jim Peterson wrote that he'd never seen so many ducks in his

life. Other folks, including some from Ducks Unlimited, made similar statements.

NOVEMBER

• Ice fishermen hit the ice early at Lake Mille Lacs.

DECEMBER

• As of early December, 147 people had drowned on waters in the state, marking the worst year for drownings since 1949.

• An Eden Prairie hunter killed a white wolf that weighed 84 pounds. He shot it near Big Falls.

Ice Fishing Season 'Opens' Early at Mille Lacs

Above: Bud Grant, coach of the Minnesota Vikings, poses with two of six timber wolves that he shot during an aerial hunt in Ontario.

DUCK BANDED IN MINNESOTA SHOT IN S.A.

From the Lake Region Press

ALEXANDRIA, Minn. — Dr. Roy L. Thompson of the Rockefeller Foundation in Cali, Colombia, South America, son of Mr. and Mrs. Arnold Thompson of Hoffman, Minn., wrote to his parents in his last letter that he shot a duck in October, 1969, that was banded in Minnesota in 1965.

Dr. Thompson shot the duck while planting corn at Monteria on the north coast of Colombia. He said they raise three crops of corn per year there.

1970 — One of the biggest bands of all time, the Beatles, broke up. Each member of the band released an album by year's end.

• *The Minnesota Vikings lost in the Super Bowl to Kansas City. The score was 23-7.*

• *A first-class stamp cost 6 cents.*

• *National Guardsmen killed four students at Kent State University in Ohio. They were protesting the U.S. incursion in Cambodia.*

• *IBM introduced the first floppy disk.*

• *Monday Night Football debuted on ABC. Howard Cosell, Frank Gifford, and Don Meredith did play-by-play.*

JANUARY

• The winter was so tough the pheasants in southern Minnesota were gathering along the sides of roads. In response, the Sleepy Eye Sportsmen's Club handed out signs that said: "Slow Down! Pheasant Area!"

• DFL candidate for governor Warren Spannaus made confiscation of handguns the main plank of his gubernatorial run. Outdoor News ran a picture of Spannaus with the words "Not Wanted" above his head. (Spannaus later switched to running for attorney general.)

MARCH

• A 2-foot American eel was captured by a Department of Conservation crew on Willmar Lake. It's thought the eel swam about 4,000 miles from Bermuda, where the species spawns.

• Department of Conservation staff netted 40,000 pounds of carp from Lake Minnetonka. The carp's destination? Missouri, where they were stocked in ponds, and anglers paid to catch them.

• A hunter informed his parents, who lived in Alexandria, that he shot a duck

GIFT FOR THE SPORTSMAN
Give Him the Best— a Genuine
LOWRANCE
FISH LO-K-TOR

Easy Monthly Payments

The Fish Lo-K-Tor is the only depth finder used by the Nisswa Guides League!

MARV KOEP'S
NISSWA BAIT & TACKLE
Box 87, Nisswa, Minn.

IDEAL FOR ICE FISHING

Marv Koep's Nisswa Bait and Tackle became the "go to" place for anglers throughout the region. The shop was on the cutting edge of the fishing industry for years.

*RECORD CRAPPIE—This crappie weighed an even five pounds when caught in 1940 by the late Tom Christenson of Red Wing, Minn., in the Vermillion River. The weight and the exact measurements were recorded by Conservation Officer Phil Nordeen, who also died recently. It was 18¾ inches long and 19⅜ inches in girth. Cannon Falls taxidermist Russ Awsumb restored the fish which is on display at the OUTDOOR NEWS booth at the Sportsmen's Show. The crappie is listed the Minnesota record and ties the world record as listed by Field and Stream magazine. Awsumb's grandson, Clifford, is shown holding the fish. —Photo for Outdoor News by Russ Awsumb

 Above: Allan Hetteen, president of Polaris Industries in Roseau, Minnesota, is shown with the first snowmobile, the Sno-Traveler, first marketed in 1954. Polaris went on to become a giant in the industry, and still is to this day.

in October of 1969 in Monteria, on the north coast of Columbia, South America. The duck was banded in Minnesota in 1965.

• Conservation Department Commissioner Jarle Leirfallom presented a wolf-management plan to the annual meeting of the North American Wildlife Conference. He said the main goal was to protect wolves from extermination and that wolves would survive permanently, "at least in the Boundary Waters Canoe Area."

APRIL

• The first-ever survey of the state's wolf population pegged the number of animals at 750.

• Dick Wettersten, state director of fish and game, reported there is a difference between brush wolves and coyotes. According to game managers, brush

$595

BUYS THE NEWEST IDEA IN SNOWMOBILES... THE COMPACT ELAN!

Ski-Doo does it again! The company that invented the snowmobile invents a totally new concept . . . Elan, the compact snowmobile.

☐ Perfect for the first time snowmobiler or the family that wants more than one.
☐ Elan is an easy handling, full-performance, full size track machine.
☐ The lowest priced Ski-Doo snowmobile ever.
☐ Available with manual start . . . or electric start for $100 more.
☐ Size one up soon.

ski-doo.

The sign of the finest one stop shopping centre for snowmobiles, winter sportswear, accessories, parts and service.

*T.M. Bombardier Ltd.

EST. 1922   EASY TERMS

Elmer N. Olson Co.

OPEN WEEKDAY EVES.
ST. LOUIS PARK
4 Blks. W. of Beltline
Hwy. 7 at Wooddale
929-7823

OPEN WEEKDAY EVES.
RICHFIELD-BLOOMINGTON
7648 Lyndale Ave. S.
866-8458

OPEN MON. & THURS. EVES.
DOWNTOWN
Where 35W Ends
Downtown
500 S. 11th St.
332-8931

Game Warden Hit on Head by Fish Spear

A Sauk Centre, Minn, man pleaded guilty and was fined $300 for hitting a conservation officer (game warden) over the head with a fish spear last week, the Minnesota Conservation Department anounced Wednesday.

The man, Harlan Ilgen, 24, Route 3, Sauk Centre, also was given a 90-day jail sentence which was stayed one year during which time he is on probation. He also was fined $25 for

—Photo by the Grand Rapids Review

STRANGERS—Two ducks which rarely appear in Minnesota were shot during this fall's season by Grand Rapids, Minn., hunters. At left, Gene Hanson shows the harlequin he got at Lake Winnibigoshish, while at right Mike Gerber shows the old squaw duck he bagged on Deer Lake near Effie.

Conservation Department Gets New Name

RON LINDNER, pro fisherman from Brainerd, Minn., shows the 5 lb. 7 oz. smallmouth bass he caught in Bay Lake.
—Photo for Outdoor News by Marv Koep, Nisswa Bait & Tackle

On Jan. 4, 1971, the Minnesota Conservation Department will cease to exist. In its place will be a new "Department of Natural Resources," created by the legislature at the 1969 session.

The Conservation Department this week unveiled the new insignia that will be in use when the name change takes effect and pointed out that the law which changed the Department's name also made some changes in the Department's structure.

◄ The former Minnesota Conservation Department released the new name and logo for the Department of Natural Resources. The logo is still used to this day.

wolves are a subspecies of coyotes.

• A Sauk Centre, Minn., man pleaded guilty and was fined $300 for hitting a conservation officer over the head with a spear.

JUNE

• There was concern that when a Northern States Power plant began operations, the fishery below Monticello would be "gone forever."

• The closed pheasant season the previous year apparently led to increased rooster counts during the annual May census.

• Ruffed grouse drum counts were the highest in 22 years.

AUGUST

• The DNR announced a 16-day pheasant season in southern Minnesota (it had been closed the year before), and a two-day deer season. It also announced a 45-day duck season.

SEPTEMBER

• Lake Mille Lacs resorter Jack Maciosek and his son caught three good-sized northern pike. Then they did something unusual: They released them.

Two-Day Deer Season 'About As Expected,' Say Officials

Minnesota's two-day deer season was "about what we expected," according to preliminary reports to Dave Vesall, state supervisor of game.

Vesall said results of the Conservation Department's telephone survey and checking stations will not be announced until Thursday — too late for this week's Outdoor News.

HOWEVER, he said, "There is no doubt but what the hunting pressure was down and so was the take of deer. There were some good areas in the north, and I think the take of deer held up very well in the southern areas. A lot more corn was harvested this year in the southern part of the state which made hunting there quite a bit

easier than last year."

Vesall said he and his hunting partner got one deer while hunting in Lake of the Woods County.

MEANWHILE, reports to Outdoor News have been slight-

(Continued on Page 2)

Timber Wolf Plan Presented by Leirfallom

A true timber wolf management plan based on the premise that the wolf is "an important animal" was presented to the North American Wildlife Conference at its annual meeting in Chicago, Ill., this week by Minnesota Conservation Commissioner Jarle Leirfallom.

Leirfallom said the primary goal must be to protect the timber wolf from extermination. Secondly, he said domestic livestock must be protected and a close watch kept on the deer-wolf relationship in Minnesota. **AS A FUNDAMENTAL** first step, a census must be taken of the timber wolf annually to determine its exact numbers, said Leirfallom. He added that the first census has already been completed in the state and the result will be announced in "about a week".

• The new state record rainbow trout was caught. It weighed 15 pounds, 7 ounces, and was caught in Lake Superior.

OCTOBER

• Nine opening-day duck hunters were cited for having 88 ducks in their possession. They were hunting the Blackduck area of Dixon Lake.

NOVEMBER

• Most of the Superior National Forest was closed to the taking of timber wolves. The forest supervisor said the move was necessary to protect the last remaining breeding population of timber wolves in the contiguous United States.

FISH-EATING WOLF – This timber wolf was spotted on Upper Red Lake eating an eelpout near a fish house. Peter Olson and Don Nelson shot the animal, which despite its body size, weighed a mere 75 pounds.

• A letter writer wondered when the state would allow fishermen to use two lines.
• Conservation Department officials predicted deer hunters would kill 40,000 to 45,000 animals during the two-day season.

DECEMBER

• The state Conservation Department and the federal Superior National Forest announced agreement on a five-point cooperative wolf-management plan for the state.

• The Conservation Department, thanks to legislation passed in 1969, became officially known as the Minnesota Department of Natural Resources.

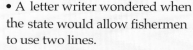

State Anglers Near Record

THESE GIANT lake trout were caught recently in Great Bear Lake, Northwest Territories, by Minnesotans. AT LEFT is the 47-pounder caught by Richard H. Fudali, 1709 Innsbruck Parkway, Minneapolis. It was 53 inches long, 1½ inches longer than the world record. AT RIGHT is the 62-pounder caught by Florian Link, 1970 Norfolk, St. Paul. It was 1 lb. 2 oz. short of the world record trout caught in 1952 in Lake Superior which was 63 lbs. 2 oz. and 51½ inches long. Fudali used a National Expert spoon, while Link had a Half-Wave spoon. Link was fishing with John Zeiss of Wayzata who caught a 22½ pound Arctic char in the Tree River on a side trip from Great Bear Lake. (See Picture, also Editorial . . . Page 2)
—Photos Special to Outdoor News

These two lake trout taken by Minnesotans on Great Bear Lake in the Nortwest Territories fell just shy of the world record taken on Lake Superior in 1952, which tipped the scales at 63 pounds, 2 ounces.

Above: This 52-pound cat was originally thought to be a lynx, but turned out to be a bobcat. It was a new state record, and there was only one in the country that was larger, a 62-pounder from Michigan.

Inventor of Spin Cast Reel Dies

MANKATO, Minn. — Lloyd E. Johnson, 57, inventor of the Johnson spin cast fishing reel, died at his home in Mankato on Feb. 20. Funeral services and burial were held in Mankato on Feb. 24.

Shortly after World War II, Johnson teamed with his fishing partner, the late H. Warren Denison, to develop a then-revolutionary new fishing reel that was free of backlash.

1971 — For the first time in many hunters' memories, the DNR didn't hold a deer-hunting season in the state.

• The voting age was lowered to 18 years old, thanks to an amendment to the U.S. Constitution.

• The U.S. Supreme Court ruled that busing of students was legal in order to achieve racial desegregation.

• Notable musicians Jim Morrison, of The Doors, and Duane Allman, of the Allman Brothers, died at 27 and 24, respectively.

• The population of the U.S. was nearly 208 million, and the average life expectancy was slightly more than 71 years.

👉 JANUARY

• Cars and trucks were driving out on 12 to 16 inches of "blue ice" on lakes in Minnesota during the last week of 1970 and the first week of 1971, and the ice was "especially good for this time of year." But not everyone was pleased, including Fisheries Supervisor Hjalmar Swenson, who said: "Mille Lacs is covered with thrown-away eelpout (burbot or mezei) and I wish conservation officers would enforce this generally-not-known law."

• New DNR Commissioner Bob Herbst, selected by Gov.-elect Wendell Anderson, received a warm reception at the Department of Conservation (the name switched to Department of Natural Resources on Jan. 4, 1971). In an editorial, Jim Peterson wrote: "Except for acting commissioners – of which Herbst was one for a short term – Minnesota has never had a genuine trained, professional conservationist as a commissioner. And, we congratulate Gov.-elect Anderson for making an extremely wise choice to one of the state's most controversial jobs." A side note: The commissioner's job paid $23,000 per year. The 35-year-old began Jan. 4, 1971.

• Dissatisfaction with the state of Minnesota's deer herd began early. Here's part of a letter from Jan. 15: *"I've hunted deer in Minnesota for over 20 years and the population*

THE ALL NEW HONDA
ATC-90

[advertisement text] limited number of these sensational new All Terrain Cycles will be available for immediate delivery. The ATC-90 is a go-anywhere, do-anything kind of machine. It is equally at home on the trail, in the snow and in the sand. The ATC-90 has power to spare. It incorporates the proven Honda CT-90 engine, complete with automatic clutch, sub-transmission (8 speeds forward) and those big flotation tires make the ride velvet smooth while delivering the ultimate in traction.

From Mighty to Mini, Honda has it all.

Three-wheelers became a popular form of entertainment and utility for sportsmen, farmers, or just weekend warriors. Over time, the industry took a hit because they were accident prone, and people were getting hurt and even killed.

GORDY PETERSON of Elmer N. Olson Co., Minneapolis, shows the 34-pound Chinook salmon he caught in Lake Michigan near Muskegon, Mich. Peterson and his son Rick, 17, fishing with Jim Borgman of Muskegon, had 14 Chinook and coho salmon totaling over 300 pounds.
—Photo Special to Outdoor News

is the lowest I've ever seen on deer and the highest population of wolves. If we don't get a bounty system soon, there won't be enough deer left to feed the wolves."

• There were 4,301 fish houses on Mille Lacs in January. That's three times as many as any of the previous three winters. Four or five years ago, there were 5,000 fish houses on the lake.

MOOSE BILL TO SUB-COMMITTEE

Three bills, each of which would permit a season on moose hunting in Minnesota, have been turned over to a sub-committee after a full hour's hearing before the House Natural Resources Committee Tuesday.

Further hearings were not announced by chairman Bob Becklin.

COUGAR SEEN IN ITASCA PARK

This summer a cougar has been seen several times by students at the Itasca Park Biological Station along the road in the Peace Pipe Springs area, the Minnesota Department of Natural Resources said this week.

MILLE LACS GETS FOGHORN

Jack Maciosek, operator of Jack's Twin Bay Resort on Mille Lacs, has set up a warning system as a public service for fishermen in co-operation with the Mille Lacs County Sheriff's Department.

Maciosek has high-powered air horns which he will sound 3 times every 15 minutes for storms and 5 times every half hour for fog from Saturday, May 15, through July 15, daylight hours only.

Camp Ripley Record Set

Bow and arrow deer hunting at Camp Ripley was the best ever this year, according to the Minnesota Department of Natural Resources.

A total of 314 deer were taken during the season, the highest number recorded since the Camp was first opened to archery hunting in 1954.

The season ran from Oct. 16—Nov. 14.

• The Minnesota Archery Association planned to push the Legislature to classify black bears as game animals, rather than varmints to be destroyed at will. The DNR and many conservation groups support the position. Much of the opposition to the change is due to bear predation on sheep. A bill passed during the session, allowing for a hunting season to be set up for bears. The season ran Sept. 18 through Oct. 1, and licenses cost $5.

FEBRUARY

• State lawmakers who sit on the Game and Fish Committee heard a bill to permit a limited moose season in northern Minnesota.

• Milo Casey was named head of DNR Game and Fish Division. Donald Fultz was named director of the Division of Enforcement and Field Service.

• An 80-year-old Arkansas woman hunting in that state reported shooting a mallard raised by members of the Lyle, Minn., Future Farmers of America.

• The Northeast Chapter of the Northern Minnesota Sportsmen's Club passed resolutions to cancel deer and moose seasons for at least two years.

• A state senator, George Conzemius of Cannon Falls, proposed creation of a citizen's advisory commission to the DNR. He said it would be a good way for citizens to provide input to the agency.

MARCH

• Two dozen deer killed by dogs running loose in Jay Cooke State Park near Duluth drew the ire of columnist Kit Bergh, who wrote:

GRAND OPENING!
Newest & Most Complete Sporting Goods Store in the Twin Cities
SATURDAY & SUNDAY
(May 1) 9 a.m. to 9 p.m. each day (May 2)
Come In and Register for Dozens of Door Prizes!
Representatives will be on hand from tackle companies, Great Bear Lodge, etc.

SPECIAL!
17-Foot Standard
GRUMMAN CANOE
$255.00

GRAND OPENING DOOR PRIZE
8 DAY TRIP TO GREAT BEAR LODGE

SPECIAL!
Rod - Reel - Line
SPIN CAST OUTFIT
$6.69

SUPER SPECIAL PRICES
LOWRANCE FISH LO-K-TORS

VISIT OUR ULTRA-MODERN GUN DEPARTMENT
RIFLES - SHOTGUNS - SMITH & WESSON, COLT, RUGER PISTOLS - AMMUNITION

Complete Camping Equipment

We Feature Top Name Brands:
Scientific Anglers, Fenwick, Cortland, Heddon, Normark, Garcia, Daiwa, Gapen, Little Joe, Lindy, Rapala, Utica-Duxbak
Vexilar, Lowrance, Browning, Weatherby, Colt, Remington, Winchester, Woods Clothing, Comfy, Alpine Design, North Face, C. C. Filson

Complete Outdoor Clothing, Boots, Rain gear

We Have the Finest Trout Fishing Department in the Upper Midwest!

Burger Bros. Inc.
4402 FRANCE AVE. S., EDINA, MINN. 55410

Above: Burger Bros. Inc., started by Ted and Bud Burger, became the backbone of sporting goods in the Twin Cities and around the state. It morphed into a very large company, eventually being acquired by and absorbed into Gander Mountain stores.

—Outdoor News Photo by Jim Peterson

RARE BEAR—Taxidermist Marv Gaston, St. Louis Park, shows the rug he made out of a pure-white black bear. It is on display at the Sportsmen's Show in the Dave's Wilderness Camp booth. The bear, which is called an albino although it did not have pink eyes, was shot by John Vande Noord, proprietor of the camp near Perrault Falls, Ontario. "I wouldn't have shot it except that it was tearing up stuff and raiding our cabins —with people in them," Vande Noord said.

BOB HERBST, newly-appointed Minnesota conservation commissioner, will take office Feb. 1 with unusually-enthusiastic acceptance.

Leech Lake Muskie Derby: This photo shows 33 muskies caught out of Walker during one of the most epic muskie fishing days in the history of the lake on August 7, 1971. Northern pike and walleyes also are mixed into the photo.

"If sportsmen are angered by the killing done by timber wolves … how much more angered must they be that their own pets – fat, pampered, blooded, affectionate family dogs – kill not for food as their wild cousins most often do, but for the pleasure of killing?"

• The March 26 issue contained the Outdoor News legislative ballot, which included boxes where readers could check "yes" or "no" to signal their support or opposition to issues such as closing the deer season, and allowing timber wolf hunting only during the deer season. Outdoor News registered as a lobbyist and shared the results with lawmakers.

• The Lake Superior Steelhead Association formed. It initially had 112 members.

APRIL

• DNR Commissioner Bob Herbst announced closure of the 1971 firearms deer season. Had a season been held, it would have been two days or less. Throughout much of the state's deer range, there were 30 to 36 inches of snow on the ground as of April 2.

• Two, and perhaps three, of the keeper-sized muskies stocked into the St. Croix River were caught and released within days of being put into the river (April 27).

MAY

• For the third consecutive year, Loral I. Delaney was named captain of Jimmy Robinson's 1971 Sports Afield All-America Women's Trapshooting Team.

• Ontario Premier William Davis announced that the government had accepted two recommendations by the Quetico Park Advisory Committee that would stop logging in the massive provincial park.

JUNE

• A massive smelt die-off occurred in Lake Superior. It's the largest since appreciable numbers of the fish appeared in the lake. More than 500,000 dead smelt washed up on beaches within 10 miles of Duluth. A fungus was thought to have caused the die-off.

JULY

• In what Jim Peterson called the biggest rampage since 1955, anglers on Leech Lake had caught a total of 21 muskies in the opening days of the Muskie Derby Days tournament. A 34-pound, 9-ounce muskie won the derby.

• The DNR, at a cost of $726,000, acquired 15,000 acres of wildlife lands in 38 counties during the 12-month time period ending June 30.

During the first moose hunting season in Minnesota in 50 years, more than 80,000 applicants took a shot at the coveted tag for the following fall. Moose numbers have since dropped dramatically, and in 2012 the season closed.

80,000 Minnesotans Apply for 1,600 Moose Licenses

TIRED OF FIGHTING WIND AND WAVES WHILE TROLLING?

Hang the NEW TROLL-MASTER BOW RUDDER* on the side of your boat and experience complete directional boat control

■ Attaches to any boat and motor in 15 minutes ■ Easily removed ■ Increases maneuverability, makes steering easier ■ Tested and proven ■ Enjoy safer boating

Spring is here! Don't go through another fishing season of fighting the wind and waves on the lake. Up until now, your steering action has always been in the stern of your boat resulting in your being constantly blown off course while trolling at slow speeds. Now, with a Troll-Master Bow Rudder*, have complete control over both stern and bow with only slight motor steering action. Great

Please send me free information and prices on the Troll-Master Bow Rudder

Name
Address
City ___ State ___ Zip Code ___
Dealer inquiries invited

TROLL-MASTER Industries

Photo for Outdoor News by Jim's Bait, Duluth

OPENERS — Although they said the weather and snow along the banks made fishing "miserable," Ted Capra, left, of Minneapolis and Butch Furtman of Duluth caught their limits of two rainbow trout each, 3 to 4¼ pounds, from Wisconsin's Brule River last weekend. They used Steelie Puff lures. "There are lots of fish in the river and more are moving in so fishing should be good next weekend," Capra said.

AUGUST

• The DNR announced a 50-day duck season, but cut the season for Canada geese to nine days. Opening day of duck season was expected to be "fair to good to excellent, depending on the weather," Peterson wrote. In the end, the opener in many spots wasn't as good as expected. One of the reasons? Too many hunters.

SEPTEMBER

• The average grouse kill on opener weekend, according to Mike Casey, state director of game and fish, was about half a bird per man per day. "Our checks ran about the same both days of opening weekend," Casey said. "Too much foliage."

NOVEMBER

• The state's pheasant season opened on Oct. 30. There were fewer hunters afield, and Peterson summed up the situation like this: "Our best is Iowa's poorest, but it wasn't always that way." Game managers found hunters average about a half a bird apiece during the season's first two days.
• The state's muskie production program reached a high mark. A total of 19,675 muskies weighing 3,200 pounds were stocked in ponds and lakes.

DECEMBER

• A federal court decision, "which gives Indians the right to hunt and fish without regard to state game laws," had DNR officials concerned. Peterson wrote that "Leech Lake fishing may be doomed." The DNR asked for clarification of the ruling.

940 POUNDS — That was the field-dressed weight of this moose, taken near Middle River, Minn., by Roger Halvorson of Fergus Falls, Minn., (third from the left). The successful party included (l. to r.) Walter Bergrud of Fergus Falls, Dale Riggles of Cass Lake, Minn., Halvorson, and Harold Riggles of Cass Lake. The moose was weighed at Frank's Mill in Cass Lake.
—Photo Special to Outdoor News

TRAGEDY OF NATURE resulted in the death of these two walleyes last week at Mille Lacs. Jack Maciosek, operator of Jack's Twin Bay Resort, north of Isle, Minn., found the two fish dead along shore. He and Conservation Officer Jim Aker (who gave Maciosek a permit to pick up the fish) deduced that the fish were spawning, and the smaller male fish was bumping the female's side — as fish do to speed up the spawning process — and ran into the larger fish's open gill. The smaller fish got stuck and both died. The larger female fish was nearly 10 pounds, the male about 2 pounds.
—Photo Special to Outdoor News

1972 — Fierce blizzards book-marked the year, closing schools in the southwest in January, and halting New Year's activities and celebrations in December.

• The first Boston Marathon is held in which women officially are allowed to compete.

• The Watergate scandal began when police apprehended five men trying to bug the headquarters of the Democratic National Committee.

• Bobby Fischer defeated Boris Spassky in a chess match in Reykjavík, Iceland, becoming the first American world chess champion.

• The world population neared 3.9 billion people.

BUD BREEZE, conservation officer at Ortonville, Minn., shows two swans killed by a trio of Minneapolis hunters. "The boys thought they had scored on snow geese," said Dennis Vieman of the Ortonville Independent. "They were somewhat shocked to see the final results which ended with appearance in a local court and a fine."
—Photo by the Ortonville Independent

JANUARY

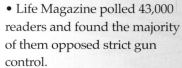

• A total of 5,470 fish houses were counted on Lake Mille Lacs on Saturday, Jan. 8, the highest number since the DNR began such surveys in 1952.

• Life Magazine polled 43,000 readers and found the majority of them opposed strict gun control.

• Outdoors News columnist Kit Bergh penned a column, after a court ruled Leech Lake tribal members could hunt and fish without regard to state game laws, that asked if Indians are game and fish hogs. He doubted it. Peterson, though, wondered what effects the court decision would have on the DNR, writing: "We sincerely believe that the Department of Natural Resources will be so much under attack that it may mean the end of it – and the end of nearly all conservation work in the state."

FEBRUARY

• DNR Commissioner Bob

TED CAPRA, fishing tackle expert from New Brighton, Minn., caught his limit of 15 crappies weighing a total of 29 lbs. 4 oz. from Woman Lake near Longville, Minn. The biggest was just over 2 pounds and all near that mark. He used Lindy jigs in shallow water, "dabbling" the lure with a cane pole.
—Photo for Outdoor News by Burger Bros.

Friday, March 31, 1972   Jim Peterson's OUTDOOR NEWS—PAGE

CRYSTAL MARINE'S SPECIALS
FOR THE
BOAT SHOW

Save $500 ON THE Family-Pack!

GLASTRON

SALE!
1972 17' GLASTRON
NEW JOHNSON 50 H.P.
$2288
3 Years to Pay

FREE!
SKI - PACKAGE

SPECIAL FACTORY PURCHASE
15' Lund 100 H.P. I.O.
$2795

HONDA HEADQUARTERS

FREE

FISHING BOAT SALE!
14 FT. LUND, 6 H.P. JOHNSON, TRAILER
$799
COMPLETE

COME SEE THE '72 HONDAS

SPECIAL FACTORY PURCHASE OF NEW
1971 KAYOT 20'
$1198

AMF ALCORT   SAILBOAT SALE!
SPECIAL FACTORY PURCHASE
NEW 1971 "MINIFISH"
Length .... 11 ft. 9 in.
Beam .... 3 ft. 10 in.
Sail Area .... 65 sq. ft.
Hull Weight .... 75 lbs.
$349

Open Monday thru Thursday 9 to 9; Friday 9-5:30; Saturday 9-5

CRYSTAL MARINE
WHERE QUALITY PRODUCTS AND THE FINEST SERVICE ASSURE SATISFACTION
2 Blocks No. of Bass Lake Road on Hwy. #52 — 533-1655

WITH A DRUGGED COYOTE under his arm, game biolog-ist Robert A. Chesness of Grand Rapids, Minn., h e a d s down a snowy trail in the Swatara area. He is working with radio-collared and ear-tagged brush wolves or coyotes in a five-year project to obtain basic ecological informa-tion about the animals.
—Photos by the Grand Rapids Herald

State Record Rainbow—16½ Lbs.

RECORD RAINBOW — Bernard Larsen of Grand Marais, Minn., caught this 16 lb. 8 oz. rainbow trout Oct. 9 in the Brule River (sometimes called the Arrowhead River) northeast of Grand Marais after a 4 1-4 hour battle. He hooked the fish on a nightcrawler at 12:15 p.m. and after breaking his rod and after sending to town for a net, the fish was landed at 4:30 p.m. It had a length of 34 inches and a girth of 19 inches and beat the former state record by 1 lb. 1 oz.

Photo by Humphrey in the Cook County News-Harald

Herbst announced he was appealing the decision of the court in the Leech Lake game and fish case. He did-n't ask for a stay in the case, but tribal officials promised "to abide by a conservation code of their own," and "police them-selves."

MARCH
• The Alexan-dria-based Viking Sports-men Club protested the May 27 bass opener, calling it too early. Club officials wanted the season delayed until June 17 or 24 – after the spawn was complete.
• 100,000 pounds of carp were removed from Buffalo Lake in one net haul.
• Viking Sportsmen Vice President May-nard Olson called carp the "sleeping death to fish-ing in Min-nesota, and nothing is being done about their control."

APRIL
• Roger Holmes was named the DNR supervisor

5,470 Houses Set Record at Mille Lacs

An aerial count of fishing shacks on Mille Lacs Saturday, Jan. 8, revealed the highest number since the surveys began in 1952, the Minnesota Depart-ment of Natural Resources reported this week.

A total of 5,470 fish houses were

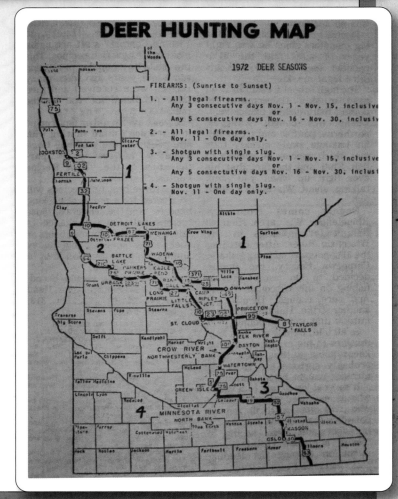

DEER HUNTING MAP

1972 DEER SEASONS

FIREARMS: (Sunrise to Sunset)

1. - All legal firearms.
   Any 3 consecutive days Nov. 1 - Nov. 15, inclusive
   or
   Any 5 consecutive days Nov. 16 - Nov. 30, inclusive

2. - All legal firearms.
   Nov. 11 - One day only.

3. - Shotgun with single slug.
   Any 3 consecutive days Nov. 1 - Nov. 15, inclusive
   or
   Any 5 consecutive days Nov. 16 - Nov. 30, inclusive

4. - Shotgun with single slug.
   Nov. 11 - One day only.

GO ONE BETTER . . . GO SKI DOO!

All Models In Stock!

The light-footed snowmobile that responds to hills, jumps, towing, racing, you name it.

PRICES START AT
$725.00

One-Week Delivery On All Models!

CROSSTOWN MARINE

6225 LYNDALE SO.   869-7585

Open 'Til 9 Every Evening; 9-5 on Saturday

'GREATEST CATCH' of northern pike in history could well be the title of this picture taken at Brabant Camp on the Mackenzie River in Northwest Territories, Canada. The fish averaged over 20 pounds each and represent only a small part of the number of 20 pounders caught and released by this group of Minnesotans. "We caught over a ton of northerns each and released everything except those shown which we filleted and took home," said Art Tourangeau of Crystal Bay, who arranged the trip. "None of the fish was wasted." Left to right are James Weinel, Wayzata; Tourangeau; Don Mensing, Cannon Falls; Carl Bergquist, Minnetonka; Robert Lampe, Northfield; Bill Tenney, Crystal Bay; John Hauschild, Minneapolis, and Harry Carlsen, Minneapolis. The group flew to Hay River, NWT, on a chartered plane piloted by Dick Morrison who took the picture as well as others shown here.
—Photo Special to Outdoor News

WORLD OF AVIATION

Sundays at 11:45 A.M.

"Flying fishing films, and aviation news in colors." Produced by Sherm Booen.

WCCO 4

Known as Mr. Walleye, Gary Roach — an Outdoor News contributor to this day — earned his stripes as an expert fisherman in the Brainerd Lakes region as one of the orignal members of the famed Nisswa Guides League. He was inducted into the Freshwater Fishing Hall of Fame in 1988.

GARY ROACH

of game.

• The price of a federal Duck Stamp increased by $2 to $5. The increase was the result of quickly increasing land prices.

JUNE

• The DNR announced that, for the first time in the state's history, all hunters who shot a deer during the firearms season would have to register the animal. Officials said the registration would give them more accurate harvest information.

• Unusually high water in the Alexandria area allowed carp to "run wild."

• Tentative agreement was reached on the three-year legal dispute over hunting, fishing, and ricing on the Leech Lake Reservation.

JULY

• After a closed pheasant season in 1969 and restricted zone hunting in 1970 and 1971, the entire state was open in 1972.

• The DNR also announced a new deer-hunting plan that allowed hunters several choices, depending on what part of the state they hunted.

• The Alexandria-based Viking Sportsmen called for a complete reorganization of the DNR after the agency announced the statewide pheasant season. The group said there weren't enough birds.

No, Mr. Spannaus, We Don't Want You to Take Guns Away From Indians, Or Whites!...Page 2

Biggest Reorganization of DNR
In 30 Years Announced by Herbst

Details of the first major reorganization of the Minnesota Department of Natural Resources in 33 years were announced Wednesday by Commissioner Robert Herbst at a press conference in St. Paul.

The new organization plan was proposed jointly by Herbst and the LEAP committee, who have been working closely with the Department of Administration, Civil Service Department and State Planning Agency. The LEAP committee was appointed by Gov. Wendell Anderson to effect greater efficiency in state government operations.

HEART OF the new organization is the decentralization of Department management supervision. Resource management respons-
(Continued on Page 5)

SEPTEMBER
• The duck-hunting season opened on a Sunday, breaking a tradition of opening on Saturdays, which had been in place for many years.

OCTOBER
• The DNR stocked more than 1,000 walleye fingerlings into the Mississippi River at Elk River and Monticello.
• Bernard Larsen of Grand Marais caught a 16-pound, 8-ounce rainbow trout in the Brule River. The fish beat the previous state record by more than a pound.

FIRST WINNER in the **Outdoor News-Normark** fish photo contest is this picture of Al Wegand of Kaukauna, Wis., with two rainbow trout from Lake Michigan near the outlet of a nuclear power plant. They weighed 16 lbs. 12 oz. and 8 lbs. 14 oz. and were caught on a No. 11S Rapala plug (a silver floater). The picture was taken by Phil Haas, 153 E. Third St., Kaukauna, Wis., 54130, who wins a Rapala Trophy Lure package and a Normark Presentation Fillet Knife worth a total of $20. The contest continues weekly through October. Fish must be caught on Rapala lures.

AT THE WINTER SPORTS SHOW SEE —
Why Johnson is more tha just another snowmobile.
The rotary engine.
Introducing Johnson's new Rotura™ rotary combustion engine... automotive power of the future. On Johnson snowmobiles today.
Up to 87½% quieter.
The 1973 Johnson Golden Ghost is up to 87½ percent quieter than most other snowmobiles. In fact, all new Johnsons meet or beat all Federal and state sound regulations. More important, they're pleasant to drive. And to be near.

Elmer N. Olson Co.
DOWNTOWN 500 S. 11th St. FE2-8931
ST. LOUIS PARK Hwy. 7 at Wooddale 929-7833

NOVEMBER
• Wildlife officials predicted new deer regulations would reduce the kill to fewer than 50,000 deer.

DECEMBER
• DNR Commissioner Bob Herbst announced the first major reorganization of the DNR in 30 years. One of the main parts of the reorganization was the creation of six regions and regional directors who oversaw all resource management in their region.

LAZY IKE

TRY ONE...
IT CATCHES FISH

fisherman all over the U.S. have proved it . . . with bass, trout, walleye, northern, salmon and panfish . . . 7 sizes . . . 24 colors . . . millions in use. Try one!

SPECIAL $2.00 OFFER
Patch - Fishing Handbook - Lure

Send for all three plus fishing contest and special award details. Just $2.00.

LAZY IKE

FORT DODGE, IOWA 50501

1973 — Following the signing of a ceasefire, U.S. ground troops no longer were involved in the Vietnam War.

• *President Richard Nixon went on national television to accept responsibility, but not blame, for the Watergate scandal.*

• *The U.S. Supreme Court ruled on the Roe v. Wade case, which legalized abortion in the first trimester of pregnancy.*

• *American thoroughbred racehorse Secretariat became the first U.S. Triple Crown winner in 25 years. The horse set records in all three races — the Kentucky Derby, Preakness Stakes, and Belmont Stakes.*

• *Median household income: $10,512.*

HERE IS the string of bass taken by Ted Capra and Al Lindner from Lake Johanna, the **Outdoor News** Lake of the Week. (see story).
—Photo for Outdoor News by Lindy's, Brainerd, Minn.

 JANUARY

• Outdoor News published a dozen pictures of speared – harpooned, in the parlance of the time – northern pike. In his editorial, Jim Peterson explained his opposition to spearing, and why the paper didn't typically publish pictures of speared fish: *"Besides being legally classed as non-sporting under federal tax laws, spearing is wrong for many other reasons. Among them are the use of 1,000-pound-test harpoons and ropes on fish which do not have to bite to be killed, jabbed in the back at a range of three feet or slightly more. Wounded fish are impossible to recover – and about 90 percent which shake off a spear die. Many hundreds of muskies, bass, and walleyes are speared illegally by those who jab first and see what they got next."*

• A federal district court in Duluth ruled that mineral mining and exploration would not be permissable in the Boundary Waters Canoe Area Wilderness.

FEBRUARY

• The DNR received $1,000 for wetland acquisition from W.J. McCabe, Jr., of Duluth. The contribution marked the largest the state ever had received to buy wetlands.

MARCH

• A legislative hearing was set for the so-called Leech Lake Indian "deal," which would give tribal members nearly unlimited game and fish rights in the Leech Lake

Polar Bear, Walrus Hunting Banned by U.S.

WASHINGTON, D.C. — With polar bear and walrus hunting in Alaska ended Dec. 21, as the Marine Mammal Protection Act of 1972 became law, the U.S. Fish and Wildlife Service announced that it does not expect to grant any exceptions under the "undue economic hardship" clause.

Congress Nears Total Ban on Wolves

By LEN LIBBEY

The U.S. Congress has all but closed the door on hunting or trapping of timber wolves, except for scientific and management purposes.

On Sept. 18, the House of Representatives passed H.R. 37, "The Endangered and Threatened Species Conservation Act of 1973," which prohibits the taking of any form of fish or wildlife in danger of, or threatened with, extinction—according to a federal Department of the Interior list.

THE EASTERN Timber Wolf is considered by the federal agency to be in danger of extinction, even though wolf researchers and the Minnesota Department of Natural Resources feel otherwise. Minnesota has the largest population of timber wolves of any state except Alaska.

H.R. 37 passed the House by an overwhelming vote: 390 to 12. A similar bill, S. 1983, passed the Senate on July 24.

BOTH BILLS now go to a Joint Conference Committee, which must iron out differences between them. The conference committee has not yet acted, but a final vote by the House and

(Continued on Page 3)

HEADLINES

Couple Nabbed for Gill-Netting

An Illinois couple, arrested by state conservation officers during the Memorial Day weekend, have been convicted of charges involving the wholesale taking of fish from a Crow Wing County lake.

Marvin and Dixie Williams of Peoria, Ill., were apprehended after officers conducted an all night "stake out" of the couple's camp on remote Stewart Lake.

Officers made the arrest on the morning of May 30 after observing the two remove 600 feet of gill net and 1,000 feet of trot or set lines from the lake. The net and the trot lines were confiscated along with numerous fish, including several 9-pound walleyes.

The pair were fined a total of $300.

Unity, 'Common Voice' Urged

By LEN LIBBEY

A call for unity and a warning against the growing anti-hunting movement were highlights of the Minnesota Game Protective League members adopted four main resolutions at a general meeting in the afternoon. They

'Trophy Buck' Season Asked for Minnesota

From the Grand Rapids Review

GRAND RAPIDS, Minn. — A trophy buck season will be proposed to the state legislature this week, secretary James Carter of the Northern Minnesota Sportsmen's club said Tuesday.

Carter's proposal would authorize the commissioner of the Department of Natural Resources to designate, at his discretion, a trophy buck season, annually, as an alternate choice

Irate Moose Attacks, Hurts Grouse Hunter

From the Thief River Falls Times

THIEF RIVER FALLS, Minn.— Mark Liden, son of Mr. and Mrs Kenton Liden of Thief River Falls, was nursing a headache and bruises after being attacked by a cow moose while hunting grouse.

SOME MORE HARPOONED FISH IN MINNESOTA THIS SEASON

HERE ARE A FEW of the big northern pike which have been harpooned in Minnesota, most of them in the first two weeks of the season which opened Dec. 1 and runs through Feb. 15 for residents only. All but three of the fish pictured in this issue were from 20 to 30 pounds each. The largest was 30 lbs. 1 oz. These pictures were published in a few local papers which accept pictures of harpooned fish. Many, like **Outdoor News**, do not. (See Editorials, Page Two).

Friday, Jan. 5, 1973   Jim Peterson's OUTDOOR NEWS—PAGE 3

area and elsewhere, and would charge state hunters and anglers as much as 50 percent more for their hunting and fishing licenses.

• A gun control bill from State Attorney General Warren Spannaus was introduced in the Legislature. The bill would require all handguns to be registered, and require all gun owners to get a permit from the commissioner of public safety, who would need to approve the permit application.

• A U.S. district court judge dismissed a lawsuit from the Humane Society of the United States that would have stopped hunting on three federal wildlife areas.

• In an Outdoor News Legislative Ballot, which included 1,000 responses, 98 percent opposed Spannaus' gun bill. Just more than 2 percent of respondents were in favor of it.

• The 13th and 14th issues of Outdoor News – published during the annual Northwest Boat, Sports and Travel Show – were 24 pages apiece, marking the largest in Outdoor News' history.

▲ OUTDOOR NEWS Supported a campaign to have sportsmen vote for any other candidate than Spannaus because of his anti-gun stance.

Pictures of Gov. Wendell Anderson hoisting fish became nationally renown when he hoisted a northern pike for a Time magazine cover. Here he has a small walleye but a big smile.

Biggest Bear . . .

LARGEST BEAR reported so far this season was shot by Lou Marturano of Burnsville, Minn. near Cook, Minn. It weighed 420 lbs. field dressed. The hide is being made into a rug by taxidermist Marv Gaston.
—Photo for Outdoor News by Marv Gaston

APRIL
• Attorney General Warren Spannaus' gun registration bill was voted down in the House by a vote of 76 to 57.

MAY
• Joe Fellegy wrote for the first time in Outdoor News. The headline was "Mille Lacs Study: Fish Are There." Fellegy would become a full-time columnist for the paper in the late 1990s.

JUNE
• A massive, 51-pound, 1-ounce muskie was the third-largest ever caught in Minnesota waters, and the second-largest caught in the state's inland wa-

A SPOTTED BUCK, weighing about 90 pounds, was taken by Lerry Serreym, Pipestone, Minn., from South of Deer Lake, Minn. The deer had large white markings on the head, neck and flank.
—Photo from the Grand Rapids Review

ters.

• State conservation officers arrested an Illinois couple after watching them remove 600 feet of gill net and 1,000 feet of trot lines from Stewart Lake in Crow Wing County. The couple was convicted and fined $300.

JULY
• The DNR set an 18-day, bucks-only deer-hunting zone in east-central Minnesota.

OCTOBER
• The U.S. House passed "The Endangered and Threatened Species Conservation Act of 1973" in September. It was similar to a Senate bill passed earlier in the year and

Fishing Hall of Fame Plans Set

An artist's rendering depicts the grounds of the Hayward, Wis.-based National Freshwater Fishing Hall of Fame, an international headquarters for education, recognition, and promotion of fresh water sportfishing. The 143-foot muskie highlights the six-acre grounds and facilities, which were constructed in 1976.

Outdoor News-Normark Photo Contest Weekly Prize

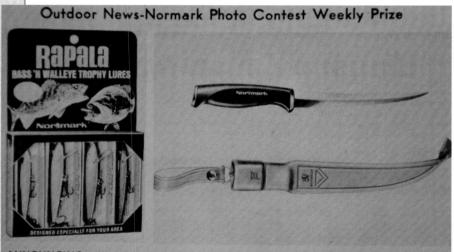

ANNOUNCING — the second annual **Outdoor News-Normark** photo contest for pictures of fish caught on Rapala Lures, starting immediately. Rules of the contest are the same as last year: pictures must be suitable for reproduction in **Outdoor News**; the fish must be caught on Rapala lures during the 1973 season and all pictures winning weekly prizes become the property of Normark Corp. Non-winning pictures will be returned if a self-addressed stamped envelope is included with the entry. Pictures may be taken with any camera — including Polaroids — and must be at least "snapshot" size. Color prints may be accepted but not color transparencies. Each weekly winner will receive a Rapala Trophy Lure Package, containing four Rapala plugs, plus a Normark Presentation Fillet Knife. The prize, shown above, is worth a total of $20. The contest runs through October. That's 25 weeks for a total value of $500. Send picture to **Photo Contest, Outdoor News, Box 27145, Golden Valley, Minn. 55427.**

▲ The Outdoor News and Rapala (then Normark) photo contest has been ongoing in the newspaper for more than four decades, and today continues in all Outdoor News Publications across seven states.

would close the door to hunting and trapping of timber wolves.

• Charles Burrows, who joined the DNR in 1947, was named fisheries supervisor. He replaced Hjalmer Swenson, who served in the position for more than 25 years.

NOVEMBER

• Jerry Liemandt took over as the state's chief game warden.

• Bills were moving through the state House and Senate to require hunters and trappers to wear blaze orange while afield.

DECEMBER

• The DNR reported that its request for $707,000 in federal aid had been approved for a fish hatching and rearing facility at French River near Duluth.

CHARGED by this 600-pound black bear after it was wounded by an arrow, Tom Lane ot Elk River, Minn., was "rescued" by guide Bob Himes of Ray, Minn., who killed the roaring beast with a rifle from 15 feet away. "Bob tracked this animal for a good 1½ miles," Lane said. "The big brute let us get within 30 yards and then came for us with a roar."

— Photo Special to Outdoor News

1974 — President Richard Nixon, in the wake of the Watergate scandal, became the first U.S. president to resign the post. Gerald Ford took his place and became the nation's 38th president.

• The Symbionese Liberation Army kidnapped 19-year-old Patricia Hearst, the granddaughter of publisher William Randolph Hearst.

• Hank Aaron became the all-time MLB home run leader with his 715th long ball. He broke Babe Ruth's record in Atlanta vs. the L.A. Dodgers.

• Miami defeated the Minnesota Vikings in the Super Bowl by a score of 24-7.

• "People Magazine" debuted. Mia Farrow was on the magazine's cover.

• India successfully tested an atomic device and became the sixth nuclear power in the world.

• The population of the U.S. grew to nearly 214 million people, and the average life expectancy increased to 72 years old.

FEBRUARY

• Bills introduced in the Legislature would have made it illegal for fishermen to use electronic depthfinders in the taking of fish, and for guides to fish while taking out clients. In an editorial, Jim Peterson said the bills directly targeted the Nisswa Guides League. "Local people are jealous of the Nisswa guides because they can't catch fish like the 'pros' do."

MARCH

• The DNR, for the first time, implied in legislation that wolves were correctly identified as endangered. The listing would give the animals federal protection.
• The House Natural Resources Committee approved a bill to ban lead shot while waterfowl hunting.

APRIL

• The DNR announced results of a

7 Lb. Bullhead State Record

By the Minnesota DNR

It wasn't a walleye or a lake trout but it was a new state record.

The largest brown bullhead on Minnesota record was taken on May 21, the Department of Natural Resources reported this week.

Fritz Johnson, fisheries biologist, who identified and weighed the fish said the 7 lb. 1 oz. specimen was caught in Shallow Lake in Itasca County by William Meyer of Holland, Iowa, who was vacationing in the area.

59 Arrested for Improper Leech License

Minnesota conservation officers and Indian game wardens arrested 59 anglers on the Leech Lake Reservation during the opening weekend of the fishing season for failure to have the proper fishing license, the Department of Natural Resources has reported.

Total Ban on Wolves Now Is In Effect

Starting Aug. 1, new regulations controlling the taking of timber wolves went into effect in Minnesota.

The Department of Natural Resources said the regulations will apply on an interim basis pending the development and approval of a cooperative agreement on endangered species with the U.S. Secretary of Interior.

THE NEW regulations result from a law passed at the last legislative session which amended the existing state statutes to comply with the federal Endangered Species Act of 1973.

Bill Advances to Ban Lead Shot

By LEN LIBBEY

Minnesota gunners would be required to use steel shot by July 1, 1975, if a bill that passed the House Natural Resources Committee becomes law.

H.F. 2143, banning lead shot for waterfowl hunting, is authored by

Rep. Glen Sherwood (DFL-Pine River). Sherwood's bill is presently in the House Rules Committee, where it will probably remain until the session ends unless its Senate companion measure gets a hearing and

Outdoor News Moves Into New Offices

This week Outdoor News is moving into our brand new editorial-advertising offices. We know we will be able to serve you better from our new quarters, and we will continue to strive for the highest possible quality in, we think, the best outdoor publication in the North Central States — if not the world.

Our new address is:
Outdoor News, Inc.
3410 Winnetka Ave. N.
Minneapolis, Minn. 55427

We also have a new phone number, and we regret any confusion this may cause at first. Our new number is:

546-4251

We hope to complete the move by the end of this week.

For our regular advertisers and subscribers, our mailing address for all correspondence remains the same: Outdoor News, Inc., Box 27145, Golden Valley, Minn. 55427. And, our mailing service remains the same: Central Mailing Service, 535 North Fourth Street, Minneapolis; Phone 335-3139.

Huge Rack Likely New State Bow Record

ORTONVILLE, Minn. — An 18-point whitetail deer, killed with bow and arrow in the Odessa, Minn., area Nov. 26, is expected to be a new Minnesota archery record when official measurements are taken after the required 60-day drying period for the antlers, the Ortonville Independent reported.

Steve Karels, 35-year-old Long Lake, Minn., house painter and a former resident of Rosen, Minn., 10 miles south of Ortonville, bagged the deer in the Minnesota River bottoms near Odessa.

THE ANTLERS were measured last week by Douglas West of the U.S. Fish and Wildlife Service, Fort Snelling, who is an official Pope and Young bow hunting record book scorer. They scored 207.4 which is considerably above the current record of 198. However, the official scoring cannot be done until after the required waiting period.

The world record for non-typical whitetails is 279 points.

KARELS was tracking a deer out of the cover of some woods and into an area of knee-high grass when he spotted a movement in a nearby swampy area. Out stepped the largest deer he had ever seen followed by a doe, he told the Independent reporter.

Since he was standing out in the open, Karels dropped to his knees and tried to hide behind his bow, the only cover available. The deer walked straight toward him from 55 yards away. Steve managed to pull an arrow from his quiver, and, when the deer moved within 35 yards, about five minutes later, he released his arrow.

The deer spun, ran for 40 yards and toppled over.

three-year study of stocking pheasants. The study showed stocking was not an effective means of restoring pheasant populations.

• Outdoor News first began publishing "Actiongraphs" on the front page of the paper. The graphs aimed to help hunters and anglers determine when game and fish were most active. The graphs moved to the inside of the paper later in the year.

MAY

• Anti-hunters won a "major victory" when the state Legislature approved a bill classifying timber wolves as endangered.

JUNE

• A 7-pound, 1-ounce brown bullhead that measured more than 24 inches in length was recognized as a state record. An Iowa angler caught the fish in Itasca County's Shallow Lake.

• The first Chinook salmon were stocked into the Baptism, Cascade, and French rivers, which are tributaries to Lake Superior. A total of 200,000 salmon were released.

JULY

• Outdoor News moved to a new office on Winnetka Avenue in New Hope.

• The U.S. Fish and Wildlife Service announced it would pub-

PHOTO CONTEST WINNER

14 Lb. LARGEMOUTH BASS was taken on Lake Griffin in Florida two weeks ago by Donald Witte, 1049 Pleasant, St. Paul, Minn. 55102. It was caught on a Rapala plug and wins this week's **Outdoor News-Normark** Fish Photo Contest. He was also a winner in last year's contest and says that Rapalas work just as well in Florida as they do here.

Pair Fined $1,000 for Killing, Then Leaving 4 Moose

From the Twin Valley Times

Two men pleaded guilty in Norman County District Court at Ada, Minn., recently to charges of illegally shooting four moose last November.

Donald Chaika, 42, Fessenden, N.D., formerly of Ogema, Minn., was fined $700 and placed on unsupervised probation for one year. Terry Sullivan, 29, White Earth, Minn., was fined $300; no probation was ordered for him.

Chaika and Sullivan pleaded guilty to complaints charging each of them with two counts of illegally shooting moose Nov. 4, 1973 in the Syre, Minn., area. The charges are gross misdemeanors.

WARNING SIGNS at the entrances to Leech Lake Indian Reservation will be placed before the start of the fishing season. (See Story).

—Photo special to Outdoor News

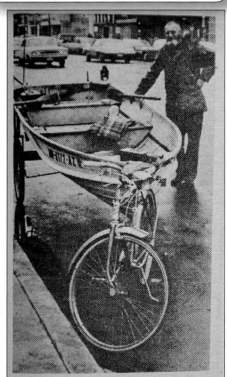

BEATING THE PROBLEMS of air pollution and fuel prices, fightng inflation, and getting some exercise is Wayne Muth of International Falls, Minn., with his boat-bike rig for nearby fishing. Using a trailer hitch on the bike and old bike wheels clamped to the boat, he says the whole rig-excluding the boat and bike-cost $8.47.

lish in the Federal Register a proposal to ban lead shot for waterfowl hunting throughout much of the United States.

AUGUST

• Timber wolves, just added to the Endangered Species list, became illegal to hunt or trap.

SEPTEMBER

• Federal Cartridge Corporation announced it would sell steel shot for use in the Tamarac National Wildlife Refuge in 1974. The U.S. Fish and Wildlife Service previously said duck hunters in that refuge had to use

ONE FOR THE WALL caught by Harry Fankhanel of Minneapolis from the Yellowstone River south of Livingston, Mont. The 14 lb. 14 oz. brown trout is the largest of 300 fish to be mounted on the Fishermen's Wall of Fame in a local fly Shop. (See Editorials, Page 2.)

—Photo special to Outdoor News

LARGEST WALLEYE EVER CAUGHT?

WAS THIS THE SIZE of fish caught in the Battle Lake, Minn., area in earlier days? Sander Swanson, Battle Lake druggist at the time and photography buff, printed the above picture.
—Photo from the Battle Lake Review

Thanks to modern digital photography, Outdoor News occasionally receives altered and sometimes humorous images from readers. This one, which Publisher Jim Peterson reprinted in 1974, clearly pre-dated the Photoshop era!

steel shot during that season.

NOVEMBER

• The DNR announced that ice fishermen, except those on designated trout lakes, would be able to fish with two lines.

DECEMBER

• A man hunting near Odessa – Steve Karels of Long Lake – killed an 18-point buck that was likely to become a new state record for deer taken via bow and arrow.

LAURI RAPALA, creator of famous Rapala lures, of Riihilahti, Finland, passed away Oct. 20 at the age of 68. His lures were invented out of necessity during the hard, lean years of the 1930s to put food on the table for his family, and have now become the world's largest selling fishing plug. He had been semi-retired the last few years, spending his time on development of new lures and fishing Atlantic salmon in Lapland.
—Photo Special to Outdoor News

Two-Line Law Now In Effect for Ice Anglers

Minnesota anglers may use two lines for ice fishing this winter and do not have to wait until Jan. 1, 1975, the Department of Natural Resources has reported.

In its announcement of the 1975 fishing regulations, the DNR's news release indicated that two line ice fishing would not be allowed until Jan. 1, 1975.

A spokesman said this is an error, since the law authorizing two line ice fishing was passed at the last legislative session and took effect at once.

Bill Would Curtail Electronic Depth Finders

WEEK'S SNOW DEPTH REPORT

Here are this week's snow depths as reported from around Minnesota by the U.S. Weather Bureau and other sources for use by snowmobilers, ice fishermen, cross country skiers and other outdoorsmen as of Outdoor News' press time:

Aitkin ....36 inches
Alexandria ....40 inches
Duluth.............32 inches
Hibbing ....40 inches
Twin Cities ....18 inches
Hayward, Wis......26 inches

DEPTH SOUNDER BILL LAID OVER

Two bills which would have established minimum size limits on fish, and one which would have made a Saturday opening on duck hunting mandatory, were killed by the Minnesota legislature Monday.

A bill to outlaw graph-type electronic depth sounders was laid over until next Tuesday, April 3, when Rep. Glen Sherwood, the bill's author, was snowbound.

TIP-UPS STILL ARE ILLEGAL

Minnesota ice fishermen may use two lines, but tip-ups are still illegal.

State Fisheries Director Chuck Burrows said tip-ups are specifically prohibited in the Game and Fish Code.

Another provision in the law also prevents the use of tip-ups, he added. It states that an angler's line must be visible to him at all times.

Burrows said that the Department of Natural Resources would look into the possibility of legalizing tip-ups for ice fishing if no enforcement problems arising from the two-line fishing are experienced.

1975 — Some of the worst recorded blizzards and storms struck the state in January, killing multiple people and closing some roads for more than 10 days.

- *The Vietnam War ended on April 30.*
- *President Gerald Ford survived two assassination attempts in a span of 17 days.*
- *The Pittsburgh Steelers defeated the Minnesota Vikings in the Super Bowl by a score of 16-6.*
- *Saturday Night Live premiered on NBC. George Carlin hosted the first show.*
- *The world's first homemade videotape systems — VCRs — were developed in Japan.*
- *A severe winter storm in November sank the Edmund Fitzgerald ship on Lake Superior.*

JANUARY

- Muskies, Inc. reported releasing a total of 7,012 muskies into Minnesota lakes during the fall of 1974. The vast majority of those fish – 5,132 – went into Lake Minnetonka.
- A blizzard called the worst of the century hit, and officials feared it may have wiped out pheasant populations and severely hurt deer, ruffed grouse, song birds and fish. Jim Peterson, in an editorial, wrote: "The future of Minnesota hunting is at its lowest point in history following last weekend's killer blizzard."
- Drainage continued to be a hot topic in the state. Farmers and drainage proponents said acquiring drainage permits was dif-

53-POUND LAKE TROUT was caught from Great Bear Lake in the Northwest Territory by Jim Buckles of Davenport, Iowa, who recently returned from fishing the lake with a group of Minnesota fishermen. Helping him lift the trophy is his Indian guide. —Photo from the Ortonville Independent

FIRST MUSKIE FROM MILLE LACS

11-LB., 36-INCH MUSKIE, first reported of legal size from Mille Lacs was caught in Isle Bay by Bruce Paulsen of Isle, Minn. Jack Maciosek of Jack's Twin Bay Resort comments that "I figure that this must be one from the first planting in 1969. We have another collection for muskie planting this year, and anyone interested could send donations to: Muskie Fund, Jack's Twin Bay Resort, Isle, Minn. 56342. I would like to encourage the fishermen not to take these fish even though they are of legal size so they have a chance to reproduce." —Photo from the Mille Lacs Messenger

CRAPPIES WERE BITING on Gull Lake for Lee Rudsenske (left) and Jeff Zernov, members of Al Linder's "In' Fisherman" staff. This limit of "slabs" was taken on 1/16 oz. "Teeny Twisters."
— Photo special to Outdoor News

SHOWING 22 ILLEGALLY SPEARED northerns taken from Wright County is Consevation Officer Pat McGuire of Buffalo, Minn. Six persons were caught in the act of spearing these northerns by conservation officers recently. Five of them were fined $300 plus 90 days in jail with $100 and the jail term suspended on the condition that they had no game fish violations within one year in Minnesota. One man pleaded not guilty. McGuire said that each of the northerns shown represented a potential 1500 fish. (See "Letters," page 2).
— Photo from the Wright Co. Journal-Press

ficult or impossible, and asked that approval of drainage projects be taken out of the DNR's hands.

Alaska to Use Planes to Thin Down Wolves

Special to Outdoor News

FAIRBANKS, Alaska — Beginning in late February, the Alaska Department of Fish and Game plans to remove a substantial number of wolves from an area south of Fairbanks.

FEBRUARY

• A bill that would virtually end trapping was introduced at the state Legislature. The bill, called the Humane Trapping Bill, would have outlawed any trap unless it "painlessly captured" or "instantly killed" the animal.

MARCH

• DNR officials, concerned about the winter's effect on pheasants' ability to find food, asked sportsmen's clubs to conduct artificial feeding in areas where pheasants were experiencing problems.
• Deer that were struggling with winter conditions also had something else to be wary of: dogs. The DNR reported dogs don't chase and kill deer for food. Instead, they do it for sport.
• Aerial surveys in the northwestern part of the state confirmed that moose populations there continued to rise. The estimate for northwest Minnesota was 3,540 moose, up from 2,760 the year before.

APRIL

• Voyageurs National Park officially was designated as the nation's 36th national park. The legislation that created the park was approved in 1971.

JIM L. PETERSON, left, assistant editor of OUTDOOR NEWS, won the Press Division of the Fish-O-Rama Crappie Tournament at Lake Minnetonka last Saturday (May 3) with an 8-ounce catch. W. O. Herbst of the sponsoring Johnson Reel Co., right, presented him with a check for $100, while Doc Wellman, co-director of the tourney, looked on. (See Editorials).
— Outdoor News Photo by Jim Peterson

Jim Peterson's Outdoor News
The Sportsman's Weekly

Published weekly by Jim Peterson's Outdoor News, Inc., at 3410 Winnetka Avenue N., Minneapolis, Minn. 55427. Second Class postage paid at Minneapolis, Minn. 55401.

PHONE: 546-4251
AREA CODE: 612

Mail all correspondence and address changes to:

OUTDOOR NEWS
P.O. BOX 27145
GOLDEN VALLEY, MINN.
55427

Editor and Publisher.... Jim Peterson
Assistant Editor...... Jim L. Peterson
Columnists......... Gary Bennyhoff
Kit Bergh
F.N. Cosgrove
Fred Daugs
John Henricksson
Steve Henry
Jack Hoene
Rae Oetting
Gerry Peterson
Jimmy Robinson
Lynn Schultz

ASSOCIATE FOUNDER
AGLOW
ACTIVE MEMBER
ACTIVE MEMBER

Copyright © Jim Peterson's Outdoor News, Incorporated, 1975

▲
The masthead above listed the staff and columnists working on the Outdoor News weekly newspaper in 1975. The names have changed many times over the years, and the 2014 version lists 26 staffers working to publish the Minnesota edition.

MAY
• Jim Peterson's son, Jim L. Peterson, appeared on the masthead as assistant editor.
• Fishermen and writer Ted Capra relayed a story in which he and his son, Dean, were fishing on Eagle Lake in Canada when their boat took on water and began sinking. The two were wearing heavy clothes and didn't have life jackets on board. Capra's message: Wear a life jacket under your foul-weather gear.
• A bill that would have put a one-year moratorium on the use of graph-type depthfinders died at the Legislature.

JUNE
• Al Lindner won two consecutive walleye tournaments. The first was on the St. Croix River while fishing with his brother, Ron. The next weekend, Al Lindner won on Lake Mille Lacs.

AUGUST
• Controversy about the Boundary Waters Canoe Area Wilderness raged. The question: Should the state enact a law outlawing logging and related activities in the BWCA?

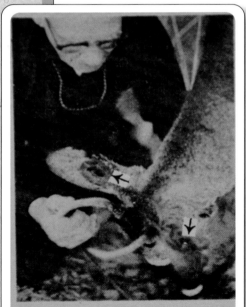
NO BULLET HOLES could be found on the body or head of the deer shot by Bill Huntley near Markville, Minn. Here is a closeup showing the two holes in the deer's ears. (See Editorials at Left).
—Outdoor News Photo by Jim Peterson

DECOY COLLECTING is a most interesting (and possibly lucrative) hobby for John "Super Swede" Lindgren, left, of Minneapolis who showed part of his collection to members of the Fur, Fin and Feather Club last week at their meeting at the Elks Club, Golden Valley. At right is Ken Burglund, club president. The decoys they are holding are worth $750 each, while the pair of Canadian honkers in the background is worth more than $3,500. Lindgren said he never sells decoys but trades them with other collectors. He has more than 3,000 decoys which, plus "some of my guns", are insured for $80,000.
—Outdoor News Photo by Jim Peterson

—Outdoor News Photo by Jim Peterson

ENSIO RAPALA, left, from Finland, tackle company executive and son of the late Lauri Rapala who invented the famed fishing lure, and Erkki Norell, also of the Rapala firm, visited Minneapolis last week for the Normark Corp. sales meetings. Below, Ensio Rapala shows a 45-pound Atlantic salmon he caught recently on the Teno River on the border between Finland and Norway. He used a No. 9 jointed gold Rapala plug.

NORTHERN weighing 23 pounds was caught recently from Mille Lacs Lake by Dick Gripp of Minneapolis. The 45 inch fish had swallowed a perch that had taken his minnow first; he had to squeeze the northern through the hole in his fish house.

—Photo special to Outdoor News

OCTOBER

• The DNR sought hunters for pilot "hunter education courses." The DNR planned to expand the program if the pilot courses were successful.

• The DNR received 400,000 chinook salmon eggs for the second round of salmon stocking in state waters.

NOVEMBER

• A hunter failed in his attempt to outrun a bear. The animal caught up to the man and clawed him, but his hunting companion killed the bear, which stood more than 6 feet, 7 inches tall, with one shot.

• DNR officials expressed concern about Iowa's stocking of grass carp. They said it posed a threat to Minnesota's lakes, streams, and tourist industry.

DECEMBER

• A U.S. House subcommittee passed a bill to increase the cost for firearms dealers to gain federal licenses. Licenses would increase from $10 a year to $250 a year for dealers who sold only rifles and shotguns. Those who sold handguns would have to pay another $200.

Outdoor News printed this photo of an 18-pound northern pike that "drowned" as a result of getting a 1-pound eelpout lodged in its gills.

Mille Lacs '76 Yield: 2½ Tons Per Day

Mille Lacs Lake has been yielding an average of 2½ tons of walleyes per day this season, according to a Minnesota Department of Natural Resources creel census, Outdoor News learned Tuesday.

The census, conducted May 15 through July 31 by Dennis Schupp, biologist from the DNR's Brainerd, Minn., office, also showed that the fish averaged 2.35 pounds each.

"The yield amounts to about 3 pounds per acre," commented Dick Sternberg of the St. Paul DNR office. "That, plus the unusual size of the fish, is almost unbelievable for such a short time. Most good walleye lakes have a yield of 3 pounds per acre for the entire year."

 JANUARY

• The state issued 750 moose-hunting licenses last fall for the northwest and northeast zones. Hunters killed 676 moose, for a success rate of 90 percent.

• The number of people who died on Minnesota waters dropped from 123 in 1974 to 110 in 1975. DNR officials say greater awareness of water safety may have led to the decline.

• A timber wolf recovery plan aimed for a statewide population of 1,500 wolves.

1976 — The nation celebrated its bicentennial.

• *Jimmy Carter was elected as the president of the United States.*

• *The U.S. Supreme Court ruled the death penalty was an acceptable form of punishment.*

• *A mysterious disease – later called Legionnaire's Disease – struck more than 180 people at an American Legion convention; 29 died.*

• *For the third consecutive year, the world population was higher than 4 billion people. The population was 4.16 billion. The U.S. population was 218 million.*

• *The median household income in the United States. was $12,686. The rate of unemployment was 7.7 percent.*

State Water Death Toll Shows Decline

Minnesota's water death toll has dropped significantly over the past year, according to Kim Elverum, Boat and Water Safety coordinator for the Minnesota Department of Natural Resources.

According to preliminary statistics, 110 persons lost their lives on and in Minnesota's waters in 1975, as compared to 123 in 1974. The total is broken down as follows:

• 56 lost their lives in boating-related mishaps with capsizing and falling overboard being the two biggest causes of death in this category;

• 35 died in swimming or wading accidents where overestimation of ability or lack of youngster supervision were the leading factors;

• 13 persons drowned as a result of falling into the water unexpectedly. Most victims in this category were very young or elderly;

• 6 died as a result of falling through thin ice. All of these deaths occurred during December.

Elverum said that the drop in water related deaths this past year may be due in part to an increased awareness of water safety by the public.

JIMMY ROBINSON, right, dean of Minnesota's outdoor writers, was honored as the Conservation Editorialist of the Year. Ron Schara of the Minneapolis Tribune made the presentation.

Proposed License Increases

	Proposed fee change	Amount of proposed fee increase
Resident fishing	$ 4.00-$5.00	$ 1.00
Resident combination fishing	6.00- 8.00	2.00
Resident spearing	3.00- 5.00	2.00
Nonresident individual fishing	6.50-10.00	3.50
Nonresident combination fishing	10.00-15.00	5.00
Nonresident short term	3.00- 5.00	2.00
Resident dark house or shelter	3.00-	0.00
Resident dark house or shelter rental	6.00-10.00	4.00
Resident small game	4.00- 5.00+	1.00
Resident deer, firearms	7.50-10.00	2.50
Resident deer & bear, bow and arrow	7.50-10.00	2.50
Resident bear	5.00- 7.50	2.50
Nonresident shooting preserve	4.00- 5.00+	1.00
Nonresident deer & bear bow and arrow	10.25-25.00	14.75
Trapping	3.00- 5.00	2.00

+ In addition there is a $2.00 surcharge for wildlife land acquisition.

Note: The above fees are for restricted licenses valid statewide except on the Leech Lake Indian Reservation where an appropriate unrestricted license or restricted licese with a Leech Lake Reservation stamp is required.

STOLEN GUNS

The following guns, all owned by the late W. R. "Bill" Beamish, were stolen recently. Any person providing information leading to the recovery of any or all of them will get a generous reward.

W.R. "Bill" Beamish Guns

1—Ithaca 2000 Grade, double barrel, single trigger, initial R L S. Serial No. 376103. Lots of engraving.

2—Ithaca No. 7-20 gauge, double barrel No. 12 ventilated rib. Serial No. 360255. Lots of engraving.

3—Browning Trap—12 gauge special stock ventilated over and under. Pidgeon grade. Serial No. 9678.

4—Winchester Model 12, Poly choke. Serial No. 1334120.

5—Remington Deer Rifle, .35, automatic, scope. Serial No. 27105.

6—Browning Over-under double barrel, modified, full choke. Serial No. 60456.

7—Browning Live Bird Game trap, modified full choke. Serial No. 3996.

8—Remington 28 gauge, automatic, ventilated rib, modified. Model 11, serial No. 4003918

Phone M. Beamish (612) 933-0594 or the Edina Police (612) 925-2233.

FEBRUARY

• The U.S. Fish and Wildlife Service finalized an environmental statement on the use of lead shot for waterfowl, proposing the ban begin in the Atlantic Flyway in 1976, in the Mississippi in 1977, and into the Central and Pacific flyways in 1978.

• The DNR proposed increasing fishing and hunting license fees. A resident fishing license would increase from $4 to $5, while a resident deer license would go from $7.50 to $10. The agency said the increases were necessary to maintain a quality fish and wildlife management program.

MARCH

• Harvey Nelson, a Minnesota native who joined the U.S. Fish and Wildlife Service in 1950, was named associate director of fish and wildlife management by the federal agency.

ALBINO BUCK WHITETAIL DEER, having pink eyes and white feet, while the body was half white, was shot by Ray Flesch and registered in the Hackensack, Minn. area.

— Photo for Outdoor News by Swanson's Minnows, Hackensack, Minn.

60,000 Pheasant Chicks Produced at Carlos Avery
By the Minnesota DNR

The DNR's Carlos Avery Game Farm produced 60,000 pheasant chicks this spring for distribution to Future Farmers of America chapters, sportsmens clubs and 4-H groups, according to game farm manager Lloyd Knudsen.

The groups raise the chicks until they are seven weeks of age and then release them into the wild.

APRIL

• The state Legislature approved a bill that allowed moose hunting to continue in the state. The state House also approved of the DNR's plan to increase license fees for fishing and hunting.

• The In-Fisherman Society offered a pamphlet, free of charge. In-Fisherman, of course, went on to become one of the nation's most popular fishing magazines.

• Gov. Wendell Anderson vetoed a bill that would have created a state duck stamp.

JUNE

• The DNR's Carlos Avery Game Farm raised 60,000 pheasant chicks for release into the wild.

LES KOUBA, nationally known wildlife artist and Ducks Unlimited Artist of the Year, displays his 8-pound walleye caught on a Lindy Rig and leech combination from 20 feet of water on Whitefish Lake.
—Photo for Outdoor News by Marv Koep, Nisswa Bait & Tackle, Inc.

Hunting, Fishing Ban Issued

By the Minnesota DNR

Commissioner of Natural Resources Robert Herbst last week announced that all hunting, fishing and trapping has been suspended until further notice in the northern two-thirds of Minnesota, and other outdoor activities curtailed.

Herbst said he was acting with the approval of Governor Wendell Anderson and in response to increasing forest fire danger in the northern part of the state.

• A U.S. Fish and Wildlife Service biologist brought up the idea of hunting mourning doves in Minnesota. He noted their importance as a migratory game bird, and that hunters in 31 other states could hunt them.

JULY

• Due to large population declines, the DNR announced that deer hunters in much of the state would be allowed to shoot only bucks.

1976 STATE DEER HUNTING ZONES MAP

The state map showing hunting zones for white-tailed deer has changed dramatically from this 1976 version. Notice how Zone 1 then extended from eastern Kittson County all the way into southeastern Minnesota.

1976 Deer Seasons

FIREARMS: (Sunrise to sunset)
Zone 1   Nov. 1-14 .... Antlered Buck Only
Zones 2-9   Nov. 6- 7 .... Antlered Buck Only
                          OR
Zones 2-9   Nov. 19-20 .... Antlered Buck Only
                                              plus Antlerless quota

BOW & ARROW: (Sunrise to sunset)
Statewide   Oct. 2-31 .... Either Sex
Statewide   Nov. 1-14 .... Antlered Buck Only
Zones 2-9   Nov. 19-20 .... Antlered Buck Only
Southeast   Dec. 1-14 .... Either Sex
                 All dates inclusive

ONE OF THE WORLD'S TOP 10 BULL ELKS was bagged by Vince Kvidera, Ortonville, Minn., while hunting near Rand., Colo. recently with bow and arrow. Under the "green measurement" system, they say it is certain this elk will rank in the top 10 of the world, possibly in the top five. Included in the hunting party were (left to right) Dick Verheul, Minneapolis; Don Verheul, Ortonville; Kvidera, and Bob Carlson, Ortonville.
—Photo from the Ortonville Independent

52-POUND STURGEON was taken in the mouth of the Little Fork River recently by Chuck Nuthak of South International Falls, Minn. The sturgeon season in the Minnesota-Canada boundary waters remains open until June 1.
—Photo from the International Falls Daily Journal

Meyer to Head Area Enforcement

Donald M. Carlson, administrator for the Department of Natural Resources' Metro Region has announced the appointment of Orville C. Meyer to the position of Area Law Enforcement Manager.

Meyer replaces James Nickisch who was recently appointed Regional Law Enforcement Supervisor for DNR's Southwest Region.

AUGUST

• According to a Mille Lacs creel census between May 15 and July 31, anglers on the lake were taking an average of 2.5 tons of walleyes per day. The fish averaged 2.35 pounds apiece.

OCTOBER

• The DNR announced that all hunting, fishing and trapping in the northern two-thirds of the state was suspended until further notice. The reason: forest fire danger. As of Oct. 5, there were 230 active forest fires burning in the state.

NOVEMBER

• The DNR announced plans to hold a wild turkey hunting season in the state, noting the birds were doing very well in the southeastern part of Minnesota. The population estimate at the time was 2,000.

CRAPPIE TOURNEY TO DRAW 10,000

About 10,000 crappie fishermen are expected to invade Lake Minnetonka again Saturday, April 24, for the annual Fish-O-Rama tournament sponsored by Johnson Reels and Holiday Stores.

Contestants must register at one of the Holiday Stores in Minneapolis on or before Friday, April 23, to be eligible for one of the prizes, topped by a boat-motor-trailer combination. Headquarters for the tournament again is Paul's Landing, on Smith's Bay, Lake Minnetonka. Weigh-in is at 2 p.m. Saturday.

BIGGEST OF THE SEASON so far reported to **Outdoor News** is this 34 lb. 10⅓ oz. muskie caught from Leech Lake by Roger Larson of Waltham, Minn. The trophy measured 56 inches long with a girth of 21 inches.

1977 — The Minnesota Vikings made it to another Super Bowl, but lost once again, this time by a score of 32-14 to Oakland.

• Fifteen countries, including the U.S. and USSR, signed a nuclear-proliferation pact aimed at curbing the spread of nuclear weapons.

• President Jimmy Carter pardoned people who evaded the Vietnam War draft.

• Walter Mondale, who served as a U.S. senator from Minnesota from 1964 to 1977, was tapped as President Carter's vice president.

• Musician Elvis Presley died at the age of 42 at his Graceland home in Memphis, Tenn.

• The movie Star Wars was shown for the first time in theaters.

• The U.S. population climbed to more than 220 million people, the life expectancy increased to 73.3 years, and median household income rose to $13,572.

Court Says Steel Shot Rule Okay

WASHINGTON, D.C. — U.S. Department of Interior regulations requiring steel shot to be used for waterfowl hunting have been upheld by a U. S. District Court decision at Washington, D.C., supporting efforts by the federal government and the National Wildlife Federation to save an estimated 2 million waterfowl a year from death by lead shot poisoning.

The decision, by Judge Joseph C. Waddy, dismissed a suit filed by the National Rifle Association

JANUARY

• A district court judge in Washington, D.C., upheld U.S. Department of the Interior plans to require steel shot for waterfowl hunting. In doing so, the judge dismissed a lawsuit filed by the National Rifle Association.

• The Minnesota Waterfowl Association lent its support to creation of a state duck stamp.

FEBRUARY

• DNR Commissioner Bob Herbst, 41, was named assistant secretary of the Interior. The job involved overseeing the U.S. Fish and Wildlife Service, National Parks Service, and the Bureau of Outdoor Recreation. Five "protectionist, anti-hunting groups," according to Outdoor News Publisher, Jim Peterson, began a campaign opposing his appointment.

• Bills were introduced in the state House and Senate to establish a dove-hunting season. The DNR supported the hunt.

• John Uldrich, of Minneapolis, who founded the Vektor game and fish charts, introduced his firm's Vexilar video

Fish Finder Bill Is Rewritten

By LEN LIBBEY

H. F. 352, legislation to ban sophisticated fish finding devices, was completely reworded at a Minnesota Senate subcommittee hearing, March 16, at the state capitol in St. Paul.

The Senate Fish and Wildlife Subcommittee concluded nearly four hours of debate and discussion on the House-passed measure when it reported out the bill to the full Natural Resources Committee on a vote of 3 to 2. At least 15 witnesses from outside state government testified against the bill at the two hearings.

Duck Stamp, Muzzle Loading Bills Advance

Bills providing for a Minnesota state waterfowl stamp and a special deer hunting season with muzzle-loading firearms were reported out of a committee of the Minnesota Legislature, April 21.

First Gun Registration Bill Passed

State Supreme Court Rules Leech Lake Indian 'Deal' Legal

We Finally Visit KaBeeLo Lodge . . . Page 2

Publisher Jim Peterson traveled extensively on fishing trips and shared his success stories with readers.

Jim Peterson's Outdoor News
The Sportsman's Weekly

25¢

HUNTING • FISHING • SHOOTING • DOGS • CAMPING • BOATING • TIPS

depth sounder at the National Sporting Goods Association show in Chicago.

MARCH

• Bob Lessard, a freshman state senator from International Falls, favored a ban on graph-style depth finders. Lessard would go on to become a long-time chair of the Senate Environment and Natural Resources Committee.

• A bill to ban graph-style depthfinders failed in the Environment and Natural Resources Committee on a 10-7 vote.

Gun Control, Duck Stamp, 'Omnibus' Bills Signed

Three important bills affecting Minnesota sportsmen were signed into law by Gov. Rudy Perpich late last week. They are:

• The Spannaus gun control bill, which, for the first time, sets up a permit-registration system and a 7-day waiting period for handgun purchases from dealers. Effective date: Aug. 2.

• The state duck stamp bill, which establishes a $3 state fee for next fall's duck season, plus the regular small game license and the federal duck stamp.

• The "omnibus" game and fish bill which sets up a wild turkey season (probably next spring), a "sportsman's" license at a reduced rate, and takes bobcat, fox and fisher off the list of "unprotected" animals.

'BIGGER THAN THIS ONE' is the way Al Lindner described the 10 lb. 4 oz. bass he caught to help him win the Virginia Invitational bass tournament last week. He is pictured with a mounted bass at the Burger Brothers Fishing Clinic Tuesday.

—Outdoor News Photo by Jim Peterson

17-Pound Walleye No Record

From the Cook County News-Herald

GRAND MARAIS, Minn.—A lunker walleye, landed recently in Saganaga Lake, was probably the largest ever caught in Minnesota.

It will never be listed in the record books, however, because the fish was frozen before being weighed.

THE FISH was caught by Arthur Nelson of Makinen, who said he had it frozen to preserve it for a taxidermist.

The state record for a walleye is 16 pounds, 11 ounces, while Nelson's fish, frozen, weighed 17 pounds.

"I WISH I'd have known that was the state record then,'' Nelson said later.

LARGEST NORTHERN PIKE REPORTED TO **OUTDOOR NEWS** this past ice fishing season (caught by hook and line, of course) is this 28-pound trophy caught by Jim Markovich, Ely, Minn. He was fishing on Farm Lake and battled the fish, which hit his large sucker minnow, for over 15 minutes. "I couldn't believe it when I pulled it through the ice,'' he exclaimed later.
—Photo from the Ely Echo

• The DNR and the Minnesota Chapter of Safari Club International investigated the feasibility of reintroducing woodland caribou into northern Minnesota.

APRIL

• The state House Environment and Natural Resources Committee approved bills to create a state duck stamp, and a special muzzleloader deer-hunting season.

MAY

• The state Senate approved legislation to require registration of handguns purchased from federally licensed gun dealers. The requirement was a watered-down version of previous gun-control bills.

• Gov. Rudy Perpich signed into law the aforementioned handgun-regis-

LINDY/LITTLE JOE fishing pro Randy Amenrud and his son, Todd, show walleyes caught on the "mud" flats of Mille Lacs Lake.
—Photo special to Outdoor News

MOST UNUSUAL TROPHY BUCK was taken on the opening day of the Minnesota season by Tom Thurstin of Cohasset Minn. He was hunting in his hometown area and shot the buck through the right front leg; the deer ran about three and one half to four miles and he tracked it for three to four hours. He scared the buck up while it was resting and it was shot by Gail Englehart, Grand Rapids, Minn., through the shoulder. Upon examining the whitetail, the hunters discovered that the right rear leg had apparently been shot off some time in the past and had healed over. "He must have been running on two left legs,'' Thurstin exclaimed.
—Photo from the Grand Rapids Herald

WHITE AMUR, more commonly called grass carp, has been found in a been found in a southeastern Minnesota trout pond. The Minnesota DNR is trying to keep the carp out of Minnesota, while some other states are actually stocking the fish as a weed control measure, (**See Story**).

—Photo special to Outdoor News

★ ★ ★ ★

Grass Carp Found in S.E. Minnesota

William B. Nye was named new commissioner of the Minnesota DNR replacing Bob Herbst who left the agency to take a job in Washington D.C.

tration bill, as well as the bill creating the state duck stamp, which was priced at $3.

JUNE
• Bill Nye, of Ohio, was named DNR commissioner. The previous commissioner, Bob Herbst, supported Nye's appointment.

JULY
• Loral I Delaney, Jimmy Robinson and Lowell King were inducted into the Minnesota Trapshooting Hall of Fame.
• Grass carp were discovered in a trout pond in southeastern Minnesota.

TED CAPRA, well-known Minneapolis "pro" fisherman, shows his two trophies he won in the Minnesota Open Bass Tournament at Farm Island and Bay Lakes last weekend. The big trophy on the right is for the top two-day catch, while the smaller trophy is one of the two given to the top two-man team. (**See Story**).

SEPTEMBER
• A picture of a 71-pound muskie, which would have been a world record, was posted in the Cass Lake Chamber of Commerce building. The fish had been speared "about 10 or 12 years ago."

OCTOBER
• The Minnesota Supreme Court ruled the "Leech Lake Agreement," which required non-Indians to pay a fee to hunt or fish on the Leech Lake Reservation, was constitutional.

NOVEMBER
• A 17-pound walleye caught in Lake Saganaga would have been a state record had it not been frozen. As a result, a 16-pound, 11-ounce walleye remained the state record.

IN THE NEWS AT THE NSGA SHOW—John Uldrich, left, Minneapolis showed his firm's latest Vexilar "video" depth sounder and checked a copy of **Outdoor News** for word of legislative action to ban them, and, at right, Dave Yeager, Anoka, Minn., five times world skeet champion, shows boxes of new controversial steel shot from his firm, Federal Cartridge Corp. They were exhibitors at the National Sporting Goods Association show at McCormick Place, Chicago.

—Outdoor News Photos by Jim Peterson

DNR Officer Injured While Blowing Dam

David Carpenter, 29, a Staples, Minn., conservation officer, was hospitalized Jan. 25 as a result of injuries he suffered when an explosive device he was using, accidentally blew up in his face.

Carpenter suffered injuries to one eye, two broken eardrums and shrapnel wounds to his face and legs.

THE ACCIDENT happened near Wilderness Park in Cass County as Carpenter was preparing to blow up a beaver dam in Section 33, Moose Lake Township.

According to Fred Hammer, area enforcement officer for the DNR, Carpenter had been using a device called a "Kinipac" to blow up the dam.

THE DEVICE uses a powder chemical in a tube, which does not become explosive until mixed with another chemical.

The device is ignited by using a blasting cap attached to a primer cord. Hammer said.

The cap went off, and the cord went off but the Kinipac did not, Hammer stated.

1978 — Prominent Minnesota politician Hubert H. Humphrey, who served as vice president of the United States from 1965 to 1969, died at the age of 66. In 1948, he was the first Democrat from Minnesota ever to be elected to the U.S. Senate.

• President Jimmy Carter led a 13-day summit at Camp David that resulted in Egypt President Anwar Sadat and Israeli Premier Menachem Begin signing the "Framework for Peace." The latter two won the 1978 Nobel Peace Prize.

• Sony introduced the first portable stereo, which it called the Walkman.

• Norman Rockwell, one of America's favorite artists whose works captured small-town life in America, died at the age of 84. For more than four decades, he created the cover illustrations for the Saturday Evening Post.

☞ JANUARY

• Babe Winkelman, a well-known professional fisherman, author and lecturer, joined the Outdoor News staff as fishing columnist. His column was called "Fishin' Hole."

• The DNR accepted applications for the state's first wild turkey hunting season.

• Wildlife artist Les Kouba won the first state duck stamp contest with his oil painting of two bluebills (lesser scaup) flying over a storm-tossed northern Minnesota lake.

• A photo of Outdoor News Assistant Editor Jim L. Peterson's wedding appeared in the paper. Part of the caption beneath it: "The *only* wedding picture you'll probably

841 Moose Bagged in Minnesota

Minnesota's fourth moose hunting season in recent years proved highly successful for most of the 930 hunting parties who participated, the Department of Natural Resources reported this week.

Wolf Gets New Rating by U.S.

By the U.S. Fish and Wildlife Service

WASHINGTON, D.C. — The Minnesota population of the gray wolf (timber wolf) has been reclassified by the U.S. Fish and Wildlife Service from the endangered species category to that of a threatened species, following public comment on a rulemaking proposal issued June 9, 1977.

New Steel Rules Go Into Effect

One change has been made in the steel shot requirement for waterfowl hunting during the season which opens Oct. 1, the Minnesota Department of Natural Resources reported this week.

Included in the lead shot ban this year will be a Mississippi River zone east of Highway 61, Highway 16 and Highway 26 between Hastings, Minn., and the Iowa border.

LES KOUBA won the competition for the 1978 Minnesota Migratory Waterfowl Stamp with this oil painting of bluebills over a northern Minnesota lake. **(See Story).** —Special to Outdoor News

Kouba Wins First State Duck Stamp Contest

Award-winning wildlife artist Les Kouba of Minneapolis has done it again. Kouba's oil painting of lesser scaup ducks (bluebills) captured first place in the Minnesota Migratory Waterfowl Stamp contest last Friday (Dec. 30) at the Department of Natural Resources.

Kouba's design features two bluebills flying over the st

RAPALA CONTEST WINNER

38½-Pound Chinook Breaks State Record

By JIM PETERSON

A Minnesota state record has been shattered, **Outdoor News** learned this week, when a 38 lb. 8 oz. chinook salmon was caught at the mouth of the Baptism River on the North Shore of Lake Superior.

Tom Quay, 1337 Arkwright, St. Paul, said he caught the monster at (approximately) 6:45 a.m. on the morning of May 22.

HE USED a No. 11 GFR Rapala plug and thus becomes the winner of the **Outdoor News-Normark** weekly contest for fish caught on Rapala plugs.

Quay said it took him between 45 minutes and an hour to land the big salmon, using a Quick 700

(Continued on Page 10)

38-POUND, 8-OUNCE CHINOOK salmon, almost twice as big as the former Minnesota record, is shown by Tom Quay, 1337 Arkwright, St. Paul, Minn. 55101, who caught it on a Rapala plug at the mouth of the Baptism River on the North Shore. Quay thus wins the **Outdoor News-Normark** weekly photo contest for fish caught on Rapala lures. **(See Story).**

ever see in Outdoor News."

• In the newspaper's Comments section, Outdoor News Publisher Jim Peterson and Park Rapids Enterprise Editor Doug Hirsch squared off on a variety of topics, including spearing northern pike.

• State Sen. Collin Peterson, DFL-Detroit Lakes, passed a bill out of the Fish and Wildlife Subcommittee to create a state trout stamp.

FEBRUARY

• Burger Brothers sponsored a seminar in Minneapolis about wild turkey hunting. The seminar drew 600 people and included speakers Ron Schara and John Hauer.

MARCH

• The U.S. Fish and Wildlife Service reclassified the state's timber wolf population from endangered to threatened. The move followed public comment that began in June of 1977.

MAY

• DNR Commissioner Bill Nye resigned the post. A main reason for the move was

WINTER FISHING is rapidly approaching, and scenes like this will be repeated many times (well, maybe with not as big a lake trout) throughout the North Central states. Snowmobiles and winter fishing equipment are on display at the SNOW WORLD '78 Show at the Minneapolis Auditorium, Thursday through Sunday.
—Photo special to Outdoor News

TIP-UPS ARE NOW LEGAL

Tip-ups are legal for ice fishing for the first time in Minnesota's history, Minnesota DNR officials said Tuesday.

The 1978 Legislature passed a law legalizing two tip-ups per person, used not more than 80 feet away from the person. The law was passed after the 1978 fishing laws synopsis was printed, so the new regulations do not appear there.

(A tip-up is a device which activates a flag or other signal when a fish bites).

MISSISSIPPI RIVER FISHING below the Red Wing, Minn., dam is going strong now, as shown by this good stringer of four walleyes and two saugers caught by Larry Bollig, fishing "pro" for Maynard's Tackle. The largest walleye weighed 7 ½ pounds, while the stringer totaled 28 pounds, all caught on a fluorescent yellow jig two miles below the dam last Thursday.
—Photo special to Outdoor News

3 LB. 9 OZ. CRAPPIE—one of the largest ever pictured in **Outdoor News**—was caught from Whaletail Lake, west of Lake Minnetonka, by Dorothy Byholm of Richfield, Minn. She was fishing in 3 feet of water with a jig and minnow.
—Photo for Outdoor News by Taxidermy Unlimited, Burnsville, Minn.

that Nye issued retroactive trapping permits to three Voyageurs National Park officials who had been charged with game law violations, according to Gov. Rudy Perpich. In a statement, Nye also said that, as an environmentalist, he was uncomfortable with some compromises he had to make.

• Joe Alexander was named DNR commissioner. The 54-year-old Alexander had been a state conservation officer for 21 years. Jim Peterson cheered the move in an editorial, saying Perpich chose the best man for the job.

JUNE

• A 38.5-pound Chinook salmon caught at the mouth of the North Shore's Baptism River set a new state record. The fish was nearly double

POSSIBLE RECORD for Minnesota bow and arrow deer hunting could be this 15-point, 220-pound buck shot at Lac qui Parle by Mary Baruells of Montevideo, Minn. An unofficial Pope and Young measurement of 183 was scored, with the official measurement to be made after a 60-day drying period.

—Photo for Outdoor News by Mitlyng's Bait & Tackle, Watson, Minn.

THE ONLY wedding picture you'll probably ever see in **Outdoor News** is this one: Jim L. Peterson, assistant editor, and Barb Zander, secretary, were married last Thursday, Dec. 29. **(See Editorials)**.

—Outdoor News photo by Jim Peterson

▲

Assistant Editor Jim L. Peterson, son of publisher Jim T. Peterson, later tragically lost his life as a result of an automobile accident caused by a drunk driver in December 1979.

94 HUNTERS BAG TURKEYS

A total of 94 turkeys were bagged by 420 hunters during Minnesota's first wild turkey hunting season in history, DNR officials announced.

The success ratio was 22 percent, higher than the 10 to 15 percent predicted.

The season closed last Sunday, May 7.

the weight of the previous state record, which weighed 20 pounds.

SEPTEMBER
• The Minnesota DNR added a new area to the parts of the state in which lead shot was banned for waterfowl hunting. That was the Mississippi River Zone in the southeastern part of the state.

NOVEMBER
• Outdoor News printed its first four-color photo. It was on the front page and showed an ice fisherman exiting his portable fish house holding a lake trout.

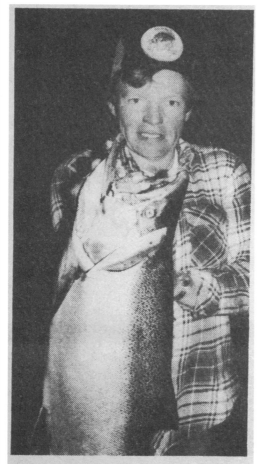

DICK STERNBERG, Minnesota DNR fisheries biologist, caught this chinook salmon, estimated at between 28 and 30 pounds, in Lake Michigan near Two Rivers, Wis. (See Editorials).

1979 — A nuclear accident at the Three Mile Island nuclear power plant near Harrisburg, Pa., released radiation. It's still considered the worst U.S. nuclear accident to date.

• The overthrown Shah left Iran, and Islamic leader Ayatollah Ruhollah Khomeini, along with revolutionary forces, took over.

• Margaret Thatcher became the new prime minister of Great Britain.

• Mother Theresa of Calcutta (India) won the Nobel Peace Prize.

• The Soviet Union invaded Afghanistan, which led to protests across the world.

• Unemployment in the United States dropped below 6 percent.

JANUARY

• DNR Fish and Wildlife Division Director Dave Vesall, who had been with the DNR since 1939 and was a founder of the Save the Wetlands program, retired from the agency. Earl Lhotka, a DNR employee for 31 years and Enforcement Division director since 1976, retired later in the month.

FEBRUARY

• The DNR received a federal grant of $768,000 to continue its Dutch elm disease program, which was designed to test various control methods.

• Despite a tough winter, Iowa officials reported that road-killed pheasants in the state show no evidence of starvation.

'Mr. Walleye' Shows His 14 Pounder

BIG STONE LAKE produced this 14-pound walleye for Gerhardt Block, known as "Mr. Walleye" in Ortonville, Minn., for his dozens of trophy fish over 10 pounds. Block, who also caught an 11 lb. 12 oz. walleye last week, was casting a Hellcat plug from shore into open water near a power plant. (See Lake of the Week Story). —Photo for Outdoor News by the Ortonville Independent

541,202 Boats in Minnesota

The state of Minnesota registered 541,202 boats in 1978, an increase of 2.8 per cent over the previous year, according to figures just released by the National Association of Engine and Boat Manufacturers.

This places the state second to California's 548,880 in total number of boats registered among the 50 states and U.S. Territories.

THERE WERE 8,034,905 boats registered nationally last year, an overall increase of 0.7 per cent. In addition, 49,183 larger boats were documented, an increase of 9 per cent over the year before.

RARE ARCTIC FOX was shot by Dick Henry of rural Lake Benton, Minn., who said the pure white fox was preying on his wild Canada goose flock. Henry, who has hunted foxes for 30 years, said it was definitely an Arctic fox and not an albino red fox, because of the short ears. DNR officials said it was not illegal to shoot an Arctic fox in Minnesota.

—Photo from the Lake Benton Valley Journal.

• After serving as acting DNR commissioner since July of 1978, Joe Alexander was officially installed as the agency's commissioner.

JOE ALEXANDER

MARCH

• DNR Fisheries supervisor Chuck Burrows was appointed as director of the Fish and Wildlife Division. A 32-year agency veteran, Jerome Kuehn, replaced him as Fisheries supervisor.

APRIL

• A federal judge rejected a claim by the Red Lake Indian Band that its hunting, fishing, and ricing rights extended beyond the boundaries of its reservation. The U.S. Department of the Interior brought the suit on behalf of the band in 1976.
• Bemidji conservation officer Richard Tarte was named new director of the Enforcement Division.
• The DNR announced it would sue the federal government in an attempt to reaffirm its jurisdiction over waters within the Boundary Waters Canoe Area Wilderness.

MAY

• Evansville, Minn., native Harvey Nelson was appointed regional director of the U.S. Fish and Wildlife Service's Great Lakes Regional Office at Fort Snelling. He had been with the Fish and Wildlife Service since 1950.
• LeRoy Chiovitte of Hermantown, Minn., caught a 17-pound, 8-ounce walleye in the Seagull River near Saganaga Lake on May 13. The massive fish set a new state record. It replaced the previous record of 16 pounds, 11 ounces. Scale samples from Chiovitte's state record fish showed it was between 21 and 25 years old.

RECORD WALLEYE 21 YEARS OLD

The Minnesota record walleye, 17 lbs. 8 oz., caught by LeRoy Chiovitte of Hermantown, Minn., in the Sea Gull River near the end of the Gunflint Trail, was between 21 and 25 years old, Don Woods, assistant DNR Fisheries chief, said Tuesday.

"We got a good look at scale samples, and they had good ring definition," he said. "We did re-measure the fish and found it was 33.3 inches long, not 35 inches. Evidently it was measured around the curve of the body, not the straight-line length." Other measurements were accurate.

5,317 Fish Houses at Mille Lacs

From the Mille Lacs Messenger

Isle, Minn.—A total of 5,317 fish houses, the second highest number on record, were counted on Mille Lacs Lake by the Department of Natural Resources during its annual aerial count on Sunday, Jan. 7.

BEST TOURNAMENT CATCH of walleyes ever made in Minnesota is this limit of 12 weighing a total of 47 lbs. 7¼ oz. by Duane Betker, left, and Doug Thompson to win the $1,750 first prize in the Lino Lakes Lions Club contest at Mille Lacs Lake last weekend. **(See Story).**
—Photo special to Outdoor News

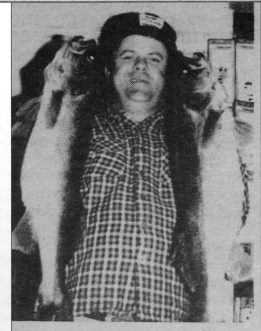

RANDY AMENRUD, pro fisherman and *Outdoor News* columnist, caught these 8½ and 9¼-pound walleyes on Lindy Rigs and nightcrawlers in Island Lake near Park Rapids, Minn.
—Photo special to Outdoor New

JUNE
• The U.S. Fish and Wildlife Service, amid rising demand for crop production, irrigation, and social changes in agriculture, announced it would crack down on people violating wetlands regulations.

AUGUST
• A Minnesota Supreme Court decision exempted White Earth Reservation Indians on reservation lands from state hunting and fishing regulations.
• Muskies, Inc. held its third-annual challenge tournament on Dryberry Lake in Ontario. All of the muskies caught were released.

OCTOBER
• Ten resorts requested a buy-out from the U.S. Forest Service under the 1978 Boundary Waters Canoe Area Wilderness Act.

Huge Trout Stolen from Hatchery

The Minnesota Department of Natural Resources reported that 30 large trout used to propagate fish for stocking purposes were stolen from an outdoor pond at the Lanesboro fish hatchery in southeastern Minnesota the night of Aug. 12.

NOVEMBER
• With poor deer hunting returns coming from many areas of the state, Publisher Jim Peterson called the 1979 deer season "pretty much a bust."
• The DNR announced the creation of a Trails and Waterways Unit.

DECEMBER
• In what some people called the most sweeping anti-gun legislation ever, Sen. Edward Kennedy introduced an 84-page anti-gun bill.
• Publisher Jim Peterson addressed the death of his son, Jim L. Peterson, in his column. The younger Peterson was driving on Highway 10 west of Elk River when a wrong-way driver collided with his vehicle. Both drivers were killed instantly. Peterson was survived by his wife and young daughter.

GOVERNOR Al Quie happily displays his 1980 opening-day catch on Otter Tail Lake with guide Hans Hanebuth.

1980 — Following the late 1979 overthrow of the Shah of Iran, the Iran Hostage Crisis developed, which led to hundreds of American embassy staffers being held hostage in Iran, and President Carter breaking diplomatic ties with the country.

• Former Hollywood actor and California Gov. Ronald Reagan was elected president of the United States.

• Beatles member John Lennon was shot and killed outside of his apartment building in New York.

• Ted Turner launched CNN, the first 24-hour news network.

• The population of the United States topped more than 227 million people, the average life expectancy was nearly 74 years, and the median household income was $17,710.

JANUARY

• The state filed suit against the federal government, seeking to retain control of the water rights in the Boundary Waters Canoe Area. According to the suit, the secretary of the Department of Agriculture was enforcing the BWCA Wilderness Act of 1978 on lakes over which the federal government had no authority.

• An 8-pound, 11-ounce eelpout caught at Walker's International Eelpout Festival not only took the festival's top prize, it also set a new state record for the species.

• During 1979, 93 boaters lost their lives on Minnesota waters. While that was seven more than died in 1978, it was fewer than before 1977, when DNR data show more than 100 were dying each year.

FEBRUARY

• Ron Schara, writing in the Star Tribune, wrote about spearing in

MILK CARTON FISH HOUSE appeared on Mille Lacs Lake ice—and it was no joke. Al Zakarariasen and Paul Bosquez (shown) of Minneapolis built it out of wood framing and 3,500 empty half-gallon milk cartons furnished by Clover Leaf Dairy. The house is 14 x 14 feet by 10 feet high, has four holes, four bunks, gas range and heater and battery-powered electric lights. "The milk cartons provide excellent insulation," Zakariasen said. "The house is light and strong. I can stand on the roof, and I weigh 218 pounds."
—Photo special to Outdoor News

STATE RECORD chinook salmon, 21 lbs. 4 oz., was caught in Lake Superior, outside the entrance to the Grand Marais, Minn., harbor by A.J. Niedorf, retired conservation officer from Cambridge, Minn. —Photo for Outdoor News by the Cook County News-Herald

Minnesota, and included Outdoor News Publisher Jim Peterson in the story.

• A bill to allow dove hunting in the state narrowly cleared a House subcommittee. The issue of hunting doves proved to be an emotional one, and in an editorial, Jim Peterson wrote he received more letters from sportsmen on the dove hunt than on any other issue before the Legislature.

MARCH

• Jim Peterson regularly ran photos of people who speared northern

RANDY AMENRUD, **Outdoor News** columnist, and his Lindy-Little Joe teammate, Gary Roach, caught this string of walleyes totalling 64 lbs. 5 oz., with the largest 11 lbs. 7 oz., in Gull Lake near Nisswa, Minn., using Lindy Rigs and leeches in 15 to 20 feet of water. This Saturday (July 12), Amenrud will be the "professor" at Bemidji State University's Fishing for Fun seminar and contest.
—Photo for Outdoor News by Nisswa Bait & Tackle

pike – and blacked out the spearers' eyes. But until now, he hadn't run any pictures of kids with speared northern pike. But he didn't spare them, either; their eyes were blacked out.

• Columnist Babe Winkelman wrote a column about catch-and-release fishing, which, at that point, was a novel concept. He relayed a story of a man getting mad at him as he released bass after a tournament.

• A man from Brooklyn Park, Minn., pleaded guilty to setting an illegal bear trap. The trap, referred to as a dangerous device, weighed 50 pounds and had teeth-studded jaws. The man had concealed the trap in the middle of a well-used trail north of Floodwood, and baited the trap with honey. A Bovey man had tripped on the trap's chain, which anchored it to a tree.

APRIL

• Minnesota joined the ranks of states to allow handguns for hunting small- and big-game animals. Besides Minnesota, 44 states allowed handguns for small game, 32 for big game. According to the legislation, which the Legislature approved and the governor signed, hunters could use any caliber for small game, and .357-, .41-, and .44-caliber for big game.

• A new requirement took hold for waterfowl hunters: In steel shot zones, they

5,474 BOATS ON MILLE LACS

Fishing pressure on Mille Lacs Lake on opening day was equal or slightly higher than usual Saturday. A Minnesota Department of Natural Resources aerial census team counted 5,474 boats at one time on the lake.

Top Eelpout of Derby Is New Record

When Diane Maas of Walker, Minn., caught an 8 lb. 11 oz. eelpout to win the International Eelpout Festival's top prize, she also set a new Minnesota record for the species.

Last Friday, Jan. 11, the Minnesota Department of Natural Resources held its first awards ceremony for fishermen who set Minnesota records for fish caught in 1979. Six fishermen attended to get framed citations from DNR

14 Lb. 1 Oz. Eelpout Is State Mark

A 14 lb. 1 oz. eelpout (burbot) is a state record, according to Minnesota Department of Natural Resources officials.

The fish was caught Feb. 2 by Leonard Lundeen of 1227 E. 8th Street, Duluth, in Deer Lake, Itasca County. Lundeen, who was walleye fishing at the time, had his record eelpout weighed in Deer River before witnesses.

MAC DAVIS, right, one of the country's most popular singers who was appearing recently in Minneapolis, took a break to go fishing with his friend, Lisa Geard, left, and 16-year-old Kevin Koep, son of Marv Koep of Nisswa Bait & Tackle and the Nisswa Guides League. Davis asked for Kevin, runnerup in the Northstar Bassmasters Classic, to guide him. They fished backwoods lakes for northerns and bass. —Photo special to Outdoor News

To the Editor:
Enclosed is a picture of a 31-pound carp my son Troy caught on the evening of May 19. I know it isn't a game fish, but he fought this fish for 2½ hours before I netted it. He hooked it just before dark on our dock on a green fluorescent jig tipped with a crawler and 6-pound test line. He was running out of line on the dock so my wife and I got him in a rowboat and the fish towed the boat about three blocks before he finally tired enough to net him.
—Roger Mathway, Idle Wave Resort, Rt. 2, Lake Washington, Dassel, Minn. 55325.

had to use steel shot in all shotguns, regardless of the gauge. Previously, the steel shot requirement applied only to 12-gauge shotguns.

MAY
• Thanks to a bill passed by the Legislature, when filing their 1980 tax returns, citizens could donate $1 or more of their refunds to benefit non-game wildlife conservation. The donation became known as the "chickadee check-off."

JULY
• The DNR swore in the first two women ever to

LARGEST BASS reported in Minnesota this year and the largest ever to be weighed in at Sport Stop, Inc., in Shakopee, Minn., is this 8 lb. 3 oz. largemouth, caught on a plastic worm by Ted Bodeen of Shakopee in Lake Waconia. It was 23½ inches long and 18¾ inches in girth. —Photo for Outdoor News by Sport Stop, Inc.

serve as conservation officers. They were Cathy Hayes and Joyce Minor.
• The Minnesota Deer Hunters Association formed.

OCTOBER
• Two conservation officers – Gary Westby and Dan Book – were injured as they tried to apprehend two suspects for stealing gas. Westby's foot was run over, and his car later went into the ditch. Book's arm was broken during the accident.

First Women Conservation Officers Are Sworn In

The first female conservation officers hired by the State of Minnesota were sworn into service on July 2 along with 15 men, the Department of Natural Resources reported this week.

Richard Tarte, Director of the DNR Enforcement Division, said

Cathy L. Hayes, 22, of Lake Elmo, Minn., and Joyce A. Minor, 28, of Fridley, Minn.

Tarte said the women were required to pass the same written examination, physical agility tests, oral examinations, back-

(Continued on page 4)

LORAL I DELANEY, the nation's top woman trapshooter from Anoka, Minn., shows the Captain Billy Fawcett Memorial Handicap trophy which she won at the Minneapolis Gun Club while competing against leading male shooters. (**See Jimmy Robinson's Column on Page 4**).
—Outdoor News photo by Jim Peterson

1981 — Just two months after taking the oath of office as the 40th president of the United States, President Ronald Reagan was shot in the left lung by a gunman. He survived the assassination attempt.

• More than a foot of heavy, wet snow caused the fabric atop the new Metrodome to rip and collapse.

• An agreement between the United States and Iran resulted in 52 hostages being freed from the country and returned home.

• President Reagan nominated Arizona's Sandra Day O'Connor to the U.S. Supreme Court. It was the first time a woman had served on the court.

• The New York Islanders defeated the Minnesota North Stars in the Stanley Cup championship, four games to one.

• A new music television (MTV) channel began airing, showing music videos around the clock.

JANUARY

• Under a system agreed to by the state and the Leech Lake Indians, state fishermen, hunters and trappers no longer had to buy a special license to hunt, fish or trap on the reservation. Instead, the state sent 5 percent of the sales of all state fishing, hunting and trapping licenses to the band.

• Minnesota retained its position as one of the top states for boat registration. As of the end of 1980, there were 580,393 boats registered in the state.

MARCH

• During fiscal year 1980, the DNR paid $4.7 million to counties. Those funds were in lieu of prop-

BOATING AND FISHING TRENDS and tips were discussed by Roland Martin, left, all-time top B.A.S.S. tournament money winner, and by Forrest Wood, third from left, the "father of bass boats," at Crystal Marine's All Star Open House last Saturday, Jan. 17. Second from left is Herb Heichert and at right is Gordy Peterson of Crystal Marine. (**See Editorials, Page Two**).
—Outdoor News photo by Jim Peterson

HEADLINES

Hearing Tuesday on Dove Bills

The Minnesota Senate Natural Resources Committee will hold a hearing on two mourning dove bills at 3 p.m. Tuesday, March 24, in Room 15 of the State Capitol.

S.F. 138 would permit hunting of doves; S.F. 407 would permanently ban their hunting.

Bull Elk Killed in N.W. Minn.

From the Greenbush Tribune

GREENBUSH, Minn. — DNR Conservation Officer Stewart Benson and DNR Forestry Officer Gordon Saul, reported a bull elk which was killed near Grygla, Minn., during hunting season.

The elk, which may have been the largest of three bulls in the herd, was discovered by a local airplane pilot in a clearing about seven miles north of Grygla in Veldt Township. Grygla DNR officers were notified.

AN INVESTIGATION showed that the elk was killed instantly with one shot in the neck. Benson believes that there is no doubt that the animal was shot intentionally.

79,000 Geese Set Record at Lac qui Parle

A total of 79,000 geese were counted at Lac qui Parle Refuge this week for a new record for that state wildlife management area near Milan and Watson, Minn.

To the Editor:

Have enjoyed **Outdoor News** for several years but I have had it with your biased editorials on winter spearing. Cancel my subscription.

Why don't you get on the fishermen who use (tax free) radar equipment to locate and catch fish, or are you one of them?
—W.S. Nesset, 41 Horn Blvd., Silver Bay, Minn. 55614.

EDITOR'S NOTE: As we've said many times before, sonar (not radar) equipment never has and never will kill a fish. The use of this equipment is not considered unsporting anywhere in the world. But, the use of harpoons IS CONSIDERED UNSPORTING all over the world!

33-POUND lake trout caught by Dennis Westlin and Jim Hinds on a Swedish Pimple while fishing on Knife Lake near Ely.

erty taxes on natural resource lands.

MAY

• The state House approved an appropriations bill for a variety of agencies, including the DNR. One part of the bill included a 30-percent hike in the price of hunting, fishing, and other licenses issued by the DNR. The Senate committee passed a similar bill the same day.

• An anti-poaching program that rewarded people for reporting violations of wildlife laws began. Its name: Turn In Poach-

MINNESOTA MUSKIE champion for 1980, Patty Bushie was presented the Muskies Inc., trophy by Jim Peterson of *Outdoor News*. Bushie's muskie weighed 39 pounds, 15 ounces.

ers. A private non-profit group, TIP, Inc., sponsored the program in cooperation with the DNR's Enforcement Division.

JUNE

• Three launches that departed from the Baudette, Minn., area, as well as a large amount of fishing equipment, were seized by authorities from the Ontario Ministry of Natural Resources and held in Morson, Ontario. The three boats and equipment were seized for alleged fishing violations in Canadian waters.

JULY

• The three launches seized in June by Canadian authorities were returned to their owners, but not before fines were levied on the owners and passengers. Fines and costs for each totaled between $986 and $1,496.

WORLD RECORD BOOK DEER was shot during the 1980 Minnesota season by Gino Maccario of Coon Rapids, Minn., near Squaw Lake, Minn. It field dressed at 260 pounds, and the preliminary scoring of the antlers indicates it will be in the top 20 in the Boone & Crockett world records. (**See Letters, Page Two**).
—Photo special to Outdoor News

Jail, $4,400 In Fines for 1,886 Fish

A family of tourists from Iowa and Illinois were apprehended by Minnesota conservation officers on Saturday, Aug. 15, with an estimated 1,886 filleted and frozen fish taken from Elm Island Lake in Aitkin County.

Officers, who had the family of four under surveillance for several days, said the packages of frozen fish weighed 237 pounds. Nearly 90 percent of the fish confiscated were crappies.

AUGUST

• The U.S. Fish and Wildlife Service rejected the state's wolf-management plan, largely due to the state's proposal to harvest 50 wolves per year.

OCTOBER

• The Save Our Game Fish Committee, which ultimately played a key role

MOOSE ESTIMATED AT 1,100 POUNDS and with near-record-book antlers, was shot near Ely, Minn., by Mike Vipond, right. Also in the party were Don Oaches, Dave Vipond and Les Vipond.

—Photo from the Ely Echo

in getting commercial fishing banned in state waters of Lake of the Woods and Rainy Lake, called for an overhaul of the DNR Fisheries Division. "We need to clean out the DNR Fisheries Division," said Moorhead's Dick Knutson, a co-chairman of the committee. "Fire them all and bring in guys looking to the future." Outdoor News supported the committee's goals.

DECEMBER

• During the month of November, 58 arrests were the result of the new Turn in Poachers program. From the time TIP began – Sept. 1 – information resulting from TIP calls resulted in 144 arrests.

FIFTIETH ANNIVERSARY of the Minnesota Department of Natural Resources was celebrated last Wednesday, July 1, at the DNR offices in the Centennial Building, St. Paul. Three former commissioners and the present commissioner got together for the picture. Left to right are Wayne Olson, Bob Herbst, Joe Alexander (present commissioner) and Jarle Lierfallom.

—Outdoor News photo by Jim Peterson

BOB MUNSON became the first Minnesotan in 60 years to win the North American Clay Target championship at the Grand American, while his wife, Lou Ann Munson, was second among the ladies, and the couple won the Husband and Wife title.
—Photo special to Outdoor News

1982 — For the first time in history, a permanent artificial heart was placed in a human. The procedure took place at the Utah Medical Center.

• Michael Jackson released Thriller, his sixth record and one of the top-selling albums ever.

• Actor and comedian John Belushi died of a heroin overdose at the age of 33.

• The man who shot President Reagan, John Hinckley, Jr., was found not guilty by reason of insanity.

• The Chicago Tylenol murders occur when seven people in the Chicago area die after ingesting capsules laced with potassium cyanide.

 JANUARY

• Deer hunters in 1981 killed a total of 101,000 animals, which was the highest harvest since 1968. The increased success was due to a higher deer population, which was the result of three mild winters and hunting regulations that limited doe take.

• Tom Zenanko, an outdoors lecturer, writer, photographer, and radio broadcaster joined the staff of Outdoor News.

• A blizzard wiped out between 20 and 50 percent of the state's pheasant population. The southwestern and west-central parts of the state were hit the hardest. The DNR asked sportsmen's clubs and individuals to feed pheasants as they could.

FEBRUARY

• A Lake Hubert couple gifted the DNR a 190-acre

LOUIE'S ORIGINAL WALLEYE RIG

Fish more ways, and fish summer & winter with the same rig. For walleye, northern, bass, crappie & other game fish.

Pat. in U.S. & Canada, Patented double hooks, locked-on spinner, locked-on 1/8 oz. sinker on end of strong mono. Approx. 22" long. Good instructions with Rig. Ask your dealer or send check or money order for $1.95—includes postage & handling to: LOUIS A. FLOREK MFG. CO., P.O. Box 84, Wayzata, Minn. 55391

 MINNOW

 NITE CRAWLER

 LEECH

DEALER INQUIRIES INVITED

State Given 4,754 Feet on Gull Lake

The Minnesota Department of Natural Resources has announced the acquisition by gift of a 190-acre tract of land adjacent to Gull Lake near Brainerd, Minn., including 4,754 feet of shoreline on the west side of the lake in Cass County.

The land was donated to the state by Mr. & Mrs. R. F. Brownlee Cote of Lake Hubert with the stipulation that the land be made a part of the Pillsbury State Forest.

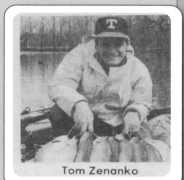

Tom Zenanko

DNR Fur Sale Set Saturday

The Minnesota Department of Natural Resources will hold a sale of furs at the Centennial Building in St. Paul on Saturday, March 20.

The furs are those that have been confiscated from violators.

The furs that will be offered include 17 beaver, 272 otter, 37 raccoon, 15 red fox, 144 muskrat, 119 fisher, 51 mink, 6 bob cat, 1 coyote, 208 pine marten and 2 lynx.

First U.S. 'Game Fair' Will Be Held Labor Day Weekend Near Anoka

40-Lb., 13-Oz. Muskie!

Gets 'Hi

Jim Peterson's

TED BURGER of Burger Brothers Sporting Goods, Bloomington, Minn., caught this 40 lb. 13 oz. muskie on a lure of his own invention, Ted's Bucktail, in Leech Lake last Sunday, July 4. He was fishing with his brother, Bud, who clubbed the monster, then gaffed it and slid it into the boat. (See Story). —Photo special to Outdoor News

tract of land adjacent to Gull Lake in Brainerd. The land included 4,754 feet of shoreline on the lake's west side.

• The DNR announced deer feeding would begin on Feb. 19 due to severe winter weather.

MARCH

• State Sen. Keith Langseth, of Glyndon, introduced a bill that would ban gill-netting of fish in all waters of the state, except for Lake Superior and waters controlled by the Chippewa bands.

• The DNR began a deer-feeding program in portions of north-central and northeastern Minnesota where concentrations of deer had little food. Many of the areas had more than 20 inches of snow.

• Howard Hansen, with long-term involvement in groups such as Ducks Unlimited and the Minnesota Waterfowl

FROZEN PHEASANTS are being found following last week's two record storms; all in the same position, facing the wind so their feathers will stay in position, but with beaks clogged with ice.
—Photo for Outdoor News by New London-Spicer Times

NEW 'GHOST' JITTERBUG

Association, served as first president of Walleyes Unlimited, which was created to improve fishing in Minnesota.

• The 25th million Lindy Rig was purchased in 1981. The rigs first were introduced in 1968.

• The DNR reminded contractors and shoreline owners that they needed permits before working in a lake, marsh or stream.

BIGGEST DEER reported to **Outdoor News** this season is this 15-point, 265-pound buck shot with a slug by Todd Nelson of Ortonville, Minn., who was hunting northeast of that city.

—Photo from the Ortonville Independent

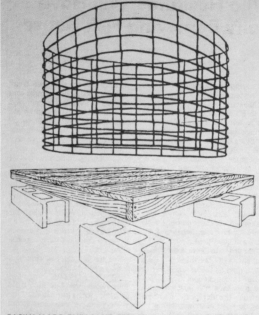

EASILY-MADE PHEASANT FEEDER is constructed of a 4' x 4' wooden platform set on cement blocks (or rocks) with ear corn placed in the woven wire fencing (12' of fencing).

Pat Laib of Spicer won the Minnesota State Doubles Trapshooting championship in 1982 with 97x100. He answers reader questions in a gunsmithing column for Outdoor News.

APRIL

• A record 200,000 people were expected to visit the Northwest Sportshow during its 10-day, 50th anniversary event. When it was all said and done, the total was even higher: 215,412. The previous record had been 199,000.

• The battle over gill nets in Lake of the Woods reached a boiling point after lines on the lake map showing where commercial netting would be allowed were changed. The Save Our Game Fish Committee told DNR Commissioner Joe Alexander he no longer was invited to be a guest speaker at an event in Greenbush, and said, "your recent actions are a disgrace to the people of Minnesota." Alexander responded that no DNR employees would be permitted at the event, and said the allegations of bribery and wrong-doing made against him were felonious and must be reported and investigated.

JUNE

• The state of Wisconsin began studying "bear ticks," which are better known as deer ticks.

JULY

• The first Game Fair was slated to be held in Anoka over the three days of Labor Day Weekend.

AUGUST

• Wisconsin announced its first wild turkey hunting season would begin April 23, 1983 in two western areas of the state.

• The nonprofit group Pheasants Forever began, and was slated to debut at Game Fair. Dennis Anderson, outdoors writer at the St. Paul Dispatch-Pioneer Press, was instrumental in creation of the group, which, among other things, sought to promote pas-

State Record Moose was shot by Len Holtegaard (left) of St. Charles, Minn., on Dec. 5, 1981, near Isabella, Minn. The antlers were officially scored for Boone & Crockett records at 199-6/8, well above the minimum to make the world record book. The antlers had a spread of 60-6/8 inches. Also in the party to the right of Holtegaard were Phil Nietz, Rollie Smith and Bill Nessler.
—Photo special to Outdoor News

sage of a bill to create a state pheasant stamp.

NOVEMBER

• In an editorial, Jim Peterson wrote that Gov. Rudy Perpich should not re-appoint Joe Alexander as commissioner of the DNR. Sportsmen in the northern part of the state were especially upset about Alexander's support of walleye gill-netting in Lake of the Woods and Rainy Lake, and had been letting Perpich know their feelings.

JANUARY
• The DNR stocked 63 tons of walleye fingerlings into more than 500 lakes across the state in the fall of 1982. "This is the largest walleye stocking operation in the nation," DNR Fisheries Chief Richard Hassinger said.

• The first Minnesota Sportfishing Congress, headlined by Minnesota Vikings coach Bud Grant, was a huge success, organizers reported. The event, held to protest poor fishing in the state, drew 800 people, including 30 legislators, as well as dozens of DNR officials and leading sportsmen.

• The DNR surveyed a sample of the state's 2,000 resorts, and found their numbers were declining. Most of the lost resorts were the "Ma and Pa" variety.

1983 — In Beirut, Lebanon, 237 U.S. Marines stationed there were killed in a terrorist attack.

• Thirty-two-year-old Sally Ride became the first woman in space as a crew member aboard the space shuttle Challenger.

• A South Korean commercial flight apparently strayed into Soviet airspace on its way to Seoul. A Soviet fighter jet shot down the plane, killing all of the 269 people on board.

• The U.S. invaded Grenada.

• The decline of long-play (LP) records began with the introduction of compact discs.

• The last episode of M*A*S*H was televised, attracting more than 125 million viewers.

• The world population approached 4.7 billion.

FEBRUARY
• The Minnesota Wildlife Heritage Foundation announced plans to hold the first Minnesota Deer Classic April 23-24. The event was to become the first annual gathering of deer hunters in Minnesota.

MARCH
• A 55-pound, 15¾-ounce northern pike was authenticated by the National Fishing Hall of Fame in Hayward, Wis. The fish, which hit a minnow, was caught in the Lipno Reservoir in Czechoslovakia on Dec. 9, 1979.

APRIL
• In his editorial, Jim Peterson called for Joe Fellegy, pres-

Minn. Bass Record Now 9 Lbs. 4 Oz.

The state's new official angling record for largemouth bass is 9 lbs. 4 oz., the Minnnesota Department of Natural Resources reports.

Officials at the DNR's Fisheries Section said considerable research went into determining a new record for bass after the previously accepted record of 10 lbs. 2 oz. could not be verified.

The new record holder is Fritz Schneider of Madison Lake, Minn., who caught the fish on a jointed Rapala in Lake Washington, LeSueur County, in 1978.

First Pheasant Banquet April 15

The first banquet to be held by Pheasants Forever, the new organization dedicated to help Minnesota pheasants and their habitat, will have pheasant (naturally) as the main course. The dinner will be held Friday, April 15, at the Prom Center, St. Paul.

The pheasants to be eaten will be game-farm birds, but the proceeds of the event will go toward boosting the population of wild ringnecks.

For ticket and other information see ad on page 10 or phone Jeff Finden at (612) 222-5011, Ext. 316, days; or 429-8689, evenings.

BUD GRANT AND LES KOUBA, a rookie artist and an old pro, team up to create an "all-star" watercolor, "Lac qui Parle Honkers", which will be sold as limited edition prints by TIP, Inc., at the SPORTSHOW. Grant is honorary chairman of TIP.
—Photo special to Outdoor News

RAPALA CONTEST WINNER

LAKE PEPIN in southeastern Minnesota produced this string of 10¼ to 18 lb. 1 oz. northern pike, all caught on 11 CM floating Rapala plugs by Curt Weibusch, RR 2, Box 223L, Eyota, Minn. 55934 and Doug Weibusch, of Zumbro Falls, Minn., to win this week's Outdoor News-Normark Corp. contest.

13 Hunters - 13 Buck Deer

DURING THE THREE DAY BUCK DEER season, a party of 13 hunters working an area about 10 miles southwest of Madison, Minn., were successful in getting 13 buck deer. One had 11 points, two had 10 points, six had 8 points, one had 7 points, one had 6 points, one had 5 points and one 4 points. Hunters in the group included Duane Schmidt, David Schmidt, Duane Croatt, Scott Hanson, Tom Ludvigson, Paul Weber, Reid Jurgenson, Russ Jurgenson, Randy Jurgenson, Dean Bertamus, Scott Fernholz, Deren Stamp and Joe Stoks.　—Photo from the Western guard, Madison, Minn.

ident of the Lake Mille Lacs Advisory Association, to resign (Fellegy later became an Outdoor News columnist). Peterson was upset about Fellegy's, and the DNR's, support for banning night fishing on Lake Mille Lacs during a portion of the summer.

• The first Minnesota Deer Classic, which included more than 500 trophy deer heads, also included 23 seminars by deer-hunting experts and nearly 100 outdoor product displays.

• Legislation requiring hunters and trappers to wear blaze orange during the firearms deer season was moving toward passage in the Minnesota House and Senate.

MAY

• Jim Peterson called on DNR Commissioner Joe Alexander and Fisheries Chief Richard Hassinger to resign, citing their "incredible war against sportfish-

500 POUND black bear, with an estimated live weight of over 600 pounds, was shot about 25 miles north of Grand Marais, Minn., by Bruce Nadue of Red Wing, Minn. The bear measured 7 ft. 3¼ in. from nose to tail. —Photo for Outdoor News by John Renschen

THIN ICE caused trouble for this doe which had fallen through on Poke-gama Lake, near Grand Rapids, Minn., Dec. 6. Deputy Sheriffs Bob Serich (left) and Stan Plonske used a safety line and small boat to reach the struggling deer. Once on land, it regained the use of its legs and bounded into the woods.
—Photo from the Grand Rapids (Minn.) Herald-Review

ermen and tourists." If the two refused to resign, Peterson wrote, then Gov. Rudy Perpich should fire them. Peterson went on to write that "Minnesota is rapidly gaining the reputation as a state where sportfishermen are not wanted."

• *Outdoor News* gave the title of Top Sportsman of the Year at Mille Lacs to Mike Meleen, of Foreston, Minn. He caught a 9-pound, 10-ounce walleye at Mille Lacs and released it.

JULY

• Under new fish transport regulations, all fish being shipped or transported by Minnesota residents must be packed and wrapped in a way that they can readily be unpacked, counted, and examined. Other requirements are a patch of skin for identification, and all undressed fish must have heads, tails, fins and gills intact.

• A storm smashed through the Carlos Avery Wildlife Management area, leveling trees and affecting about 1,000 acres.

BUD GRANT, Minnesota Vikings Coach, was one of the main speakers at the Minnesota Sportfishing Congress meeting at Mankato last Tuesday, March 15. He is shown here with Fritz Schneider of Madison Lake, Minn., whose 9 lb. 4 oz. largemouth bass from Lake Washington was declared the official Minnesota record recently when the previous record fish was disallowed.
—Photo special to Outdoor News

AUGUST

• During the media preview for Game Fair, Chuck and Loral I Delaney introduced the first sporting clays range ever in the Western Hemisphere. The Delaneys had shot sporting clays in Europe.

SEPTEMBER

• Changes in U.S. Fish and Wildlife Service regulations governing timber wolves will allow the state to implement its wolf-management plan. There was a stable population of 1,200 to 1,400 wolves in northern Minnesota at the time.

NOVEMBER

• Minnesota U.S. Senator Dave Durenberger introduced a bill to reduce acid rain by taxing major air polluters for their emissions.
• The DNR announced the appointment of Larry R. Shannon, from Sacramento, Calif., as the new DNR Fish and Wildlife director.

DECEMBER

• The mild winter of 1982-'83 contributed to the state's all-time high ice-related death toll of 20 fatalities, according to the DNR. Alcohol consumption and nighttime operation of snowmobiles were major contributors.
• The DNR and Pheasants Forever joined forces to distribute food to feed pheasants. There was concern that high numbers of birds would starve and die because of deep snow and sub-zero temperatures.
• The opening weekend of Wisconsin's deer season was disappointing with rain sweeping the state. The kill was 25 percent below average.

STATE SENATOR BOB LESSARD of International Falls, Minn., caught this 24-lb. 10 oz. northern pike in Ontario's Crooked Lake to take the lead in the International Falls Daily Journal season-long fishing contest in that category. He used a spinner and minnow combination for bait.

Trophy at Deer Classic

ROBIN IDOL of Seely Lake, Mont., is shown holding a set of antlers from a Minnesota deer killed in 1955. The antlers scored 186 inches and were ranked 43 in the Boone and Crocket record book.

TOP MUSKIE caught in the Mississippi near Little Falls by Rev. James Boesel of Hicksville, N.Y., weighed in at 42 pounds.

1984 — *A blizzard struck southwestern Minnesota. Though only a few inches of snow fell, there were very low windchills and heavy winds, which caused 16 deaths and left many people stranded in fish houses and vehicles.*

• *Former vice president and U.S. senator from Minnesota, Walter Mondale was nominated as the Democratic presidential candidate. Mondale lost to President Reagan, who got 59 percent of the vote.*

• *What many consider the most popular TV show of the 1980s, The Cosby Show, debuted.*

• *The U.S. Supreme Court ruled people who used their VCRs to tape television shows weren't violating copyright laws.*

• *The U.S. and the Vatican exchanged diplomats for the first time in 116 years.*

• *The Soviet Union and other bloc nations pulled out of the Summer Olympics, held in Los Angeles .*

CONTENDER for the world record in the 10-pound line class is this 34 lb. 6 oz. brown trout caught in Lake Michigan near Arcadia, Mich., by Robert Henderson, Vestaburg, Mich.

—Photo from Huron Daily Plainsman

👉 JANUARY

• Pheasant feeding reached a fevered pitch in the state, the result of a severe winter that led some people to find birds frozen solid. Birds were unable to find food and shelter because of deep snow and freezing temperatures. Pheasants Forever chapters operated about 1,100 pheasant feeding sites across the birds' range in the state, and the DNR set up a special hotline for citizens to access help for pheasants.

• The DNR announced that the white-tailed deer kill in 1983 – about 146,000 during the firearms season – was the new high-water mark for the state. It also was 40 percent higher than the kill in 1982. The previous record was 127,000 deer, back in 1965. The DNR sold about 372,000 firearms licenses.

MARCH

• Mariner Outboards began sponsoring Muskies, Inc.'s catch-and-release program. Since the program began, Muskies, Inc. members have released 13,813 muskies over 30 inches in length. According to Bill Davis, the group's catch-and-release chairman, that's the equivalent of stocking 367,584 fingerlings. Of the sponsorship,

THIS 22 LB. 11 OZ. walleye caught by Al Nelson of Higdon, Ark., from Greers Ferry Lake set the Arkansas record in 1982. Now, studies are proposed to see if a "giant" strain of walleyes could exist in Minnesota. (See Editorials, Page Two).
—Photo special to Outdoor News

A LIVING MEMORIAL to the late Jim L. Peterson dedication was held near Brandon, Manitoba, Canada. Left to right are Lenny Samuelson; landowners John and Erma Ginter; Don Helmeke; Barb and Jeff Lutz; Jim Peterson; Dave Moran; Bob Peterson and Doreen and Neil Groves. Pictured in front is Jim L. Peterson's daughter, Heather.

Davis said, "This long-term sponsorship will free up club funds so that we can increase our stocking and research projects."

December

• A 22-year-old from Little Falls illegally speared a 49-pound muskie from the Mississippi River south of Little Falls. In his editorial, Jim Peterson quoted Frank Schneider, past president of Muskies, Inc. and the Minnesota Sportfishing Congress, as saying: "The $165 fine was not much more than a slap on the wrist". Think of all the young

1983 Water Deaths Lowest On Record

There were 80 water related deaths in Minnesota during 1983, the lowest number recorded during any of the 40 years for which the Department of Natural Resources has records.

The highest number of such fatalities, 180, occurred in 1944, and the previous low year was 1977 when 84 persons died in state waters.

Information from state agencies on issues like boating and snowmobile fatalities frequently appeared the following year.

muskies that a fish that size could produce. Hundreds of fish have been lost. Furthermore, the value of the fish being caught in the summer – if it is killed and not released – would be many thousands of dollars to the tourist industry and the economy of the state." Peterson noted several other occasions in which large muskies also were illegally speared.

• The DNR declared Lake Mille Lacs an experimental lake, and banned spearing on the lake between Dec. 1 and Dec. 20. The agency planned to hold the shortened spearing season on an experimental basis for two years.

BOB SCHRANCK, author of "Bounty Bag", a collection of wild game and fish recipes and an outdoor writer for the Minneapolis Star and Tribune, will give wild game and fish cooking demonstrations during the annual Dayton's-Bachman's spring flower show, "Minnesota Wild," which is now underway and continues through Sunday, April 8, in Dayton's Minneapolis eighth-floor auditorium.

LADY HUNTRESS FASHIONS are being shown at Game Fair '84 for the first time by designer Phyllis Rose who will hold two more fashion shows this weekend, at 2 p.m. Saturday and Sunday, at the Game Fair Seminar Tent. She also has a booth in the Exhibit Tent, displaying her new line of hunting apparel for women, plus accessories and gift items from Andersen Originals of Prior Lake, Minn.
—Outdoor News photo by Jim Peterson

NEW PRODUCTS

ARBOGAST SPUTTERBUZZ

1985 — U.S. President Ronald Reagan and Soviet leader Mikhail Gorbachev began meeting to patch up relations between the two countries.

• *An exhibition led by Dr. Robert Ballard located the wreck of the RMS Titanic in the North Atlantic.*

• *Live Aid concerts in Philadelphia and London drew many big-name musicians. The concerts aimed to benefit victims of famine in Africa.*

• *British scientists found a hole in the ozone layer over Antarctica.*

• *The U.S. population neared 238 million and the life expectancy approached 75 years of age.*

JANUARY

• The state began a buyout program of commercial fishermen on Lake of the Woods and Rainy Lake. The program is the result of legislation passed in 1983 that calls for phasing out of commercial gamefish netting on the two border waters. Commercial fishermen had the option of selling their remaining quota to the state for $1.15 per pound. Fishermen who did not sell were required to convert from gillnets to trap nets in 1987. Commercial fishermen had averaged annual catches on Lake of the Woods of 250,000 pounds of walleyes, and on Rainy Lake averaged annual catches of 18,000 pounds. The state paid for the buyout via a $2.50 surcharge on fishing licenses in 1984.

• Both U.S. Sen. Dave Durenberger and Gov. Rudy Perpich asked the U.S. government to get involved in the controversy between Minnesota and Ontario over fishery resource management of the border lakes.

BUD GRANT (L) AND HOWIE HANSON received their awards at the Fur, Fin and Feather Club's "Old Timers Party" at the Radisson South last Wednesday evening (Nov. 20). Grant, the Vikings head coach and popular outdoorsman/conservationist, was honored as "Sportsman of the Year", and Hanson, president of the Minnesota Sportfishing Congress, received the "Jimmy Robinson Badge Number One" award. **(See Editorials, Page Two).**
—Outdoor News photo by Jim Peterson

FEBRUARY

• Two bills to ban or curtail spearing were introduced in the state Legislature.

MARCH

• The Reinvest in Minnesota bill, designed to use state General Fund revenue for millions of dollars in fish and wildlife improvement programs, passed the House Natural Resources Committee.

DR. WALTER BRECKENRIDGE, left, well-known wildlife artist, photographer and lecturer, was presented the Communicator-Conservationist Award at the Sportshow last week by Harold Swanson, chairman of the Farmer-Sportsman Awards committee. —Outdoor News photos by Jim Peterson

18½-Pound Bass Caught on Rapala in Florida

Deer Hunting Licenses Set New Record

Based on estimates from county auditors, it appears that approximately 413,500 persons bought licenses to hunt deer with firearms in Minnesota during 1984, the Department of Natural Resources reported this week.

Wild Turkeys Set Record in Minnesota

Minnesota's 1985 wild turkey season was a banner hunt, setting a new record with 323 gobblers bagged this spring.

The 1985 harvest was 80 percent above the previous record of 178 set in 1984. A total of 2,750 permits were made available through a computerized drawing, and an estimated 14 percent of the hunters registered a gobbler this spring.

World Record—Almost

NEAR RECORD northern pike was caught though the ice of tiny Lake Wazeecha near Wisconsin Rapids, Wis., by Chuck "Scales" Schauer of Wisconsin Rapids who used a minnow for bait. The 48-inch fish weighed 31 lbs., 2 oz., just 11 ounces short of the 31-lb. 13 oz. northern from Saskatchewan which is the world record for northerns caught through the ice, according to the Freshwater Fishing Hall of Fame in Hayward, Wis.
—Photo from the Wisconsin Rapids Daily Tribune, Courtesy of Jim Vavrina, Wisconsin Rapids

The bill was based on the report of Gov. Rudy Perpich's "Governor's Commission to Promote Hunting and Fishing in Minnesota."

JUNE

• The DNR sent buyout agreement forms to the 17 commercial fishermen on Lake of the Woods and Rainy Lake. DNR Commissioner Joe Alexander didn't know how many would take part, but said he "wouldn't be surprised if all but three or four of them decided to hang up their nets this year."

AUGUST

• The DNR unveiled plans for a 17,000-acre non-motorized zone in the Nemadji State Forest dedicated to management of timber wolves and moose.

• Ray Ostrom, who helped Ron Weber organize Normark in the 1960s, retired as secretary/treasurer of the company. He had been with Normark for 25 years.

• DNR Deputy Commissioner Steve Thorne wrote a long letter to the editor, criticizing Jim Peterson for a variety of articles he'd written about the DNR's proposal to create a wolf and moose management area in the Nemadji State Forest. Thorne wrote that articles criti-

cizing the agency's plan "are either the result of a misreading of the Department's plan or a deliberate attempt to mislead the reader."

SEPTEMBER

• Minnesota ranked third in the nation in the number of licensed anglers in 1984. And it was fourth in the number of nonresident anglers. According to the Department of the Interior, Minnesota had nearly 1.5 million paid license holders. California had the most, with more than 2.5 million.

OCTOBER

• Minnesota conservation officers and a Beltrami County sheriff's deputy seized 4,800 feet of illegally placed gill net from Upper Red Lake. The nets were on the east end of the lake, outside of waters controlled by the Red Lake Indians.

NOVEMBER

• In an effort to reduce the risk of the state's wild turkeys breeding with inferior hybrid or pen-raised birds, the DNR required a permit to release any turkeys into the wild.

DECEMBER

• The DNR reminded ice fishermen that Lake Mille Lacs was a trophy lake, which meant fishermen could take only one walleye longer than 20 inches.

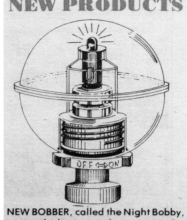

NEW PRODUCTS

NEW BOBBER, called the Night Bobby, uses calculator-type batteries and a light emitting diode (L.E.D.). The Night Bobby will last up to 24 hours and features a slip slot to allow the line to slip freely when desired.
—Photo Special to Outdoor News

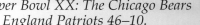

JANUARY

• A group – the Fish and Wildlife Legislative Alliance – was formed to push for the passage of the Reinvest in Minnesota bill. The alliance was a conglomeration of the state's conservation, fish and wildlife groups.

• Federal Cartridge Corporation announced its management and other investors had purchased Federal

1986 — In Super Bowl XX: The Chicago Bears defeated the New England Patriots 46–10.

• All seven astronauts aboard the space shuttle Challenger died when it exploded 73 seconds after liftoff from Cape Canaveral, Fla.

• The Statue of Liberty in New York Harbor was reopened to the public after an extensive refurbishing.

• President Reagan ordered frozen Libyan assets in the U.S., and U.S. warplanes also attacked Libya. The attacks were in response to a bombing in Berlin of a disco frequented by U.S. servicemen. Two servicemen were killed in the disco attack; 79 were injured.

• The cost of a first-class stamp was 22 cents.

Cartridge and its sister division, Hoffman Engineering, from the Olin Foundation, Inc. The new company was renamed Federal-Hoffman, Inc., though the ammunition division still operated under the Federal Cartridge name.

• The U.S. Environmental Protection Agency held four hearings in Minnesota on acid rain.

• The U.S. Fish and Wildlife Service proposed new rules for lead shot in a report that supplemented an environmental impact statement the agency published in 1976. The new rules included six alternatives, one of which was to shut down migratory bird hunting so no migratory birds died of lead poisoning.

• Conservation officers on Lake Mille Lacs reminded anglers they could not fry and eat walleyes while on the lake, due to its status as a "trophy lake."

MARCH

• The House Environment and Natural Resources Committee approved a bill to allow the Department of Agriculture to select and sell up to 10,000 acres of state land located next to wild rice beds. The bill was designed to aid the state's paddy rice industry.

• Retired Vikings coach Bud Grant became honorary chairman of the RIM Legislative Coalition, which pushed for passage of Reinvest in Minnesota.

9-Point Antlered Doe

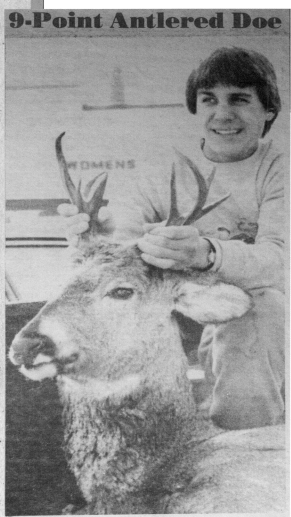

'BUCK' TURNED OUT TO BE A DOE with nine points on its well-formed antlers, surprising 16-year-old Adam Olson of Grand Rapids, Minn., who was hunting with three others near Deer River, Minn. The deer is being studied by the DNR.
—Photo from the Grand Rapids Herald-Review

HEADLINES

Pair Fined $1,330 for 66 Northerns

Two non-resident anglers from Iowa have forfeited a total of $1,330 after failing to appear in court following their arrest by Minnesota conservation officers for possessing 30 northern pike each over the legal limit of 3.

Violet and Wayne McDaniel of Muscatine, Iowa, were apprehended at a resort on Bowstring Lake near Deer River, Minn., in Itasca County.

Frog Spearers Among Latest T.I.P. Arrests

A taste for frog legs turned out to be an expensive proposition for two people in southern Minnesota.

The two were arrested for spearing giant bullfrogs following a tip to the local conservation officer, said Glenn Nyquist, president of TIP (Turn in Poachers), Inc.

"WHEN I REACHED the scene," said the arresting officer, "I found the poachers had already speared seven frogs. Some of them were close to six inches long."

Giant Buck May Be New Bow Record

From the Wright County Journal-Press

BUFFALO, Minn. — Curt Van Lith is hoping to be notified that his deer is a new state or maybe national record for a typical deer head by bow and arrow.

Curt was on his stand in a tree near a corn field between Maple Lake and Buffalo, when he saw

STATE RECORD moose, shot last fall by Don Blake of Chaska, Minn., who was hunting north of Lutsen, Minn., also is the fifth largest Canadian moose in Boone and Crockett world records. The antlers, with a spread of 59 inches, scored 229. They will be on display at the Deer Classic.

• The DNR announced that 142 hunters had been arrested in the fall of 1985 in the Lac qui Parle Goose Zone for a variety of state and federal law violations. Most of the arrests – 88 – were for using lead shot.

• The Reinvest in Minnesota bill passed on the final day of the legislative session, and was sent to Gov. Rudy Perpich for his signature. The bill, described as one of the best pieces of fish and wildlife legislation ever passed in the country, included $16 million in funding, including

LARGEST TURTLE ever weighed by the Minnesota DNR, 65 pounds, will be on display at the DNR building at the State Fair, Aug. 21 through Sept. 1. (See Story).
—Photo from the Grand Rapids Herald-Review

EDITOR'S NOTE: This is the cover of "The Best of Jimmy Robinson," the 334-page book with dozens of stories and pictures of famous people, plus several full-color art prints, published by John R. Meyer, Lakes Publishing Company, Inc., Detroit Lakes, Minn. It is one of my prized possessions, because it was signed by Jimmy: "To my good friend, Jim Peterson, one of the best friends I ever had."

$10 million to take marginal and erodible land out of production. Perpich signed the bill March 20.

• The DNR ordered 40 tons of deer pellets as part of an emergency deer-feeding measure in the International Falls and Isabella areas of northern Minnesota. Deer in other parts of the state fared well over the winter.

April

• The DNR's budget was cut by about $4.3 million, the result of unallotments Gov. Rudy Perpich used to make up the state's expected revenue shortfall.
• A U.S. District Court judge in Alaska ruled that Alaska natives – Eskimos – could hunt migratory waterfowl during any season of the year. The headline in Outdoor News? "Year-Round Eskimo Hunting May Wipe Out Some Species."
• The DNR added rock reefs to walleye-spawning areas on Lake Winnibigoshish and Dixon Lake.
• Gov. Rudy Perpich signed into law a rule that requires motorboat operators suspected of being intoxicated to submit to a blood or breath test, or be fined.

CLIFF LETTY'S cartoons ran in Outdoor News for many years.

May

• DNR walleye researcher Dennis Schupp reported fishermen could substantially increase the number of larger walleyes in future years by releasing smaller fish.

June

• The DNR and University of Minnesota collaborated on a project to gather goose eggs from the city, hatch them, and then give the goslings to sportsmen's groups in Carver, Dakota and Itasca counties. The idea was to slow the expansion of the metro goose population, and establish resident flocks in outstate areas.
• Outdoor News and Sports Afield writer Jimmy Robinson died at 88 years old. The headline in Outdoor News read: "Sportsman of the Century Jimmy Robinson is Dead." He was one of the founders of Ducks Unlimited, and that group's officials estimated he was responsible for obtaining more than $10 million

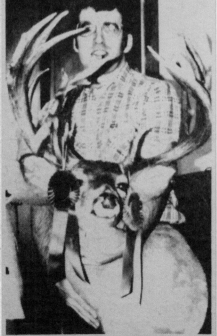

BEST OF SHOW non-typical whitetail in the historical division at the Deer Classic was shown by Roy Ober of Cloquet, Minn., whose grandfather, Peter Antonson, shot this trophy which scored 233 3/8, in 1938.
—Outdoor News photo by Jim Peterson

WORLD RECORD lake sturgeon, caught on hook-and-line, by James M. DeOtis of Maple Grove, Minn., on Sept. 11. The National Fresh Water Fishing Hall of Fame certified the 92-pound 4-ounce fish was caught on 15-pound-test line.

in donations.

AUGUST

• Gerald Kittridge was named director of the DNR Enforcement Division. He replaced Fred Hammer, who had been director since 1980.

• The DNR reported that 43 of the 50 trumpeter swan eggs gathered in Alaska had been successfully hatched. The eggs were part of an effort to restore the birds in Minnesota.

• The DNR opened the state's largest boat access in Two Harbors. It provided public access to Lake Superior via Agate Bay. The access included three launch ramps and parking for 98 vehicles.

SEPTEMBER

• A 12-year-old caught the new state record bass, which weighed 8 pounds, 4 ounces, in Kego Lake near Longville. Another youth, a 15-year-old who was hunting near Mizpah, killed a 687-pound black bear that measured 7 feet, 7 inches in length. It was thought to be the biggest Minnesota black bear on record. The next Outdoor News contained a photo of a new record black bear – 758 pounds live weight, shot near Flour Lake off the Gunflint Trail – and a new state record bass – an 8-pound, 9½-ounce fish caught in Fountain Lake in Albert Lea.

OCTOBER

• The National Freshwater Fishing Hall of Fame certified a 92-pound, 4-ounce sturgeon caught in the Kettle River as a new world record.

• The DNR announced plans to try to remove a herd of

Eelpout: Haute Cuisine?

Anyone who has taken the trouble to fillet one of the ugly, slimy eelpout has found it to be a real gourmet's delight with a "salt-water" flavor. It is often called poor-man's lobster by those who have tried it.

Getting somebody to try it is the real chore.

Here's how I make the cleaning chore a little bit easier: I take the frozen fish down to the laundry tub in my basement, turn the water on as hot as it will go and wash the slime off the fish with a scrub brush. At the same time, the flesh is thawed about a quarter to a half inch below the skin, making it easy to make the cuts down the back, sides and tail. Then I take a pliers and pull off the skin and cut out the "tenderloin" meat along the backbone. (Throw the belly meat away).

I cut the strips of meat in chunks and put them in a pot of boiling water with some onions, celery and a couple of bay leaves. I let the water come back to a full boil for one minute. Then I take out the chunks of meat and place them under a broiler, basting them with seasoned lemon butter, for three to five minutes or until done.

Try it sometime — and you'll never throw away another eelpout!

In his Jan. 10, 1986, column, Publisher Jim Peterson lamented the wanton waste of eelpout (burbot) on Mille Lacs and other large lakes, and he offered his tips for cooking what he called "a real gourmet's delight."

40 elk that was damaging crops in the Grygla area of northwestern Minnesota. The agency had tried removing them twice before.

NOVEMBER

• A bowhunter killed a 264-pound buck near Buffalo that had a preliminary Pope & Young score of 198. It was thought it may have scored high enough to be a new state or national record.

• The DNR announced a two-day post-season deer hunt for early December in the northwestern part of the state. A blizzard during the regular season prevented enough deer being killed there during the regular season.

DECEMBER

• The deaths of 1,500 Canada geese at the Lac qui Parle Wildlife Management Area were a mystery after testing indicated lead didn't kill them.

• The DNR announced plans to use federal sharpshooters to reduce deer numbers in the Minnesota River valley. Deer density in the area was estimated at 69 deer per square mile. The density manageable for habitat and safety – 15 to 25 deer per square mile.

• Dorothy Molter, the last resident of the Boundary Waters Canoe Area Wilderness, died at her cabin on Knife Lake, which is along the international border near Ely. One newspaper story referred to her as "The Loneliest Woman in America."

HUGE CRAPPIE, weighing 3 lbs. 8 oz., was caught Jan. 17 in Bald Eagle Lake, the **Outdoor News** Lake of the Week on Jan. 10, by Craig Oldenburg of Ham Lake, Minn. **(See Letters, Page Two)**
—Photo for Outdoor News by The Outdoorsman, Forest Lake, Minn.

40-Pound

muskie was caught in the Mississippi River near Cohasset, Minn., by Jim Funk of Grand Rapids, Minn., who was using a homemade lure. The trophy was 52 inches long and 23½ inches in girth.
—Photo from the Grand Rapids Herald-Review

1987 — For the first time in history, the world population exceeded 5 billion people. The U.S. population was more than 242 million.

    • Iraq President Saddam Hussein apologized after an Iraqi missile attack killed 37 people aboard a U.S. frigate in the Persian Gulf.

    • The Minnesota Twins baseball team won its first World Series, defeating the St. Louis Cardinals four games to three.

    • Congress held a number of hearings regarding the Iran-Contra scandal; President Reagan accepted responsibility for the policy going astray.

    • British Prime Minister Margaret Thatcher won a third term.

JANUARY

    • Federal Cartridge executive Bob Ehlen died at the age of 81. Ehlen worked for Federal for 60 years, beginning as an office boy and groundskeeper when he was 16 years old. His pay at the time? Less than 23 cents an hour. Ehlen retired from Federal in 1981. At the time, he was chairman of the board.

• An experimental spearing ban that began in 1984, and became a total ban two years later, worked. According to guide and pro fisherman Jerry Anderson: "A number of northern pike in the 20-pound class have been caught by anglers in recent weeks. Trophy fishing for northerns will continue to get even better."

• Taxpayers donated a record amount to the 1986 Nongame Wildlife Checkoff – nearly $800,000. The average donation was $5.06, and the DNR was able to fund more than 90 projects.

• At an international meeting, the United States and Mexico agreed to join forces on conservation efforts to benefit snow geese and endangered masked bobwhite quails.

• C.B. Bylander, who had been assistant managing editor of the Winona Daily News, was named regional public affairs coordinator for the DNR in Brainerd.

• Ron Nargang, who had been director of the Minnesota Soil and Water Conservation Board, was named director of the DNR Division of Waters.

• Through January, 70 vehicles

GRITS GRESHAM (right), famous national television outdoorsman, visited Game Fair '87 and was presented the Game Fair Appreciaton Award by Chuck Delaney.

ROBERT B. "BOB" EHLEN, who died last week at age 81, is pictured when he received the Sportsman of the Year Award in 1982. (See Editorials).
—Outdoor News Photo

TWELVE-POUND LARGEMOUTH bass was caught March 26 by 7-year-old Michael Pendzimas, 16721 Valley Drive, Andover, Minn., while vacationing at Lake Toho near Kissimmee, Fla., with his taxidermist father, Mike, who will, of course, mount the fish.
—Photo Special to Outdoor News

World's First Ice Trolling Contest Held at Grand Rapids

From the Grand Rapids Herald-Review

GRAND RAPIDS, Minn. — Watch the record books.

A perch, little bigger than the bait it was caught on, just may be the largest fish ever caught while ice trolling.

You see, it was also the only fish caught during the world premiere of the winter event on Forest Lake in Grand Rapids Saturday, Jan. 24.

ICE TROLLING is the brain-child of Grand Rapids business-man Al Kruger and was made a part of the Grand Vinterslass celebration.

The concept is simple: cut a trench in the ice and troll along its edge with a snowmobile, much as one would troll from a boat. There, however, the similarities end.

AFTER ALL, when one is troll-
(Continued on Page 6)

ICE TROLLING from a snowmobile being driven along a trench in the ice, part of the Grand Vinterslass celebration at Grand Rapids, Minn., is believed to be the first such event in the world. Patrick Basten tries his luck while his father trolls down the ice of Grand Rapids' Forest Lake.

ICE TROLLING TRENCH on Grand Rapids' Forest Lake can be seen clearly in this picture as Lee Wagner and Jeff Oakley try their luck. (See Story).
—Photos from the Grand Rapids Herald-Review

had fallen through the ice, and seven people had died after going through the ice. That was more than double the number for the entire previous winter.

FEBRUARY
• The highest number of deer ever killed by accidents – mostly via cars – in the seven-county metro region occurred in 1986. The total: 2,818.

MARCH
• The Senate Agriculture Committee approved a bill to allow tilapia fish farming in the state. Tilapia is a fast-growing African food fish. The DNR and sportsmen's groups opposed the bill.
• The DNR designated Lake Minnetonka for experimental northern pike and muskie management. As a result, spearing was banned on the lake between Dec. 1 and Feb. 15.
• The DNR announced that placing in the water any artificial product, including a plastic tree designed to attract fish, was illegal.

13 Lb. 3 Oz. Walleye

MINNESOTA RIVER FISHING, from boats in open water, was the "strangest in anyone's memory, with many, many anglers getting limits of walleyes," said Curtis B. Warnke, editor/publisher of the Wood Lake, (Minn.) News. Included in the catches were the 13 lb. 3 oz. walleye caught Feb. 15 by Jeff Jertson of Granite Falls, Minn., (ABOVE) and the 10 lb. 2 oz. walleye caught by Mark Phinney on Feb. 14 (BELOW), by casting jigs from a boat. (SEE LETTERS, PAGE TWO). —Photos from the Wood Lake News

APRIL

• The Fisheries Division of the DNR, in part because of the tilapia bill in the Legislature, announced plans to continue with strict controls on the importation and rearing of fish in the state in order to protect native populations.

MAY

• Both the state House and Senate voted to increase the cost of hunting and fishing licenses. The house also dropped a portion of legislation that would have mandated the use of ethanol in unleaded gasoline.

JULY

• The DNR announced plans for the state's first elk hunt in nearly a century. The idea behind the season, to be held in the Grygla area, was to resolve long-standing elk depredation problems. The DNR planned to make five licenses available for the season.

AUGUST

• The DNR announced plans to hold a special goose

STATE ARCHERY RECORD whitetail head and what may be the second largest in Pope & Young's national records, was shown by Curt Van Lith of rural Wright County at a recent Fur, Fin and Feather Club luncheon where he was the guest of Hugh Price, right, director of the Deer Classic. The head will be on display at this weekend's exposition at the St. Paul Civic Center.
—Outdoor News Photo by Jim Peterson

Metro Goose Hunt: 'Partnership in Action' . . . Editorials, Page 2

CAPABLE PARTNERS' METRO GOOSE HUNT produced these big honkers for a group hunting in Brooklyn Park in cooperation with the Brooklyn Park Police Dept. The group, which included (L-R) Greg Burgins, Gary Hite, Chris Commins, Don Kindom and Tom Kindom, show the results of the hunt which enabled handicapped hunters to have an outing with a Capable Partner. (See Editorials, Page Two). —Photo Special to Outdoor News

JOHN SATTERWHITE, the "world's greatest shot," again will perform his unbelievable shotgun feats twice daily at Game Fair '87. He is best known for picking up seven clay targets, tossing them in the air, then breaking all seven before they hit the water of Game Fair Lake (1.8 seconds). —Outdoor News Photo by Jim Peterson

hunt in the seven-county metro area to reduce goose numbers. The season was to be held Sept. 1-10. The Canada goose flock in the metro numbered about 15,000 at the time, and wildlife officials worried it could double by 1991.

SEPTEMBER

• Thirty-seven muskies were caught during the 20th anniversary International Muskies, Inc. tournament in the Longville, Walker, and Cass Lake areas. Anglers released 35 of the fish. A total of 688 anglers competed in the three-day event.

• Lead poisoning was confirmed as the cause of death for 75 mallards in Traverse County's Mud Lake.

OCTOBER

• The DNR announced plans to hold a special late December Canada goose hunt in the seven-county metro area. The hunt was to be held Dec. 18-27, and like the special September season, was designed to control metro goose numbers.

• Grass carp, one species of Asian carp, were found to have been illegally imported and stocked into three private ponds in the metro region. A golf course has purchased 50 of the weed-destroying fish from a private outstate hatchery.

• A hunter killed a moose with a 69-inch rack near Greenwood Lake. It was thought to have been one of the largest moose ever taken in the state.

• Lake Christina was treated with the fish-killing rotenone in an effort to rehabilitate the lake. Cost for the project, thought to be the largest waterfowl lake reclamation in the country, was $300,000.

NOVEMBER

• The DNR announced it was designating Cass Lake for northern pike and muskie management, which meant it was closing to spearing. The agency planned to evaluate the regulation after 10

years. "Cass Lake is a muskie lake that could provide some of the greatest muskie fishing in the world," DNR Commissioner Joe Alexander said.

DECEMBER

• Glenn Meyer bought Outdoor News and became the newspaper's publisher. Jim Peterson stayed on as editor/publisher emeritus.

• Ely was selected as the home for the International Wolf Center.

• Steve Carney began writing an Outdoor News column.

After 20 years, Outdoor News ownership changed hands. Glenn Meyer bought the business in December 1987.

Jim Peterson's Outdoor News *The Sportsman's Weekly*

Published weekly (52 times a year) by Jim Peterson's Outdoor News, Inc., at 3410 Winnetka Avenue N., Minneapolis, Minn. 55427. Second Class postage paid at Minneapolis, Minn. 55401. (USPS 286-440)

PHONE: 546-4251   AREA CODE: 612

Outdoor News welcomes unsolicited fishing and hunting photographs; enclose a self-addressed stamped envelope for return. Subscription rates: $9 per ½ year, $17 per year, $30 for 2 years. Single copy price: 75¢. Mail all subscriptions, correspondence, address changes and postmaster notice of undeliverable copies to:

**OUTDOOR NEWS, INC.
P.O. BOX 27145
GOLDEN VALLEY, MINN. 55427**

EDITOR AND PUBLISHER
Glenn A. Meyer
EDITOR/PUBLISHER EMERITUS
Jim Peterson

OFFICE MANAGER
Wanda Smith
COLUMNISTS
Wes Broer
Gene Cooper
Fred Daugs
Butch Furtman
Jack Hoene
Len Libbey
Phyllis Rose
Claude E. Titus
PRODUCTION DEPT.
Leo Torola
Esther Torola
Barb Korkko

ASSOCIATE FOUNDER   CHARTER MEMBER

Copyright 1987   Jim Peterson's Outdoor News, Incorporated

By JIM PETERSON

Fred Daugs, Outdoor News columnist, has set a new world record!

This week Daugs received notification that his 15.03 pound rainbow trout, which he caught in Waterloo Creek, Alamakee County, Iowa, on April 9, has been certified as the new world record for rainbow trout caught on fly-fishing tackle with a 2-pound-test tippet.

DAUGS, WHO now lives in Monona, Iowa, after having retired from his teaching position at Carl Sandburg Junior High in Golden Valley, submitted affidavits, pictures and line samples to the National Fishing Hall of Fame in Hayward, Wis., after catching

(Continued on Page 9)

ALLEGED FOUL PLAY SUSPECTED WITH WINNING FISH IN MINNETONKA CRAPPIE CONTEST . . . SEE PAGE 5

JIM PETERSON shows good northern, one of thousands released to be enjoyed by other anglers on another day. Jim's belief is to take enough fish for a lunch and release the rest, especially the big females. —Photo Special to Outdoor News

1988 — A multi-year drought that began in 1988 became one of the worst in history, covering 45 percent of the nation. Precipitation in Minnesota was 6.61 inches from May to July, which was the second-driest of the past 100 years.

• The Iran–Iraq War ends, with an estimated one million lives lost.

• In a terrorist act, Pan Am Flight 103 exploded over Lockerbie, Scotland, killing the 259 people on board.

• Wildfires in Yellowstone National Park burn 750,000 acres (36 percent of the park) before firefighters take control.

ONE OF THE BEST trophy whitetails reported to the **Outdoor News** this past season. Steve Sperl's 15 point, 240 pound buck shot with slug in Stearns County. You'll see this one at the Deer Classic in February. —Photo Special to Outdoor News

JANUARY

• The Outdoor News Fishing Report first appeared on the front page of the paper.

• The front page of Outdoor News carried a story headlined: "Outdoor News 20th Anniversary 'Look Back' to the beginning – 1968." Contributing Editor Steve Grooms wrote the story.

• The U.S. Fish and Wildlife Service had to destroy 4,000 lake trout brood fish and 5.5 million fry at its Iron River National Fish Hatchery near Iron River, Wis. An unidentified infectious agent caused the fish losses.

FEBRUARY

• The first "Outdoor Calendar" appeared in Outdoor News. It listed a variety of items, including special events, fishing contests, banquets and seminars.

• Mike Travis became the new editor of Outdoor News.

• The state of Minnesota and the three Chippewa Indian bands with rights in the 1854 Treaty area of northeastern Minnesota reached a tentative agreement whereby the state would give them annual payments in return for the bands not exercising some of their hunting and fishing rights. The state Legislature had to approve the agreement, which included a $5.05 million payment the first year.

• State Rep. Willard Munger and Sen. Roger Moe announced legislation for a constitutional amendment to establish an Environment and Natural Resources Trust Fund. The two planned to fund the account via state appropriations, including 2 cents from each pack of cigarettes sold. The story was written by Outdoor News' new legislative reporter Dorothy Waltz.

MARCH

• Outdoor News launched a "World Class Sweepstakes." In the sweepstakes, anyone who filled out a card – subscribers and

OFFICER Jim Morowczynski of the Orono Police Department with the 9.9 h.p. Johnson outboard motor that Steve Holland of Chaska, Minn., returned to him on May 19. —Outdoor News photo by Mike Travis

Chuck Schultz with the new archery record Minnesota moose. The animal was estimated at 1,000 to 1,200 pounds field dressed. Its rack measured 62½ inches and scored an impressive 181 points to take the title.

non-subscribers alike – were entered in a contest in which the grand prize was a seven-day guided big-game trophy hunt in British Columbia. Four additional prizes also were awarded.

• In response to a series of articles called "Empty Skies: America's Ducks in Crisis" written in the St. Paul Pioneer Press-Dispatch by that paper's outdoor editor, Dennis Anderson, Outdoor News launched a "Helicopter Hanky" to help raise the $650,000 necessary to buy a helicopter for the U.S. Fish and Wildlife Service to use in nabbing duck poachers in Louisiana.

• The Committee for an International Wolf Center submitted a $2.5 million request to the Legislature to build the center in Ely.

APRIL

• Nearly 500 people attended a

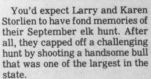

Minnesota Elk Hunter "Glad It's Over"

By STEVE GROOMS

You'd expect Larry and Karen Storlien to have fond memories of their September elk hunt. After all, they capped off a challenging hunt by shooting a handsome bull that was one of the largest in the state.

Unfortunately, the memories that stick with the Storliens are mostly of the circus atmosphere surrounding the hunt and the extreme pressure put on them by environmental groups to not go through with the hunt. "That really spoiled the hunt for us," said Larry Storlien. "I don't really envy the next person who gets a permit."

THERE MAY or may not be another season. According to LeRoy Rutske, the DNR's big game specialist, no firm decision has been made about having another elk season. "Our managers up there are in favor of it, but a lot of people have an interest in this issue, so you never know," Rutske said. He said the DNR was pleased with the success of the first hunt, which went just as expected. "Nobody here expected this would be an easy hunt. We guessed about half the hunters would get an elk, and that's what happened."

There were two seasons in the state's first legal elk hunt since

(Continued on Page 6)

waterfowl symposium at the Edina Community Center. Officials from the Minnesota DNR, U.S. Fish and Wildlife Service, and a whole host of other agencies and nonprofit groups involved in duck conservation attended. Editor Mike Travis wrote that it was an "extremely worthwhile gathering."

• Publisher Glenn Meyer wrote his first editorial in Outdoor News. The topics: Handing out newspapers at the Northwest Sportshow, and Dennis Anderson's Empty Skies series.

• Outdoor News, for the first time, devoted nearly an entire page of the newspaper to running Reader Shots – hunting and fishing pictures submitted by readers.

• New Outdoor News writer Tim Lesmeister filed a story on the Holiday/Johnson Crappie Contest on Lake Minnetonka. But some details of the winning fish – a 1-pound, 14.9-ounce crappie – drew some suspicion, and Outdoor News sought more information about the potential that the crappie actually had been caught two days before in Lake Mille Lacs.

MAY

• The DNR announced plans to release four trumpeter swans on Swan Lake at the Nicollet Conservation Club. It marked the second consecutive year of swan releases.

• A wide variety of media outlets reported on the "Crappie Caper" story that Outdoor News broke. Additionally, the Orono Police Department launched a formal investigation. The man who said he caught the crappie that day in Lake Minnetonka, Steve Holland, wasn't talking.

• DNR Commissioner Joe Alexander announced he was working with Ontario to match the state's and province's respective walleye laws governing the Rainy River border area.

• The Crappie Caper saga concluded. Steve Holland returned the 9.9-horsepower motor he "won" at the crappie tournament. For returning the motor and making a public statement, he was not charged. His statement was this: "I'm giving the motor back to get this matter settled! I retract all my prior statements and will make no further comment, period. I waive any claim for prizes or awards from this or any future Holiday contests."

JUNE

• Former Minnesota Viking Bill Brown drew the names for the World Class Sweepstakes. There were thousands of entries.

This One Bird

Can Help Thousands of These Birds

The Helicopter Fund is in response to Dennis Anderson's "Empty Skies" articles in the St. Paul Pioneer Press Dispatch. The series focused on the excessive illegal harvest of waterfowl in the wintering grounds of Louisiana's coastal marshes. Federal enforcement agents say they need a helicopter to stop this slaughter of ducks and geese. $650,000 is needed to get them a chopper. **Let's make this bird fly!**

Send a minimum of $10 with the coupon below and receive the **Outdoor News Helicopter Hanky.** About $2 of the amount will be used for the cost of the hanky, mailing package and postage. Allow 4-6 weeks for delivery. The **Helicopter Hanky** is a public service of **Outdoor News** newspaper — absolutely no money is kept for profit.

Permission is granted to reprint this ad in its entirety. — Courtesy of Outdoor News, Minneapolis, Minn.

I AM PLEASED TO ANNOUNCE POPULAR SEMINAR SPEAKER, TERRY TUMA HAS TAKEN A FULL TIME POSITION WITH OUTDOOR NEWS AS ADVERTISING MANAGER.

TERRY TUMA

Terry, his wife Karen and sons Troy and Travis make their home in Lakeville, Minn. Terry is best known in the Upper Midwest for his seminars and TV and radio show "Fishing — An Inside Look".

He has written many articles on the subject of fishing and plans to do some writing for this fine publication in the future. While he is considered by many to be an expert on fishing panfish, he is an accomplished walleye and northern fisherman.

Terry will continue his schedule of seminars. If your club or organization would like to talk to Terry about seminars please contact him here at **Outdoor News, Ph. 546-4251.**

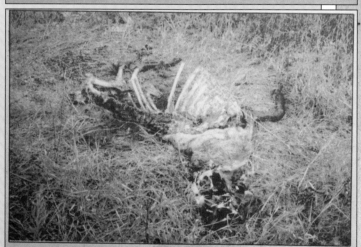

A CLOSER VIEW of the mature bull elk. The initial report to the DNR, although quite vague, said that the animal had at least a 5 X 5 polished rack. Sometime between when the DNR was told about the animal and when they finally found it, someone removed the antlers. The carcass was not as deteriorated as the first three elk, which means that this animal was killed at another time, probably two or three weeks later.

JULY

• Lee Eggen caught a 105-pound sturgeon from the Moose Horn River near Moose Lake, Minn. The fish was more than 12 pounds heavier than the state record lake sturgeon at the time. Just days later, following some media attention on the catch, the fish was stolen. It also turned out the fish wasn't eligible for the record, as three brothers had taken turns reeling it in.

AUGUST

• Several United States senators, including Minnesota's Rudy Boschwitz and Dave Durenberger, sent a letter asking a conference committee dealing with federal budgets to consider providing the U.S. Fish and Wildlife Service with a $400,000 challenge grant for the purchase, maintenance and operation of a helicopter to be used for waterfowl law enforcement in the nation's southern wintering grounds.

SEPTEMBER

• Publisher Glenn Meyer wrote about Geese Unlimited, which had a mission to take surplus metro geese and transplant them elsewhere in the state.

• Two committees were created to work for passage of the Environment and Natural Resources Trust Fund. One group, created by Gov. Rudy Perpich, included former governors Elmer Anderson and Wendell Anderson. Another, a political action committee created by Sen. Roger Moe, featured Bud Grant as the honorary chairman.

• A new law required duck hunters to have personal flotation devices in their duck boats.

OCTOBER

• Four elk were killed illegally in northwestern Minnesota. Turn in Poachers offered a $1,000 reward for information leading to the arrest of the poacher(s).

• Curt Wells began covering North Dakota outdoors for Outdoor News.

• The reward to find the elk poachers rose to $5,100, which included $500 from Outdoor News.

1988 FIRST BEST BUCK CONTEST

Outdoor News launched its popular (and ongoing) Best Buck Contest in 1988. Through the years, the newspaper has printed thousands of entries and winners.

NOVEMBER

• The drive to purchase a helicopter for use in stopping duck poaching in Louisiana ended with success. Enough money was raised via individual and corporate donations – $250,000 – and appropriated to the U.S. Fish and Wildlife Service – $341,000 – to buy a Bell JetRanger helicopter.

• Voters approved establishment of the Environment and Natural Resources Trust Fund. Of those people who voted, 73 percent favored it.

DECEMBER

• Babe Winkelman sued In-Fisherman for its use of the phrase "Teaching America to Fish." In-Fisherman said it had been using that phrase, and variations of it, since 1974. In-Fisherman also sued Winkelman for copyright infringement and plagiarism.

1989 — More than 10,000 Chinese students took over Tiananmen Square in Beijing to rally for democracy. Others – totalling more than 1 million – joined them. The government took a hard line and thousands of protesters were killed.

• The Berlin Wall opened, allowing easterners into West Germany.

• George Herbert Walker Bush inaugurated as 41st president of the U.S.

• The Exxon Valdez oil tanker ruptured, sending 11 million gallons of crude oil into Alaska's Prince William Sound.

• An earthquake struck the San Francisco Bay area, killing 67.

Three Pound Pike is so Unusual That Fish Specialists Won't Even Guess at the Odds

By Mike Travis

When Tom Voigt and Mark Mastin of Park Rapids, Minn., walked into Jerry Matzen's bait shop in Nevis, Minn., on Sunday afternoon of opening weekend 1988 with a pail of northerns they wanted to get weighed — that wasn't unusual. Matzen told **Outdoor News** that these guys always catch fish.

What did gain his attention was when Voigt held up a strange looking fish that appeared to be a northern, except there was hardly any color to it, and said, "Jerry, we got this for you, we can't eat it."

Matzen took a glance at the fish and exclaimed, "Get it in the tank!" to Voigt. The tank Matzen was referring to, is a huge aquarium in his place of business where he keeps fish from area lakes, rang-

THIS IS A photograph of the "white" northern when it was still alive in Jerry Matzen's fish tank at his bait shop.

👉 JANUARY

• At the Minnesota Sportsmen's Boat, Camping and Vacation Show, Outdoor News at its booth had a 3-pound, mutant "white" northern on display. Caught in the Park Rapids area, the fish was translucent and when it was alive, it was possible to see bones through the fish's flesh. Biologists said the pike was neither a silver pike, nor a true albino pike.

• A northern pike caught in Anoka County had an overall golden hue, and a distinct golden color that ran across the top of its back.

• Lake Minnetonka became the first lake in the state to be infested with Eurasian watermilfoil. According to the article, "In the long run, the spread of the weed to other Minnesota lakes is almost inevitable."

MARCH

• The DNR announced it would begin feeding deer in the northern half of the state, which had been covered in more than 18 inches of snow since January. Most deer were in good to fair condition, but officials didn't want things to get worse. It was estimated the feeding could cost as much as $500,000.

• The Izaak Walton League of America and four other conservation groups were slated to go to court in April in an attempt to stop military jet training over the Boundary Waters Canoe Area Wilderness.

• Outdoor News began its Wood Duck Challenge as part of an effort to get kids involved in conservation and the outdoors.

The first-ever Outdoor News Best Buck Grand Prize winner appeared in the Jan. 13, 1989, edition.

GRAND PRIZE WINNER

Bruce Johnson of Cleveland, Minn., hunted near New York Mills, Minn., in Becker County. As he sat in his stand with his Remington .308 Model 6, his thoughts were interrupted by a familiar sensation . . . he was not alone in the woods. Turning slowly, he caught sight of a nervous doe, tail twitching and constantly looking back. Another deer had to be behind her. Sure enough there it was — nose down, neck extended — the buck was trailing the doe. Johnson's thoughts were on the buck. The 12 point buck weighed 235 pounds and the rack had a 21-3/8 inch inside spread.

APRIL

• The state's trap and transplant program for wild turkeys was deemed a success, having transplanted more than 500 birds to contribute to a total state population of between 9,000 and 15,000 wild turkeys.

• The state House Judiciary Committee voted 15-8 against an assault rifle ban, and laid it over for study.

MAY

• The look of the front page changed, thanks to a smaller Outdoor News logo that took up less of the page.

• Harold Cleveland, of Harris, Minn., caught a rare blue walleye in the Boundary Waters Canoe Area Wilderness. Cleveland had the fish mounted, but originally caught it in December of 1988.

GORDY MIKKELSON DAY
WEDNESDAY DEC. 27

One of Minnesota's leading conservationists and outdoorsman, Gordon Mikkelson of Minneapolis and Akeley, Minnesota, received the Minnesota DNR's highest honor on December 18. The Meritorious Service Award was presented to Mikkelson by DNR Commissioner Joe Alexander and Governor Rudy Perpich declared December 27 as Gordon Mikkelson Day. A special Environmental Educators Award was presented by the Fur, Fin and Feather Club and WCCO radio bestowed its "Good Neighbor" award on Mikkelson.   Pg. 2

Outdoor Notes...
By Glenn Meyer, Publisher

THE HELICOPTER WILL FLY SOON! Over a year has passed since Dennis Anderson and the St. Paul Pioneer Press published their provocative series, "Empty Skies; America's Ducks in Crisis." In the series, Anderson challenged sportsmen and conservationists to raise $650,000 to buy a much needed helicopter for the Fish and Wildlife Service to use in waterfowl law enforcement on the wintering grounds.

Since March 1988, over $310,000 has been donated to the Helicopter Fund by over 3,200 individuals, corporations and foundations. An additional $400,000 was authorized by Congress as the USF&WS's share of the costs. A Bell Jet Ranger with floats was ordered for delivery this fall in time for the official dedication ceremony on October 3 in Fort Worth, Texas.

Anyone doubting the effectiveness of using a helicopter to curtail the baiting and slaughtering of waterfowl on the wintering grounds, need not look at the record. Special Agent Dave Hall recently reported that the use of borrowed helicopters this past season reduced the baiting busts from 79 during the 1987 season to a mere three during the 1988 season.

"With the fear of helicopter enforcement and all of the negative publicity, they just stopped baiting," exclaimed Hall. "Maybe we've turned the corner in Louisiana."

Thanks to all our **Outdoor News** readers who contributed to the Helicopter Fund and helped make this a reality.

Youth Shoots Bull Elk By Mistake

By Nancy Lee

It's unfortunate, but it has happened again. Another Minnesota elk has been taken illegally. The elk was taken during opening day of the 1989 firearms deer season.

The 5X5 , 700 lb. bull elk was mistaken for a deer by a 15 year old hunter on Saturday, November 3, at 4:50 p.m. near Motley, Minn., in north central Minn. Foggy weather conditions may have been partially responsible for the mistaken identity. The young hunter will face a gross misdemeanor charge in juvenile court.

Conservation officer, Jeff Halverson (pictured right), out of Region 3 headquarters in Brainerd, Minn., believes this elk strayed from either the Grygla or the Red Lake, Minn. herd. Halverson said that an elk was spotted near Nimrod, Minn., in late October and possibly could be the same one that was killed last Saturday.

In October 1988, **Outdoor News** covered the elk poaching near Grygla, Minn., and helped raise the $7,000 reward posted for information leading to the arrest of the poachers. The reward has not been collected.

—Photo Courtesy of Nancy Lee

A NEAR RECORD 17 lb. 6 oz. walleye was caught by Bob Bruininks of Minneapolis, Minn., while fishing on Loon Lake in Cook County. The fish was only 2 oz. shy of the state record.

—Special to Outdoor News

JUNE

• State officials and sportsmen expressed concern about grasshopper control. Due to large grasshopper populations thanks to climatic conditions, plans were in place to spray 21 counties. Sportsmen were concerned about the potential for the insecticide to kill birds and animals. There also was some concern that pheasant chicks would suffer, due to their reliance on insects as forage.

JULY

• The bones of a 1,000-pound, 100-year-old elk were recovered from Upper Spunk Lake near Avon. The water was thought to have preserved the antlers, which measured 53 inches in length. A St. Cloud State wildlife professor believed the elk was at least 5 years old when it died.

• Bob Bruininks, of Minneapolis, caught a 17-pound, 6-ounce walleye on Loon Lake in Cook County. The fish, caught on a spinner and leech, was 2 ounces shy of the state record.

AUGUST

• In the week before the 1988 deer season, two men poached a deer and put the animal into their van. As they drove down the road with what they assumed was a dead deer, the animal came back to life. The men wrestled with the deer, which had broken the windshield, and killed it with two shots to the head with a .22 rifle. Neither man was injured, but a TIP call led to the poachers' arrest.

• Eric Meyer, son of Outdoor News Publisher Glenn Meyer, joined the paper as an advertising sales representative.

SEPTEMBER

• Through their license fees and special taxes, America's hunters and fishermen contributed more than $1 billion every year for conservation and wildlife management programs.

• The U.S. Fish and Wildlife Service was set to receive its helicopter to conduct law enforcement on duck wintering grounds. But the agency reported using borrowed helicopters during the 1988 season. The results? Baiting busts were down from 79 during the 1987 season to three in 1988. "With the fear of helicopter enforcement and all of the nega-

TRUE ALBINO BUCK AT OUTDOOR NEWS BOOTH

THIS 8 POINT albino buck was taken during a regular firearms hunting season in Minnesota. The animal was completely white, except for the forehead, and had pink eyes, nose and translucent hooves. White deer occur about one in 100,000, but the odds of a true albino is only one out of 500,000. When albino deer are discovered the majority are does, making this animal even more unique.

—Outdoor News photo by Jeff LeBaron

SHOW MAP, EXHIBITOR LIST AND SEMINAR SCHEDULE... P. 6

Prior Lake Hunter Bags Apparent World Record Moose Along B.C. River

Ernie Peacock of Prior Lake, Minnesota has taken what appears to be a world record moose near the Liard River in northern British Columbia last October 22.

Initial Boone and Crockett scoring on the bull's antlers measured 247, five points above the current record for that species posted in 1980.

Peacock, who bagged the moose at 350 yards with a 7 MM Mag, said the bull's antlers spread was over six feet. His outfitter, Ted Cobbett of Scatter River Outfitters, Ltd., in Fort Nelson, BC, immediately estimated it as a new world record. Cobbett was involved in the hunt when the current top mark was taken.

From base camp, the two men had made a grueling 9½ hour horseback trek across a sub-zero tundra and driving 60 mph winds to

ERNIE PEACOCK poses with the six-foot plus moose rack he recently took on a trip to British Columbia.　—Special to Outdoor News

RELEASING TEN wild turkeys in the 850 acre Rice County Park near Faribault, Minn., from left to right are: Glenn Cramer, Director of the Rice County Park System; John Idstrom, DNR Area Wildlife Manager; (far right) Gary Nelson, DNR Wild Turkey Specialist and his daughter Kristy.　—Outdoor News photo by Butch Owens

A EUROPEAN FISHERMAN with two zanders, a walleye-like fish North Dakota is attempting to introduce as a gamefish. The zander is considered by the Minnesota Department of Natural Resources (DNR) to be an "exotic" fish, and there are no plans to import or even begin researching the possibilities at this time. According to Jim Groebner, fish habitat and development coordinator for the Minn. DNR, "Because it's an exotic, we want to be cautious on bringing it into this state." Minnesota walleye population requires much of the department's attention, and given the possible problems an import could create, we don't see the need at this point.
—Special to Outdoor News

Poachers Sometimes Pay Twice

By Tim Lesmeister

"I'm surprised no one was killed," said Gary Thell, a Minnesota Department of Natural Resources (DNR) conservation officer. He was referring to an incident in which two men had allegedly poached a deer about a week prior to last year's opening day of the firearm season.

Responding to a call from Turn In Poachers (TIP), Thell found some unusual circumstances surrounding this particular case. "The informant said that two men had shot a deer. They shot it with a high powered rifle right through the front shoulder. They then pulled the deer into their van and took off down the road."

After the two men travelled a couple of miles down the road, "Mister buck," laughs Thell, "became a cat and decided to come back to life."

Trying to escape, the deer obviously saw the light coming through the windshield and tried to exit there. "It shattered the windshield with points of impact in five places," said Thell.

The two men panicked at that point and wrestled the deer down. While still in the van they took a .22 caliber rifle and shot the deer twice in the head to kill it.

Thell has no knowledge of anyone, other than the deer, being injured in this fracas. But, he wonders how the two men could have been so lucky. "Even with them shooting that rifle in the truck, holding down that deer and shooting it twice in the head...it's amazing neither of the men were

THE TOP TWO photos show some of the damage done to a van once the poached buck came "back" to life. The poachers wrestled the animal back to the van floor and dispatched it with a .22. A phone call to TIP was credited for allowing a Minnesota conservation officer to make the arrest.
—Photos Courtesy of Minn. DNR

tive publicity, they just stopped baiting," Special Agent Dave Hall said. "Maybe we've turned the corner in Louisiana."

OCTOBER
• An outbreak of avian cholera, the first of its kind in Minnesota, had

killed 3,000 to 4,000 Canada geese – of a flock of 167,000 – at the Lac qui Parle Refuge in western Minnesota.

NOVEMBER
• Plymouth deer hunter Harold Kloster and his hunting partners were doing a deer drive in western

Minnesota. Kloster saw movement, then saw antlers and a head. He fired a slug and the deer went down. When Kloster found the animal, he was surprised to find his one shot had killed two deer – both eight-pointers with identical racks and bodies.

• Prior Lake hunter Ernie Peacock killed what apparently was a world record moose in northern British Columbia. The rack measured more than six feet across, and scored 247, which was five points above the world record at the time.

DECEMBER
• Results from Wisconsin's first fall turkey hunting season produced a success rate of 22 percent and a total of 1,570 birds. Minnesota would hold its first fall turkey hunt in 1990.

(LEFT TO RIGHT) Nicolas and Tim Baumgartner, Shannon Kern and Michael Baumgartner all helped salvage these elk bones from Upper Spunk Lake near Avon, which is located in central Minnesota. The antlers and an assortment of these elk bones will be on display in the Outdoor News Booth No. 100 at the Minnesota Hunting and Fall Sports Show.
—Special to Outdoor News

1990 — Iraqi troops invaded the neighboring country of Kuwait, which resulted in the Persian Gulf War.

• Nelson Mandela, imprisoned for more than 27 years in South Africa, was released.

• The Berlin Wall came down, reuniting East and West Germany.

• Fox began broadcasting The Simpsons television show, which rose to quick and lasting popularity; Seinfeld debuted on NBC.

• President Bush signed the Clean Air Act, which aimed to reduce air pollution.

JANUARY

• There was a time when it was a big deal to see a Canada goose in Minnesota, let alone shoot one. But by 1988, Minnesota hunters took 85,000 geese during the hunting season, and relocation programs had been undertaken. An Outdoor News headline read: "The Rise of the Canada Goose: Too Much Of A Good Thing?"

• Entries in the 1989 Outdoor News' Best Buck Contest exceeded 1988 entries by hundreds. The winner was Dennis Kendrick of Marine, Minn., who killed a symmetrical 8-pointer near Scandia.

FEBRUARY

• Fishermen in the state set or tied 14 Minnesota fish records during the 1989 fishing season. Perhaps most impressive was a 16-pound, 12-ounce brown trout caught on Lake Superior. Other new records included: white crappie; quillback carpsucker; shovelnose sturgeon; hybrid sunfish; black bullhead; pink salmon; Chinook salmon.

• The Minnesota DNR and U.S. Fish and Wildlife Service conducted sharpshooting efforts to reduce deer numbers along the Minnesota River. The goal was to bring deer numbers in line with what habitat in portions of the Fort Snelling State Park and Minnesota Valley National Wildlife Refuge could support.

• As a 19-year-old in South Dakota in 1939, Leroy Nelson caught a 33-pound, 8-ounce northern pike. It was large enough to be the state record, but – it being the Depression – Nelson didn't have the money to get the fish mounted. So it stayed in South Dakota. His record fell in 1972. By 1989, he

Outdoor News
The Sportsman's Weekly
Published Since 1968

HUNTING • FISHING • SHOOTING • DOGS • CAMPING • BOATING • TIPS

June 26, 1990

Dear Senator/Representative:

On behalf of our State's sporting and conservation communities, **Outdoor News** would like to learn your position on a number of issues that are critical to the future of our natural resource base.

We would appreciate your response to the following questions. In turn, we will be publishing your answers in hopes of giving our readers a better understanding of your legislative objectives.

1. <u>Wetlands Protection Legislation:</u> In your opinion, what must be included in legislation to assure a no-net loss of wetlands in the future? What measures can be taken to promote the restoration of previously drained wetlands? What will you personally do to assure passage of a wetlands protection bill?

2. <u>Reinvest-In-Minnesota:</u> What level of funding will you support for RIM in the upcoming biennium? Are there particular programs within RIM that you believe should receive increased emphasis? Are there any special actions you will take to promote RIM?

3. <u>Environment and Natural Resources Trust Fund:</u> Do you support the Constitutional dedication of lottery proceeds to the Environment and Natural Resources Trust Fund? Do you believe that the Trust Fund should become the sole source of support for RIM and other natural resource programs? Once the Trust Fund has been funded, what priorities should the Legislature establish among eligible programs/projects?

4. <u>Past Accomplishments:</u> What legislative accomplishments have you achieved that have protected or improved Minnesota's environment and natural resources?

5. <u>New Ideas:</u> What new ideas for protecting and enhancing Minnesota's natural resources do you hope to bring the Legislature if you are elected in November?

On behalf of sporting men and women of Minnesota, we appreciate your time and consideration in responding to these questions. We will look forward to receiving and sharing your answers in our upcoming publications.

With best regards,

Outdoor News

Glenn Meyer

Glenn Meyer, Publisher

> Publisher Glenn Meyer sent this letter to state politicians in June 1990 and shared the responses with readers.

Helicopter Flys Because of Concerned Sportsmen

By Don "The Duckman" Helmeke

Over two years have passed since Dennis Anderson and the St. Paul Pioneer Press published their provocative series, "Empty Skies... America's Ducks In Crisis." Over two years have passed since the sportsmen and conservationists in Minnesota and across the nation had the audacity to take on the waterfowl establishment.

Over two years have passed since **Outdoor News** made the decision to join in the battle to raise $650,000 to buy a helicopter for the U.S. Fish and Wildlife Service (USFWS) to use in waterfowl law enforcement on the wintering grounds.

Last October the heralded helicopter was delivered. After yet another two months delay for installation of specialized enforcement equipment, in late December of 1989, the fearsome Bell Jet Ranger finally took to the air to patrol the vast coastal marshes of Louisiana. With but a few days remaining in the 30 day Louisiana waterfowl season. Federal agents aboard the Bell struck hard. They arrested four men for the illegal baiting and slaughtering of over 50 mallards in one morning's shoot in a marsh 20 miles west of New Orleans.

But, the story doesn't end there. This past March, New Orleans Times-Picayune outdoor writer Bob Marshall reported that the helicopter was effectively grounded due to lack of operating funds. "We're desk-bound for the remainder of the fiscal year — that means through September," said (More on Page 19)

Outdoor News salutes our military in Saudi Arabia

These servicemen and hundreds more are receiving free copies of Outdoor News as part of "Operation Stay In Touch."

Sfc. Stanley Sayers

LCpl. Jerry Eliason

Sgt. Barry Platt

Sgt. John W. Reese

Pfc. James A. Johnson

E3 Alan D. Meyer

E4 James Fink

E3 Alan Dale Seeley

AMS2 Sam Syrstad

Cpl. Scott M. Helling

was living in Cambridge, Minn. His wife and sons that year bought the fish mount from South Dakota for $462 and presented it to Nelson.

MARCH
• Outdoor News invited readers to join its "Action Team." The paper printed an entire page of information related to state and federal government, including legislators and their contact information, and asked readers to make their voices heard.
• Roger Holmes, then head of the DNR Wildlife Section and the Fish and Wildlife Division's acting director, received a Ducks Unlimited Wetlands Achievement Award.

APRIL
• The DNR announced that based on

MONSTER BULL MOOSE. Dan Volkmann, a retired game warden from Hinckley, Minn., and Chuck Moffatt of Hinckley, Minn., bagged these two moose near Upsala, Ontario during January of 1969. The larger bull scored 201-2/8 (in the Boone & Crockett Record Book), and at that time was the fourth largest bull moose recorded in Ontario.
—Special to Outdoor News

results of aerial surveys, the moose population in northeastern Minnesota had dropped by 34 percent from the previous year, and the population in the northwest had dropped by 35 percent.

• More than 1,000 blue and snow geese died in southeastern North Dakota. Avian cholera was a suspected cause. The die-off prompted calls in some quarters for higher snow and blue goose limits.

• The U.S. Fish and Wildlife Service extended by 90 days the comment period for the revised recovery plan for the eastern timber wolf. The American Farm Bureau Federation asked for the extension.

MAY

• A new law prohibits transportation of Eurasian or Northern watermilfoil on roads and highways. It also prohibited launching boats with any of the vegetation attached, and made the penalties misdemeanors.

• A northwestern Minnesota husband and wife

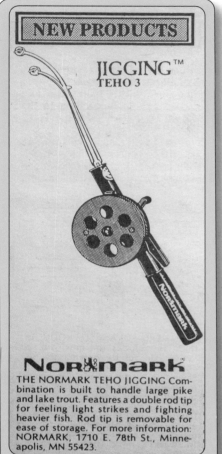

NEW PRODUCTS

JIGGING™
TEHO 3

NORMARK

THE NORMARK TEHO JIGGING Combination is built to handle large pike and lake trout. Features a double rod tip for feeling light strikes and fighting heavier fish. Rod tip is removable for ease of storage. For more information: NORMARK, 1710 E. 78th St., Minneapolis, MN 55423.

deeded 80 acres of land to the Rocky Mountain Elk Foundation. The land, adjacent to the Grygla Wildlife Management Area, then was donated to the DNR, which deemed the land critical habitat for elk.

JUNE

• John Carlson, of Hines, Minn., killed a bear with a 21-inch skull and weighed an estimated 675 pounds. The bear, killed in Beltrami County, would have made the Boone and Crockett record book, but Carlson shot it through the skull, which precluded an accurate measurement.

JULY

• DNR officials announced that they would consider changing tournament rules based on studies that showed high rates of mortality among fish brought back to tournament weigh-ins.

• The DNR asked for limited control of timber wolves after populations in the state doubled from 750 that lived in the state 20 years ago.

• Roger Holmes was named director of the DNR Fish

JIGGING FOR WALLEYES. Jason DeGeorge, age 11, of Rushford, Minn., landed a 45 lb. 7 oz. flathead catfish while fishing on the Mississippi River near Winona, Minn. The big cat was 44" long and took 30 minutes to land.

—Special to Outdoor News

Outdoors Writer Bob Schranck...

Bob Schranck, who has written in just about every section of the daily newspaper in his 33 years at the Star Tribune, is most comfortable writing about outdoor activities and issues.

A desire to make his living with words led to his first newspaper job in 1952. A year and a half later, he was working in the Madrid Bureau of Associated Press. (More on page 2)

Former Minneapolis Star Tribune scribe Bob Schranck contributed to Outdoor News during the early 1990s.

...Joins Outdoor News!

FISH - A - LIVE
" FLOATING " Collapsable Fish Bag

" Brings EM Back Alive "

✳ Attaches To Docks, Boats, Shore
✳ Works Better Than A Stringer
✳ Keeps Dozens Alive All Day
✳ Available In 2 Sizes

✳ Panfish up to 14" - $12.99
✳ Gamefish up to 19" - $19.99
✳ Float Kit Available 8" Dia. - $4.95

MN Residents add 6% Sales Tax & $2.00
For Shipping & Handling

Send Check or Money Orders To:
Fish - A - Live
P.O. Box 422
So. St. Paul, MN 55075

and Wildlife Division. Holmes had been chief of wildlife since 1972.

AUGUST

• The Mille Lacs Band of Ojibwe Indians filed suit in federal court claiming the provisions of the 1837 Treaty exempted them from state hunting and fishing regulations.

SEPTEMBER

• Candidates for governor and state offices answered a variety of questions on natural resources topics. Outdoor News sent questions to 30 candidates; half re-

sponded.

• The Minnesota Conservation Federation named DNR Commissioner Joe Alexander the "Conservationist of the Decade" for 1980 to 1990. It was the first time the federation presented such an award.

• Outdoor News threw its support behind Putting People First, a Washington, D.C.-based group created to fight animals rights activists. In a note, the paper called Putting People First, "one of the most aggressive pro-sportsman groups in the country at this time."

OCTOBER

• A two-year undercover investigation on Lake of the Woods conducted by agents with the DNR, U.S. Fish and Wildlife Service, and Ontario Ministry of Natural Resources resulted in more than 300 violations that included more than 60 individuals and 12 resorts. DNR head Joe Alexander called the illegal activities "outlaw commercialism."

NOVEMBER

• Outdoor News began "Operation Stay in Touch," which gave free subscriptions to troops stationed overseas during Operation Desert Shield.

• A district judge ruled that Babe Winkelman owned the phrase "Teaching America to Fish," but also said Al and Ron Lindner could use variations of the phrase because they, too, were in the business of teaching people to fish.

Hines Minnesota Bear Hunter Bags 675 Pound Black Bear

John Carlson is a transplant from Rochester, Minnesota — the opposite end of the state from Hines, where he lives with his wife and two girls. John is a math teacher for grades seven through 12 in Kelliher, Minnesota. He is an avid hunter and fisherman.

Hunting buddies from Rochester got John started on bear hunting. Soon he was putting out baits...and even got involved in hunting nuisance bears. Dispatching nuisance bears was not as sporting as John preferred.

The lottery worked in John's favor in 1989. He was awarded a permit.

After carefully scouting and placing the bait along the Blackduck River in Beltrami County, the hunt was on.

Watching the bait from a tree stand is similar to deer hunting. Any little sound can trigger a rapid heartbeat. John heard such a sound from his stand on Sept. 5.

When he finally identified the source, it turned out to be a great big ferocious field mouse. However, when he looked up from watching the mouse...there, in the tall grass, was his bear.

Lots of thoughts raced through his mind...Just a small bear. School has started, my time for hunting is limited. He's in a good spot — better take him.

John made a clean shot to the

neck at 30 yards with a 30.06 loaded with 220 grain Winchester Silvertips. Upon approaching the bear John noticed movement — so one final shot to the head ended it.

The bear looked bigger close up. It's enormous size was more evident when Carlson tried to roll the bear onto its back to field dress it.

With help from Loren Stromberg and his tractor, the bear was loaded into Carlson's pickup two hours later. Measurements of the bear were: nose to tail, 6'6''; chest circumference 5'6''!

675 POUND BLACK BEAR. John Carlson of Hines, Minn., won't have this prized bear recorded in the record books because of its broken skull.
—Special to Outdoor News

Because the temperature was 75°F., the hide was removed before weighing the carcass. The next day the animal's quarters were weighed — they totalled 573 lbs.!! This

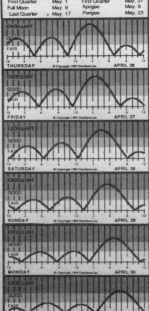

FISH & GAME FORECASTER

The information on these graphs can be helpful in predicting the optimal times of day for catching fish and hunting game. This information is based on past wildlife activity patterns and many predictable factors (sunrise, sunset, tide forces, etc.) which dictate these patterns of activity.

Apr. 26 - May 2

Sunrise/Sunset Table Northern U.S. (44°)		Moonrise/Moonset Table Northern U.S. (44°)	
Sunrise	Sunset	MoonRise	MoonSet
Apr. 26 4:59 AM	6:57 PM	Apr. 26 5:17 AM	9:17 PM
Apr. 27 4:57 AM	6:59 PM	Apr. 27 6:04 AM	10:33 PM
Apr. 28 4:56 AM	7:00 PM	Apr. 28 7:02 AM	11:36 PM
Apr. 29 4:54 AM	7:01 PM	Apr. 29 8:10 AM	
Apr. 30 4:53 AM	7:02 PM	Apr. 30 9:24 AM	12:26 AM
May. 1 4:51 AM	7:03 PM	May. 1 10:39 AM	1:03 AM
May. 2 4:50 AM	7:05 PM	May. 2 11:51 AM	1:32 AM

MOON PHASES			
First Quarter	May. 1	New Moon	May. 24
Full Moon	May. 9	First Quarter	May. 31
Last Quarter	May. 17	Apogee	May. 9
		Perigee	May. 23

EXCELLENT / GOOD / FAIR
THURSDAY — APRIL 26
FRIDAY — APRIL 27
SATURDAY — APRIL 28
SUNDAY — APRIL 29
MONDAY — APRIL 30
TUESDAY — MAY 1
WEDNESDAY — MAY 2

The Annual Fish & Game Forecaster can be purchased by sending $6.95 to Forecaster, P.O. Box 23208, Dept. ODN, Minneapolis, MN 55423. Minnesota residents add 6% sales tax. Canadian residents add $1.

1991 — The Minnesota Twins baseball team won its second World Series in five years, defeating the Atlanta Braves four games to three.

• A cease-fire ended the Persian Gulf War.

• The Pittsburgh Penguins defeated the North Stars in the Stanley Cup championships.

• Anita Hill accused Judge Clarence Thomas of sexual harassment. After contentious hearings, he was confirmed to the U.S. Supreme Court.

• The Halloween Blizzard struck, dumping more than 28 inches of snow in the Twin Cities.

 JANUARY

• In an effort to "test the waters," State Sen. Bob Lessard, DFL-International Falls and chair of the Environment and Natural Resources Committee, introduced a bill mandating that anglers use only barbless hooks beginning in 1993. Punishment for violating the law would have been a warning; beginning in 1994 it would have been a petty misdemeanor. Lessard said the bill's immediate purpose was to gauge anglers' feelings about barbless hooks.

Outdoor News led an effort to organize sportsmen statewide via an organization called SPORT — Sportsmen Protecting Outdoor Recreation Traditions — during the early 1990s. Below, Ken Burglund worked the SPORT booth in 1991 at Game Fair.

SPORT REPORT. Active volunteer, Ken "Burgie" Burglund answered questions and enlisted sportsmen into SPORT last weekend at Game Fair. SPORT was recently founded to offset the anti-hunting and animal rights movement. The response has been very good, and the organization will be at Game Fair this coming weekend, August 16-18.

Several people asked if a certain club or group was supporting SPORT and if so, they would not. There are so many organizations with as many causes, it's impossible to "vouch for" every one of them. Some national organizations have state chapters that are more aggressive in some areas of their agenda than others. It's impossible to agree 100 percent with everyone all the time ... so SPORT intends to work with as many groups as possible, so long as they help more than harm our cause.

Mutant Ninja Goldfish

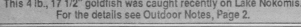

This 4 lb., 17 1/2" goldfish was caught recently on Lake Nokomis. For the details see Outdoor Notes, Page 2.

ANIMAL RIGHTS ACTIVISTS demonstrated at the Holiday Plus store in Bloomington, Minn., holding anti-hunting posters. The activists found little support for their cause. Photo two shows a bowhunter trying to figure out the convictions of one of the activists. The leader of the demonstration (photo three), is wearing leather shoes ... sending a mixed message about his attitude towards animal feelings and/or rights.

Carlson Appoints Sando

GOVERNOR Arne Carlson and Lieutenant Governor Joanell Drystad hear Rod Sando's good neighbor philosophy. Sando reveals his thoughts in Bob Schranck's column on page 3.

—Photo Courtesy of Bob Schranck

MR. MINNESOTA SPORTS-PERSON, Rollie Johnson, will be among friends at the Fur, Fin and Feather "Old Timer's Luncheon" December 11. The event will be held at the Sheraton Park Place in St. Louis Park. **Special to Outdoor News**

FEBRUARY

• Lessard, in response to responses to a questionnaire printed in Outdoor News, announced his proposed barbless hook bill was going nowhere. "I've been around here for 16 years, and never once in those years have I ever had a response from a newspaper like what my office got from the barbless hook questionnaire printed in Outdoor News."

MARCH

• Bowhunting legend Myles Keller had a 24-foot trailer that included 16 of his trophy whitetail deer heads stolen while he was at the Shooting, Hunting, Outdoor Trade (SHOT) Show in Dallas. Police believed the thieves were targeting the trailer, not the deer heads. All 16 bucks were Pope & Young animals, and represented 30 years of hunting in five states. Eight came from Keller's home state of Minnesota.

APRIL

• A significant decline in moose numbers in the northeastern part of the state led DNR officials to close the fall hunting season. While it was unclear what caused the decline, evidence pointed to high infestations of winter ticks. The DNR also announced it would hold a season in the northwestern part of the state, where the moose population was increasing.

• Lawmakers tapped portions of the Environment and Natural Resources Trust Fund and directed the money to

FISHING IN STYLE! Pat Murphy of Hastings, Minn., showed some real style and ingenuity when he constructed this igloo-shaped fishhouse. The house as a 12-foot high dome, and is 20 feet in diameter. Inside there are 10 holes, a kitchen sink, wall-to-wall carpeting and much more. Shown outside the fishhouse out of Karpen's Sunset Bay Resort are Scott Murphy and Brian Sherry.

Predator patrol — team one

OUTDOOR NEWS strongly supports trapping and shooting predators of game birds. The populations of fox, raccoon, skunk and coyote are too high, and are having a negative impact on upland birds and waterfowl. Please send **Outdoor News** photos showing the results of your predator control program!

the state's General Fund. That included $2 million from the Future Resources Fund (cigarette tax money).

MAY

• Local forestry officials in Aitkin County, as well as five conservation officers, worked a stakeout and caught three individuals who were setting fires on private property. In that area of Aitkin County, there had been wildfire problems for nine of the previous 10 years.

• Outdoor News Publisher Glenn Meyer's

TWENTY YEARS AGO THIS WEEK. On Jan. 4, 1971, the Minnesota Conservation Department had its name changed by the state legislature. A new logo was introduced as well as some departmental changes. One of those changes was to give the commissioner the authority to pay the expenses of advisory groups or individuals who have specialized knowledge on technical natural resource matters.

301 POUND BUCK

ELL-KAY FOSS of Wannaska, Minn., dropped this "super buck" that field dressed out at 301 lbs. Live weight was calculated to be over 380 lbs. —Photo Courtesy of Joy Nordby (Grygla Eagle)

brother Geoff was accidentally shot while turkey hunting in Missouri. He was hit by No. 4 shot from a distance of 30 yards and recovered at a hospital in Kirksville, Mo.

• The Minnesota Wetlands Conservation Act passed off the Senate floor with only seconds left in the 1991 legislative session. The act is considered one of the strongest wetland protection measures in the nation. According to a follow-up story: "Under the final bill, protection of wetlands will become an integral part of state and local water management planning."

JUNE

• While bow fishing on Bald Eagle Lake on May 21, Fran Michaud bagged an 85-pound carp – the largest in the state ever taken by a bow fisherman. A biologist estimated the fish, which was 46.5 inches long with a 32.5-inch girth, was 80 years old.

Outdoor Notes . . .

By Glenn Meyer, Publisher

SHOCKING ADVERTISING:

"Milwaukee ... July 1991 ...

They were drugged and dragged across the room ...

Their legs and feet were bound together ...

Their struggles and cries went unanswered ...

Then they were slaughtered
and their heads sawn off ...

Their body parts were refrigerated
to be eaten later ...

Their bones were discarded with the trash.

It's Still Going On!

That is the headline in a full page ad that appeared in the *Des Moines Register* last week. It was paid for by the People for the Ethical Treatment of Animals (PETA)!

Minnesota has new Fisheries Chief

Management changes in the Minnesota Department of Natural Resources' (DNR's) Fish and Wildlife Division have been announced by Director Roger Holmes. Richard Hassinger, formerly chief of Fisheries, has been appointed assistant to the director of Fish and Wildlife. Jack Skrypek, chief of Ecological Services, has been named acting chief of Fisheries. Both Fisheries and Ecological Services (plus Wildlife), are sections of the DNR's Fish and Wildlife Division.

Hassinger, 52, a Duluth native and 30-year DNR employee, has been Fisheries Section chief since 1982. He will tackle a wider range of problems in the new post of Fish and Wildlife Division assistant director. Holmes said, "He is tak-

ing this opportunity to get broader experience in Fish and Wildlife management by moving over to the Director's Office," Holmes said.

Among Hassinger's new duties will be serving as the DNR's representative in negotiations over Native American fishing and hunting treaty rights. Hassinger will also follow through on several new fisheries management initiatives at the division level.

"We will be able to use his excellent background of fisheries management, knowledge of the Game and Fish Fund, and expertise for the division as a whole," Holmes said of Hassinger.

Skrypek, 52, a St. Paul native and 30-year DNR employee, has been

Jack Skrypek

BURGER BROTHERS. Bud and Ted Burger caught these East Coast Atlantic salmon on the Moisie River in Quebec, Canada. The fish on the left weighed 28 lbs. and the one on the right weighed 31 lbs. The Burger's caught the salmon by using the fly fishing method. After taking the photo, the fish were released.

Photo Courtesy of Burger Brothers

AUGUST

• A group called SPORT – Sportsmen to Protect Outdoor Recreation Tradition – was created "to act as a defense line between any group or individual that poses a threat to the fishing, hunting or trapping rights and privileges of sportsmen and women in Minnesota."

• Angler Chris Sager caught the new state record tiger muskie in Lake Calhoun in Minneapolis – a 33-pound, 8-ounce fish that topped the previous record by more than 3 pounds.

Operation Stay In Touch!

CPL KOREY G. KAMPEN displays an upbeat attitude while serving our country in Saudi Arabia. Cpl Kampen is a member of the First Tank Battalion. For more photos, see page 21.

(Four Color Separation Courtesy of G.V. Graphics, Golden Valley, MN)

SEPTEMBER

• The DNR instituted a ban on baiting deer. According to the new regulation, it was illegal to place or use bait for the purpose of taking deer. The agency defined bait as grain, fruit, vegetables, nuts, hay, or other food transported and placed for the purpose of attracting or enticing deer.

OCTOBER

• Anglers fishing in Lake Nokomis caught a 4-pound goldfish that measured 17.5 inches in length.

NOVEMBER

• Avian cholera was spreading quickly among Canada geese stopping over at the Lac qui Parle Wildlife Management Area in western Minnesota. The number of birds with avian cholera increased from 100 or 150 per day to 500 per day. Officials were scrambling to find an incinerator large enough to burn all the carcasses.

• A fisherman caught a 13-pound walleye in Gull Lake.

Letter From The Gulf!

To Outdoor News:

Thank you very much for the free subscription to **Outdoor News**.

Every bit of news we receive from home is important to us here, especially the outdoors news. We had to leave the great state of Minnesota right in the middle of hunting season — the first deer hunting season I've missed in 25 years! We received refunds for our deer hunting licenses, but the antlerless permits many of us got went unused.

Being in Saudi Arabia has given all of us a deep sense of appreciation for the beautiful forests, lakes, and clean water Minnesota has. They have no deer hunting shacks, red wool, leaf-covered logging roads, 12 gauges, brook trout rivers, canoe portages, or walleye lakes.

Sand, oil and camels (no open season) are about the only things they have. Part of the reason we are here is to preserve their standard of living and OURS. I think it's worth it. Thanks again.

—Paul Rust (Saudi Arabia)

1992 — U.S. President George Bush and Russian President Boris Yeltsin declared an end to the Cold War.

• Riots and violence erupted in Los Angeles after four police officers were acquitted in the beating of Rodney King.

• Bill Clinton was elected as president.

• After 20 years, Johnny Carson hosted The Tonight Show for the final time.

• The U.S. population neared 255 million, and the life expectancy rose to nearly 76 years.

 JANUARY

• An investigation by the Board of Animal Health revealed eight herds of wild hogs (300 animals total) at farms throughout the state. The animals were imported to the state for hunting purposes. Dr. Walter Mackey, of the Board of Animal Health, said: "If Minnesota ever allows European wild hogs to become established in our woodland, we will regret it. We will never get rid of them."

• The DNR announced that anglers broke seven state records in 1991. Records that fell included those for brook trout and tiger muskies.

• The death toll due at avian cholera at Lac qui Parle Wildlife Management Area grew to more than 6,500,

POACHERS BUSTED. Conervation Officers (left to right) Tony Anderson and Scott Fritz, apprehended two adults and two juveniles who are suspected of spearing 18 northerns from a creek near Cedar Lake in Rice County. *Special to Outdoor News*

including 5,904 Canada geese. A similar outbreak in 1989 killed 7,200 geese.

MARCH

• The DNR began preparations for a court case with the Mille Lacs Band of Ojibwe Indians. Even so, the agency continued negotiations with the Band about treaty rights. In 1990, the Band filed suit against the state, arguing the 1837 Treaty gave them the right to

POTENTIAL NEW STATE RECORD!

BEST BUCK WEEKLY WINNER. Camp Ripley in Morrison County, Minn., produced a potential new state record whitetail. Michael Langin of Osceola, Wis., had the hunt of his life when he used a doe bleat to bring this 19 point buck within 25 yards of his stand. At 9 a.m. on Oct. 31, 1992, this 4-1/2 year old buck was dropped with an arrow to the spine. The antlers green score was 228 7/8 non-typical Pope & Young points. The inside spread measured 17-7/8 inches wide with the longest tine at 13-6/8 inches. If the score holds until the 60 day drying period has ended, this buck will be a new state record. *Photo Courtesy of Craig Cousins*

IRATE PROTESTER tried to upstage Bud Grant as he spoke to the crowd.

hunt, fish and rice without state regulation in the ceded territory.

APRIL

• The state filed charges against Ely bear researcher Lynn Rogers, claiming the he possessed two bear cubs that died or were killed while in his possession. Rogers disputed the version of the story contained in the complaint.

• The Save Mille Lacs Committee, formed in response to the Mille Lacs Band of Ojibwe Indians' suit against the state, continued to grow; hundreds of people attended a meeting in Bloomington.

• Hundreds of anglers, including former Vikings coach Bud Grant, descended upon the state Capitol "to bring politicians their concerns over the lawsuit filed by the Mille Lacs Band of Chippewa." DNR Commissioner Rod Sando later told the crowd the agency had reached an impasse with the Band as it related to commercial use of the resources.

JUNE

• The DNR reported that exotic species such as zebra mussels, ruffe,

WORLD RECORD SHEDS. This set of non-typical world record sheds were collected in Minnesota. The antlers with 39 points scored 334 0/8. For complete story and live photos of this wild deer, see Jeff LeBaron's column in next week's issue of Outdoor News.

Teacher suspended for forcing animal rights philosophy

School officials in Ohio have placed a teacher on leave while they investigate claims that she forced her animal rights philosophy on students, according to a recent Associated Press report.

Parents of students in Kathleen Markovich's fifth-grade class had complained that their children were being forced to perform homework assignments involving animal rights issues. Mrs. Markovich denied the charge.

24 LB. 12 OZ. NORTHERN

AITKIN COUNTY LUNKER. Cory Waskey of Anoka, Minn., had a thrill of a lifetime when this 41" 24 lb. 12 oz. northern pike nailed his shiner minnow in 7' of water on Ripple Lake. The huge pike hit the bait at 1:30 p.m. on Feb. 4, 1992 and was landed after a 30 minute battle. The fish had to be pulled through an 8" hole without the assistance of a gaff.

Photo Special To Outdoor News

SPONSORSHIP SUPPORT. Don Shelby Invitational Bass Tournament organizers Shelby, left, and Irwin Jacobs presented a silver sponsor appreciation award to **Outdoor News** staffer Terry Tuma with the help of celebrity participant Hulk Hogan, right, during one tournament banquet.   *Outdoor News Photos by Jim Linette*

and spiny waterfleas had taken hold in certain lakes and rivers in the state. The agency said boaters were one vector for spreading them, and urged boaters to be vigilant.

JULY

• Zebra mussels were discovered on a barge pulled out of the Mississippi River in St. Paul. Officials with the DNR were not surprised, as the mollusks had been found in the Mississippi River near LaCrosse, Wis., in 1991.

AUGUST

• Outdoor News launched its "Opinion" piece, to go along with Publisher Glenn Meyer's column and letters to the editor.

Capitol rally sends message

By Glenn Meyer

Anglers by the hundreds turned up on the steps of the State Capitol Thursday, April 15, to bring politicians their concerns over the lawsuit filed by the Mille Lacs band of Chippewa. The suit against the state asks for hunting and fishing rights off the reservation. The part of the suit that has sportsmen troubled, is the effect of the spearing and netting of fish in Mille Lacs Lake.

The Hunting & Angling Club sponsored the rally to ask the Governor, Attorney General and legislators to get involved in this issue, and requested the following:

1) That the state of Minnesota issue a fact sheet which fairly outlines what is at stake in this litigation, and to keep the public informed.

2) That no more secret negotiations take place giving away public resources, and that the demands and offers be made public.

3) That the state of Minnesota devote adequate attention and resources to prepare for a proper defense of this litigation.

4) That the state of Minnesota file in support of the counties right to also participate in this litigation, and file in support of the right of the local landowners to also intervene in this litigation, and file in support of the right of responsible hunting and fishing clubs to participate in this

CLYDE BELLACORT trying hard to discredit Bud Grant.

FAMILIAR PHRASE sounded often at the rally.

BIG TURNOUT at the State Capitol for the Hunting & Angling Club rally.

with legal position; and c) determine the long-term ramification

Grant was addressing the crowd, when a man began heckling him. After a call for the security did not deter the man, Grant asked him to the microphone and allowed him to address the crowd.

When Grant returned, he told the sportsmen he was there to make sure the citizens of the state were properly represented in the law suit, and asked fellow sportmen to get involved ... but to do it in a civilized manner. As he spoke a parade of vehicles pulling boats passed in front of the Capitol as the crowd cheered.

Minnesota Department of Natural Resources (DNR) Commissioner Rod Sando told the group the DNR reached an impasse in the negotiations with the tribe when it came to the commercial use of the resources. Sando said he felt very confident about the case, and that the DNR did have access to adequate resources to defend their position.

Although the DNR is preparing for a court case, Sando said the door for negotiations is still open.

Larry Peterson of Park Falls, Wisconsin, led a delegation of the group Protecting American's Rights and Resources (PARR) and told the crowd gathered on the capitol steps, that they had incompetent people handling the situation in Wisconsin, and no to let this happen here.

Outdoor Notes . . .
By Glenn Meyer, Publisher

NUMBER ONE S.P.O.R.T. AWARD. Finding a state legislator who is more pro-sportsman than Senator Bob Lessard, is tough. The northern Minnesota lawmaker is an avid hunter and fisherman himself, who knows the issues and speaks out loud and clear, when problems appear at the Capitol.

SENATOR BOB LESSARD (left) accepts the first *Number One S.P.O.R.T. Award* from S.P.O.R.T. Executive Director, Alan Robinson.   *Special to Outdoor News*

SEPTEMBER

• A federal magistrate allowed the Save Mille Lacs Association to participate in the lawsuit filed against the state by the Mille Lacs Band of Ojibwe. According to SMLA President Doug Iverson: "The *amicus curiae* will allow us to not only provide information to help the court to render a just decision, but also to show the court the level of concern of the state's sportsmen."

GIANT MUSKIE. Mike Christopherson of Bemidji, Minn., was casting a black Eagle Tail over a reef on a lake in northwest Ontario, when this enormous muskie nailed his bait. The 55 inch, 43 lb. fish was hooked at 9 a.m. on Sept. 15, 1991, and the angler kept the trophy to be mounted.

OCTOBER

• A TIP call led conservation officers to 11 anglers who were in possession of 1,846 sunfish and crappies – 1,351 fish over the limit. The anglers, from Minnesota and Illinois, were fishing Mission Lake in Crow Wing County.

• Gary Clancy began writing his "Enjoying Our Woods & Lakes" column in Outdoor News .

NOVEMBER

• The state DNR and Mille Lacs Band of Ojibwe reached a tentative settlement concerning the Band's claims to hunting, fishing and gathering rights in the ceded territory. The settlement was subject to approval of the Minnesota Legislature.

• Outdoor News unveiled *Bowhunter's Hotline*, which it called "The hottest new bowhunting publication available."

DECEMBER

• Outdoor News published a full-page, point-by-point breakdown of the Mille Lacs treaty agreement.

ALBINO WHITETAIL. This rare 8 point whitetail buck was taken by Ken Malisheski of Big Lake, Minn., on Nov. 7th at 2:30 p.m. in Kanabec County. This all white deer had pink eyes and nose. The unusual buck chased a doe past Ken's stand at 75 yards, where he made the shot with a 30.06 caliber rifle. Special to Outdoor News

MINNETONKA MULE DEER. On Nov. 26, 1992, Arlyn Hamann, of Minnetonka, Minn., discovered this oddity in his backyard. A forked horn mule deer was feeding behind his house which is located near the intersection of I-494 and County Road 7. It spent the following two days in the vicinity and on Nov. 28th, it spent the evening sleeping in the Hamann children's sand box. Special to Outdoor News

1993 — PLO leader Yasser Arafat and Israeli prime minister Yitzhak Rabin shake hands in Washington D.C., after signing a peace accord.

• Federal agents raided the Branch Davidian Complex in Waco, Texas. Four agents and 76 Branch Davidians died.

• In New York City, a van bomb parked below the North Tower of the World Trade Center explodes, killing six and injuring more than 1,000.

• A first-class stamp cost 29 cents.

COLORADO RECORD. Mike Okray of Stevens Point, Wis., bagged this 36-point, 300-pound trophy whitetail deer while hunting in Colorado last October. The buck's rack measured 258 2/8 non-typical in Boone & Crockett to set a Colorado state record. See page 7. Photo Courtesy of Greg Pile

 JANUARY

• Firearms deer hunters set a new harvest record during the 1992 season. The 230,000-deer kill was up 11 percent from 1991 – which was the previous record high. It marked the sixth time in 10 years hunters eclipsed the record.

• A British ammunition company was making bismuth shot, and some hunters pushed the U.S. Fish and Wildlife Service to allow bismuth as an alternative to steel.

• DNR Commissioner Rod Sando proposed buyouts of resorts that would be adversely affected by the treaty fishing zone the DNR and Mille Lacs Band of Ojibwe Indians agreed to as part of the negotiated settlement.

• Outdoor News began a new feature called "Remembering the Good Ol' Days." The feature included old hunting and fishing photos, and short stories accompanied the photos.

• Hundreds of people rallied at the state Capitol in opposition to the negotiated settlement between the state and Mille Lacs Band. About 30 or 40 tribal members and supporters of the settlement also were on hand.

• The 1992 bear harvest of 3,130 animals was a new state record, marking the seventh record harvest in 10 years.

FEBRUARY

• The DNR would have been combined with eight other state agencies as part of a superagency bill introduced in the Legislature by Sen. Larry Pogemiller, DFL-Minneapolis. In one issue of Outdoor News, Pogemiller wrote in favor of the bill, while Sen. Bob Lessard, DFL-International Falls, wrote against it.

• The Bureau of Alcohol, Tobacco and Firearms offered a $10,000 reward for information leading to arrest and prosecution of whoever was responsible for setting fire to and destroying five meat trucks owned by the Swanson Meat Company in Min-

GRAND KIDS AT OPENER. Winners of Outdoor News' Grand Kids Contest spent opening weekend fishing and meeting local sports and broadcasting personalities, as well as Gov. Arne Carlson (above). Photo layout on pages 8 and 9.

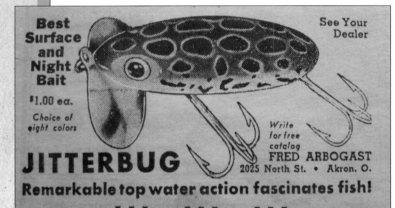

Best Surface and Night Bait

$1.00 ea.

Choice of eight colors

See Your Dealer

Write for free catalog FRED ARBOGAST 2025 North St. • Akron. O.

JITTERBUG

Remarkable top water action fascinates fish!

GOOD NEWS ... BAD NEWS. When Moses was leading his people out of the desert (back in the old days), he came across the Red Sea. Wanting to get his people to the other side, he prayed to God for help. God told Moses he had good news and bad news. To help Moses and his people, he could part the sea by just raising his hands ... that's the good news. The bad news is ... he would first have to get permission from the DNR!

neapolis. Messages were left behind claiming to support an animal rights movement.

MARCH
• Minnesota and Ontario fisheries officials met to discuss concerns and establish an advisory committee to search for ways to settle border disputes.
• Marge Anderson, chief executive for the Mille Lacs Band, vowed to seek court permission to launch a commercial netting operation on Lake Mille Lacs if the state Legislature didn't approve the negotiated settlement.

APRIL
• Bud Grant opined that the case between the state and Mille Lacs Band should be settled in court, not out of court. Grant also said sportsmen and women, by and large, were not in favor of the negotiated settlement.
• A bill was introduced in the state House to allow anglers to not have more than one walleye longer than 20 inches, and one northern pike longer than 30 inches.
• Indian officials, in testimony before the U.S. Senate Committee on Indian Affairs, requested Wallop-Breaux funding (federal excise taxes on fishing tackle) for tribal natural resource programs.
• The state House shot down a bill allowing youths ages 12 to 16 who had a firearms safety permit to receive top preference for antlerless deer permits.
• Outdoor News held "The Grand Kids Contest." The qualification process involved having kids, in 50 words or less, write why they wanted to fish the Governor's Fishing Opener with their favorite grandparent. Winners received a trip to the Governor's opener.
• Gov. Arne Carlson urged DNR Commissioner Rod Sando to develop a revised version of the negotiated

The Outdoor News staff in 1993 included: (back row) Jim Linnett, Terry Tuma, Dan Johnson, Eric Meyer, John Connelly; (front) Terry Welch, Publisher Glenn Meyer, and Sara Meyer.

GARY AND NANCY CLANCY with a stringer of walleyes taken on leeches from Lake of the Woods on opening day 1990.

Photo Courtesy of Gary Clancy

BEST BUCK WEEKLY WINNER

PIEBALD BUCK. Eric Johnson of Eagan, Minn., spotted this unique whitetail twice while scouting his southern Twin Cities metro area hunting territory. On Sept. 19 he arrowed the buck at a distance of 15 yards.

Special to Outdoor News

BOAT PARADE GOES SMOOTHLY. The Hunting & Angling Club held a boat parade in front of the State Capitol on Saturday. Many sportsmen from across the state brought their decorated boat and formed a procession in front of the Capitol in St. Paul. The intention was to send the legislators the message about the agreement. No nets ... and no agreement! The message was delivered in a peaceful manner. Even the local media had trouble finding anything negative to say.

agreement between the state and Mille Lacs Band.

• The DNR created a workshop to inform southeast Asians about opportunities and regulations related to natural resources use in Minnesota.

• Nine Indians were issued citations for attempting to spear or possessing a spear on Lake Mille Lacs. The nine, part of a spear-in, opposed the state and Mille Lacs Band negotiated settlement.

• Dan Johnson became Outdoor News editor.

MAY

• Gov. Arne Carlson signed a law that made blaze orange the only acceptable color for apparel during the firearms deer season, beginning in 1994.

• The state Legislature voted not to approve the negotiated settlement between the state and Mille Lacs Band.

JULY

• A district judge in Montana struck down that state's law protecting hunters from harassment, saying it infringes on free speech.

• The three headlines on the July 6 front page: "Adrift on Rainy Lake: Anglers survive a living nightmare;" "Metro geese roundup captures over 3,000 honkers;"

1,250-POUND MOOSE. Wildlife artist Les Kouba (kneeling) and hunting partners (left to right), Chuck Thompson, Paul Adlis and Stan Adlis, shot this huge moose north of Thief River Falls, Minn., on Oct. 9. The old moose had antlers that spanned 61 inches at the widest point. The hunters took the moose as it walked out of a small stand of woods near the Adlis farm.

Special to Outdoor News

32-year-old Metro angler struck by lightning Monday

A 32-year-old Minneapolis angler was struck by a bolt of lightning while fishing on Lake Independence during a thunderstorm Monday evening. The man is expected to survive, but remains in serious condition Tuesday, suffering from second- and third-degree burns to his hand, feet and thighs.

Reports from eyewitnesses said the man's fishing reel was burned into his hand, and the rod was completely blown away. A friend fishing in the boat with the injured man felt the jolt, but was not hurt.

Boaters are very vulnerable to lightning strikes, and should leave the water and seek shelter when thunder and lightning storms are present.

Almost a state record!

Brenda Passow of Pomeroy, Iowa almost broke the Minnesota state walleye record last Friday with this 17-pound, three-ounce trophy taken from Bad Medicine Lake near Park Rapids.

The walleye hit a homemade lure and nightcrawler combo on four-pound test line.

If the giant fish had immediately been weighed on official scales, it might have topped the 17-pound, eight-ounce record fish caught by LeRoy Chiovitte in the Sea Gull River in Cook County on May 13, 1979.

A LARGE CROWD. Approximately 600 sportsmen met on the steps of the State Capitol Sat., Jan. 9 to send a message to elected officials that they should get involved in the treaty dispute.

Special to Outdoor News

"Search for toxic barrels goes on in Lake Superior."

• The Save Lake Mille Lacs Association sought to become a full party in the lawsuit between the Mille Lacs Band and the state.

AUGUST

• A two-year, multi-agency investigation into the illegal sale of game fish revealed a pipeline of walleyes allegedly running between tribal nets in Leech and Red Lake, and to buyers in Minnesota and elsewhere. A DNR Enforcement official estimated there would be 40 arrests.

• An Iowa angler caught a 17-pound, 3-ounce walleye in Bad Medicine Lake near Park Rapids. It was 5 ounces smaller than the state record.

SEPTEMBER

• Two friends were fishing Lake Minnetonka when a muskie bit one angler's jig and broke his line. Then the muskie appeared, head above water, 30 feet from the boat. It "charged" the boat, and the two anglers netted the 18-pound fish. They released it.

• The U.S. Justice Department announced it wanted to join the treaty rights lawsuit between the state and Mille Lacs Band – on the side of the band.

OCTOBER

• A pen-raised buck attacked and killed the man who had raised it since it was a fawn.

• The U.S. Justice Department was allowed to intervene in the lawsuit between the state and Mille Lacs Band; the Save Lake Mille Lacs Association was not.

DECEMBER

• Fall turkey hunters killed 605 birds, setting a new fall harvest record.

"Rollie Johnson Remembered" event scheduled for April 1

The dean of outdoor sportscasters in the Midwest, Rollie Johnson, is gone -- but the stories linger on. Friends and fans of the late, great outdoorsman and broadcasting executive are invited to a "Rollie Johnson Remembered" stag evening in his honor April 1 at the Minneapolis Convention Center.

What tales will be told at the get-together which will be both an open house and an organizational meeting of the Rollie Johnson Remembered Society?

Although he passed away at 88 in January, the event will celebrate Rollie's accomplishments in a setting he would have enjoyed ... surrounded by friends he valued much more than his many awards and honors. As befits the occasion, the cash bar will feature "Lord and Coke" (Lord Calvert and Classic Coca Cola), the libation of his choice, plus beer. Dry hors d'oeuvres will be served.

Proceeds from the $10 admission -- at the door -- will go to the Protect Minnesota Sportfishing Legal Fund. The event will run

THE LATE ROLLIE JOHNSON. Rollie's life will be remembered by friends and fellow outdoorsmen at the Minneapolis Convention Center on April 1.

Special to Outdoor News

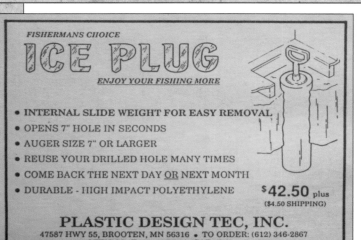

FISHERMANS CHOICE
ICE PLUG
ENJOY YOUR FISHING MORE

- INTERNAL SLIDE WEIGHT FOR EASY REMOVAL
- OPENS 7" HOLE IN SECONDS
- AUGER SIZE 7" OR LARGER
- REUSE YOUR DRILLED HOLE MANY TIMES
- COME BACK THE NEXT DAY OR NEXT MONTH
- DURABLE - HIGH IMPACT POLYETHYLENE

$42.50 plus
($4.50 SHIPPING)

PLASTIC DESIGN TEC, INC.
47587 HWY 55, BROOTEN, MN 56316 • TO ORDER: (612) 346-2867
OPEN M - F (4pm - 8 pm), SAT. (8am - 4pm)

Les Kouba (left) and Paul Adlis display their impressive moose antlers.   Special to Outdoor News

Dr. Jerry Jurgens of St. Cloud, Minn. took this 6x6 bull elk during an Oct. 1993 hunt in the Gallatin National Forest in Montana. Dr. Jurgens was guided by J.R. Buffalo Creek Outfitters from Gardiner, Mont.

1994 — Former football star O.J. Simpson was arrested in the killings of his wife and a male friend. The story, and subsequent trial, captivated the nation.

• Nancy Kerrigan, an Olympic figure skater, was attacked. Her opponent, Tonya Harding, pleaded guilty to lesser charges, but was believed to have had involvement in the attack on Kerrigan.

• Major League Baseball players went on strike; the World Series was cancelled.

☞ JANUARY

• The state of Wisconsin banned back-trolling for muskies on inland waters. Natural resources officials worried the technique provided too great of an opportunity to catch muskies.

• Outdoor News discontinued its regular editorial, substituting instead a column by Editor Dan Johnson. " … We believe that a newspaper's editorial should be used sparingly, for very special issues," Johnson wrote.

• The North Central Caribou Corp. proposed reintroducing woodland caribou into the Boundary Waters Canoe Area Wilderness. The group wanted to introduce 25 caribou a year for three years. DNR officials said reintroducing caribou would be at the bottom of their priority list, given the budget crisis.

FEBRUARY

• The state legislative auditor audited the

DNR and found the agency illegally spent at least $93,000 on administrative costs. The money, raised by the sale of fishing and hunting licenses and duck and pheasant stamps, was supposed to go to fish and game habitat.

MAY

• Animal rights group People for the Ethical Treatment of Animals threatened to sue the DNR unless the agency completed an environmental impact statement on its goose roundup program, which was designed to reduce metro goose populations.

• The Proper Economic Resources Management group sought to file for amicus status on the side of the DNR. The Fond du Lac Band of Chippewa filed the lawsuit against the state over off-reservation hunting and fishing rights across the Arrowhead portion of the state. PERM also supported a group of landowners intervening in the Mille Lacs Band of Ojibwe's treaty rights lawsuit against the state. "We feel that allowing unregulated harvest is not wise resource management, and we fear the consequences of doing so could be devastating," PERM President Mark Rotz said.

• Animal rights activitists argued that bowhunting for deer was illegal and asked the DNR to conduct an environmental assessment of bowhunting. The animal rights activists claimed a bow and arrow was not a sufficiently efficient weapon."

JUNE

• Former Vikings football coach Bud Grant, who was actively involved with Proper Economic Resources Management, updated Outdoor News readers on the Mille Lacs treaty case in a question and answer piece with Editor Dan Johnson.

ALASKAN MOOSE RACKS. (left) Brad Reddeck of Orono, Minn., and (right) Curt Fenton of Hopkins, Minn., took two moose with enormous racks while hunting the Stoney River area in Alaska. Reddeck's moose had a rack that measured 66 inches while Fenton's squeaked in at 63 inches. Photo courtesy of Mid-America Taxidermists.

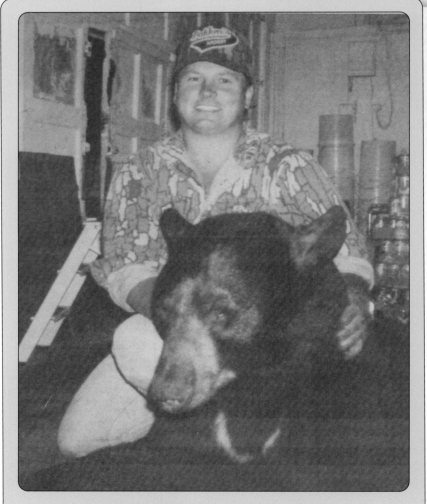

▲ Larry Latourelle with a near record black bear. Its skull green scored 21 1/16 inches.

DNR goose roundup program will likely face some difficult choices

By Scott Phippen
Outdoor News Staff

Metro residents will likely face some difficult choices in the future as Canada geese numbers continue to increase and effective control measures become harder to find.

"We keep telling the cities that a special hunt is possible in the metro area," said Jim Cooper, a University of Minnesota biologist. "We can continue to relocate them but eventually, we'll run out of places to send them. At that point, we will have to decide what can be done."

Some possible options include special goose hunts, contra-

People for the Ethical Treatment of Animals (PETA) has threatened to sue the DNR unless an Environmental Impact Statement (EIS) is done on the program.

During a goose roundup last week, PETA member Sylvia Brown videotaped the entire operation and again asked for an EIS.

"This makes me sick," Brown said. "It's like taking slaves from Africa all over again. The program doesn't work. It actually contributes to the problem once these birds return to the area. That's why we want an EIS. We

Since then, the city has had Cooper capture all but six breeding pairs and 10 goslings and the population has rarely increased over 200.

Although captured geese used to return up to 30 percent of the time, Cooper has taken steps to reduce the problem. Geese form a return instinct to the area where they learned to fly. By capturing goslings, Cooper said the geese won't have any return tendencies. Adult geese have their primary wing feather clipped. When the feathers regrow a year later, the birds will reimprint on their new home.

WHAT A TROPHY! Jerry Johnson shot this 10-point albino whitetail near his rural Cambridge, Minn. home at 10:30 a.m. on Wed., Nov. 9. Johnson saw the deer along a swamp edge and made an 80-yard shot with his .30-06 to drop the buck. He plans to have the deer mounted.

• The Mille Lacs treaty case, which began when the Mille Lacs Band of Ojibwe sued the state in 1990 for the right to hunt, fish and gather free from state regulation across territory ceded to the federal government in the treaty of 1837, began in a federal courtroom in Minneapolis.

• The DNR announced that in coming weeks, as many as 40 people would be charged with illegally selling walleyes netted in Leech and Red lakes. The case was the result of a multi-year investigation that included federal, state, and tribal officials.

JULY

• Authorities were investigating the deaths of three fishermen who were found in Leech Lake. They were believed to have drowned June 18.

• Despite the DNR's goose roundup program, goose numbers in the metro continued to increase. Officials warned they eventually would run out of places to relocate the geese. PETA, meanwhile, maintained its threat of a lawsuit, comparing the roundup program to "taking slaves from Africa all over again."

• Outdoor News began printing Mixed Bag, which included a variety of short news stories.

AUGUST

• Several anglers who had fish confiscated during their return from Ontario to Minnesota filed a lawsuit against the state over its controversial border law. According to the anglers' attorney, preventing anglers from returning with fish caught in Ontario oversteps state authority and discriminates against state residents.

• The U.S. House passed a $30 billion crime bill that banned 19 named types of assault-style firearms and scores of others deemed by the government to meet assault-style characteristics. All Minnesota congressmen voted in favor of the bill, except Republican Rod Grams, who called the bill, " … a welfare package for criminals at taxpayers expense."

SEPTEMBER

• Joe Fellegy wrote a front-page piece for Out-

Progress in walleye sting reported

A multi-agency investigation into the illegal fish trade has resulted in two Grand Forks, North Dakota businesses being charged and fined, according Bill Spence of the Minnesota Department of Natural Resources.

The Bronze Boot was fined $5,000 for violating federal law when it purchased 228 walleye fillets from the Red Lake Indian Reservation.

This picture of a piebald-looking Canada goose was taken on March 25, 1994 in Roseville.

Rodney Schmidt, of Red Wing, trapped these two white coyotes near his home in 1994.

Hinckley man lands record sturgeon
Subdues 94-pound fish after 3-hour battle

By Dan Johnson
Outdoor News Editor

Hinckley, Minn.

A light fog rolled eerily across the Kettle River's dark waters the evening of Monday, Sept. 5th, as Kim Bengtson and Bill Hegge, Jr. settled back into their lawn chairs to savor the smell of steaks on the grill and wait for the telltale bite of a sturgeon on their fishing lines.

But the men's evening would soon prove to be anything but relaxing.

The two fishermen were enjoying an evening on the riverbank, like many before, when a giant, prehistoric fish picked up one of their baits (a gob of nightcrawlers fished on the bottom) and headed for deeper water.

"I was just getting ready to flip the T-bones when it hit," said Bengtson, a 30-year-old iron worker from Hinckley.

The steaks would have to wait.

Hegge, of Minneapolis, had already landed a fish – a 42-pound lake sturgeon – on that night in St. Croix State Park, so it was

(See **Record**, Page 5)

STATE RECORD. Pictured with the 94-pound, 4-ounce lake sturgeon are (left to right) Bill Hegge Jr., Dan Hegge and Kim Bengtson. Photo courtesy DNR

door News. Known as a writer and fisherman, Fellegy also was deeply involved in the Mille Lacs treaty lawsuit and consulted for counties involved in the case. The headline of his story: "The Mille Lacs Case: A historian's perspective on the band's treaty rights."

• Hunters killed two record-book bears. One bear, taken by bow near Sandstone, green-scored 21¾₁₆ inches. The other bear, taken by gun near Ray,

weighed 617 pounds. Its skull's unofficial green score was 23⅛₁₆ inches.

OCTOBER

• A federal grand jury indicted 10 men (nine of them Minnesotans) on charges of illegally buying and selling thousands of game fish from lakes in Minnesota, Wisconsin, and Canada. The indictments came after a four-year undercover investigation that included authorities setting up an undercover wholesale foods business. Additional indictments were expected.

DECEMBER

• Six bands of Wisconsin Chippewa Indians filed motions in U.S. District Court to intervene in the Mille Lacs band's case against the state of Minnesota. The Bands signed the same 1837 treaty as did the Mille Lacs Band.

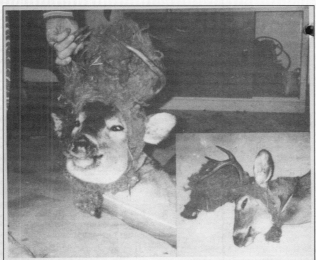

RON LYNCH of Elk River, Minn., shot this unusual deer in Sherburne County on November 9, 1994. He saw this eight-point buck earlier in the season while bowhunting, but couldn't tell what was on his head. Apparently this buck got his antlers tangled up in a round bale of hay. It must have taken him a long time to free himself because there was approximately 125 feet of twine caught in his antlers. It was also wrapped around his neck and ears.

1995 — More than 680 people were injured, and 168 died, in an act of domestic terrorism at a federal building in Oklahoma City, Okla. Timothy McVeigh and others were arrested; McVeigh, who carried out the attack, was put to death.

- *A jury in Los Angeles found O.J. Simpson not guilty of the murder charges against him. More than 150 million people across the nation watched television as the verdict was read.*

- *Jerry Garcia, the frontman of the Grateful Dead, died at the age of 53.*

- *The movie Forrest Gump, which starred Tom Hanks, won the Academy Award for Best Picture.*

- *The U.S. pumped $20 billion worth of aid into the Mexican economy.*

- *The median household income in the U.S. was $34,076; the unemployment rate was 5.6 percent.*

- *The world population grew to 5.7 billion people.*

KEVIN CRANE of Gonvick, Minn., shot this 23-point non-typical buck while hunting with his son Corey. The huge whitetail's rack measured 24-inches inside and scored 221-5/8 Boone & Crockett.

TROPHY NORTHERN. Joe Reis, of Rosemount, Minn., caught this 33.4-pound pike on Thunder Lake near Remer on May 26. He was using a rainbow chub and six-pound line when the 44½-inch trophy struck.
Photo courtesy of Kellogg's Northwoods

JANUARY

- Gun legislation in Canada changed things for hunters going there from Minnesota. Hunters had to register their guns at the border, and then de-register them when they re-entered Minnesota. Only shotguns and rifles were allowed to be brought into Canada.

- Sen. Pat Pariseau, R-Farmington, was set to introduce a bill in the Minnesota Legislature to add a right to bear arms amendment to the state constitution.

FEBRUARY

- A DNR-proposed rule change would outlaw the use of turkey decoys with beards; predominantly red or white heads; and those that exhibit strutting postures. Agency officials said the rule, which had little opposition, was necessary to prevent accidental shootings.

MARCH

- Rep. Doug Peterson, DFL-Madison, offered a bill in the Minnesota Legislature to create a hunting season in the state for mourning doves. The DNR supported establishment of the season, and officials noted it had been closed since 1947.

APRIL

• The Mille Lacs Band of Ojibwe faxed to the DNR a 14-page document detailing tribal fishing regulations on waters within the 1837 ceded area, including Lake Mille Lacs. Included in the rules was a year-round walleye gill-netting season on Mille Lacs. DNR officials said they would have any tribal members who try it arrested.

• The first slot limit in state history was put into place on Big Sand Lake. Anglers were able to keep six walleyes. The protected slot was 18 to 26 inches, and anglers could keep one fish longer than 26 inches. DNR officials said the regulation would reduce the walleye harvest by 39 percent.

JUNE

• Outdoor News columnist Fred Daugs, who specialized in trout fishing, passed away after Memorial Day. He was 71 years old. Daugs was a teacher at Carl Sandberg Junior High

Outdoor News has been a longtime sponsor of Ron Schara's Minnesota Bound, which began in 1994. Shown with Schara above is wild game chef John Schumacher.

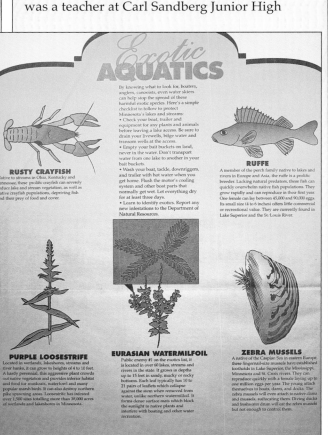

Exotic AQUATICS

By knowing what to look for, boaters, anglers, canoeists, even water skiers can help stop the spread of these harmful exotic species. Here's a simple checklist to follow to protect Minnesota's lakes and streams:
• Check your boat, trailer and equipment for any plants and animals before leaving a lake access. Be sure to drain your livewells, bilge water and transom wells at the access.
• Empty your bait buckets on land, never in the water. Don't transport water from one lake to another in your bait buckets.
• Wash your boat, tackle, downriggers, and trailer with hot water when you get home. Flush the motor's cooling system and other boat parts that normally get wet. Let everything dry for at least three days.
• Learn to identify exotics. Report any new infestations to the Department of Natural Resources.

RUSTY CRAYFISH
Native to streams in Ohio, Kentucky and Tennessee, these prolific crayfish can severely reduce lake and stream vegetation, as well as native crayfish populations, depriving fish and their prey of food and cover.

RUFFE
A member of the perch family native to lakes and rivers in Europe and Asia, the ruffe is a prolific breeder. Lacking natural predators, these fish can quickly overwhelm native fish populations. They grow rapidly and can reproduce in their first year. One female can lay between 45,000 and 90,000 eggs. Its small size (4 to 6 inches) offers little commercial or recreational value. They are currently found in Lake Superior and the St. Louis River.

PURPLE LOOSESTRIFE
Located in wetlands, lakeshores, streams and river banks, it can grow to heights of 4 to 10 feet. A hardy perennial, this aggressive plant crowds out native vegetation and provides inferior habitat and food for muskrats, waterfowl and many popular marsh birds. It can also destroy northern pike spawning areas. Loosestrife has infested over 1,500 sites totalling more than 38,000 acres of wetlands and lakeshores in Minnesota.

EURASIAN WATERMILFOIL
Public enemy #1 on the exotics list, it is located in over 60 lakes, streams and rivers in the state. It grows in depths up to 15 feet in sandy, mucky or rocky bottoms. Each leaf typically has 10 to 21 pairs of leaflets which collapse against the stem when removed from water, unlike northern watermilfoil. It forms dense surface mats which block the sunlight to native plants and interfere with boating and other water recreation.

ZEBRA MUSSELS
A native of the Caspian Sea in eastern Europe, these fingernail-size mussels have established footholds in Lake Superior, the Mississippi, Minnesota and St. Croix rivers. They can reproduce quickly with a female laying up to one million eggs per year. The young attach themselves to boats, dams, and docks. The zebra mussels will even attach to native clams and mussels, suffocating them. Diving ducks and freshwater drum will eat the zebra mussels but not enough to control them.

SPINY WATER FLEA
This exotic isn't an insect at all, but a tiny crustacean with a long, sharp, barbed tail spine. They reproduce rapidly with a female producing 10 offspring every two weeks during the summer. Their impact on the

SEA LAMPREY
These parasitic, jawless fish attach their suction-type mouth, ringed with sharp teeth to a fish. Approximately 40 pounds of fish, roughly 40 times a lamprey's body weight, are consumed by an adult lamprey during its lifetime. In Lake Superior it is estimated that sea lampreys kill an equal

RECORD-BOOK BUCK. Barry Peterson dropped this 12-point, 165-pound buck on opening day of the archery season while hunting in the metro area. The rack, which green scores 195-3/8 points and should be the second largest buck taken in the state, has an inside spread of 20 3/8 inches with the longest tines measuring 12 inches.

On a sad note

Longtime **Outdoor News** columnist Fred Daugs passed away Memorial Day after a long battle with cancer. Daugs, 71, of Monona, Iowa, specialized in trout fishing and was active in teaching youngsters to fish. A former English teacher and football coach in Robbinsdale, Minn., Daugs wrote columns for **Outdoor News** for over 20 years. He will be missed.

Reader John Acker didn't bag a buck this year but did take a photo of this albino deer in the Minneapolis metro area.

School for many years. He taught many of his student how to trout fish.

• The DNR's budget, finalized during the legislative session, included several full-time layoffs. Lawmakers also agreed to repeal the ban on returning with fish from Ontario. But the 1995 session, according to Associate Editor Scott Phippen, "lacked excitement."

• DNR conservation officers asked for help in solving a poaching case in Bloomington. The two trophy-class whitetails, which were sufficiently tame that people could take close-up photos, were killed in 1994, between Christmas and New Year's.

• Shortly after the story about the two deer poached in Bloomington ran in Outdoor News, conservation officer Mike Hammer received a tip about the deer. By the following day, he had five suspects and one set of 10-point antlers in his possession.

• A 14-year-old was bitten by a muskie at Lake Rebecca. Ron Payer, fisheries operations manager, speculated the muskie mistook the boy's hand, which was splashing the water, as food. The attack happened in waist-deep water.

JULY

• The DNR invited 50 people to serve as a sounding board for the agency during the re-

ONE OF MY FAVORITE ANTI JOKES.
From WFLA Update...
The leader of an animal rights group accompanied her husband on an African Safari. As they stalked through the tall grass, a lion suddenly pounced on the woman and began dragging her off.
The woman screamed, *"Shoot!, Shoot!"*
"I can't" he shouted.
"Why not?" came the hysterical response.
"I'm out of film!" he said.

mainder of the Mille Lacs Band of Ojibwe's treaty rights lawsuit.

• A number of people around Lake Miltona in Douglas County, including resort owners, opposed the continuation of muskie stocking in the lake. They argued it would hurt the populations of other game fish, including walleyes. The DNR said muskies would not

The Buck Castle

A portable heated deer stand that doubles as a great waterfowl blind. Designed with you in mind to give you the advantage to withstand the chilling winds, rain, and snow. Rifle or bow-hunter, this stand means you stay comfortable while you bag that trophy buck.

BUCK CASTLE

No more chilling winds, rain and snow.

The Buck Castle
• weight 28 lbs.
• platform diameter 35 1/2 in.
• setup time 3-5 minutes
• water repellent cordura and fleece

Buck Castle Heater
• foam padded seat
• stainless steel propane burner
• weight 6 lbs. without gas cylinder
• up to 30 hours per 1 lb cylinder

Time tested, hunter approved!
Field tested by the
Minnesota Deer Hunters Association
Approval rating – Very Good to Excellent

WAL-KIN Mfg.
Rt. 6 Fergus Falls, MN 56537 or call
1-800-362-6307
(call 5pm-9pm)
We accept Visa & MasterCard

COs find mile of illegal net on Upper Red Lake

By Scott Phippen
Outdoor News Staff

Thanks to a TIP (Turn In Poachers) call, state conservation officers discovered two Red Lake band members illegally netting outside the reservation on Upper Red Lake last Sunday.

The two men were tending a mile of commercial fishing net approximately a quarter of a mile outside the reservation boundary when three COs approached them. The suspects fled back onto the reservation when they were spotted, but according to CO Jeff Granger, that

(See **Illegal Net**, Page 7)

Tackle Terry
By Terry Tuma

TERRY: Is it better to fish when the barometer is rising or falling?

ANSWER: I don't think this question has ever been scientifically answered, and I believe it doesn't make a difference. However, light rain, cloudy conditions, wind, warm fronts and stable weather improve fishing. Weather conditions that cause poor fishing are thunderstorms, cold fronts, unstable weather and no winds. But, if we adapt and accept these conditions, our success will definitely improve.

The "Tackle" Terry Tuma tip of the week became a popular fishing resource for readers.

WANTED: Have you seen these racks?

By Scott Phippen
Outdoor News Staff

Two trophy-class whitetail deer were poached in Bloomington late last year and Department of Natural Resources conservation officers are asking for citizens to help solve the crimes.

The carcass of one of the deer, which was apparently killed for its large antlers, was found buried underneath freshly cut branches within 100 yards of homes along the Minnesota Valley Wildlife Refuge. The carcass was cape-dressed (skinned from back to front), and the head removed.

(See **Deer**, Page 18)

These illegally killed bucks were so tame that Bloomington residents could take close-up photos.

negatively affect other fish.

• The Minnesota Outdoor Heritage Alliance, formed in 1994 at the urging of U.S. Sen. Collin Peterson and state Sen. Bob Lessard, began to organize and inform state lawmakers about issues of importance to state fishermen, hunters, and trappers. The first order of business: A constitutional amendment guaranteeing the right to hunt, fish and trap in Minnesota.

AUGUST

• Mountain lion sightings were on the rise in Minnesota. DNR wildlife biologist Bill Berg, stationed in Grand Rapids, said he received between 60 and 70 reports each year of cougar sightings.

• A Scott County judge upheld the state's hunter harassment statute, ruling it didn't violate protesters' rights to freedom of speech. The case involved a group of high school and college students who were arrested for disrupting a special archery hunt near Savage. Nine of those arrested challenged the law and claimed it violated their rights.

OCTOBER

• Thanks to tips, state conservation officers found a mile of illegal net on Upper Red Lake that had been set by two band members outside of their reservation.

• State conservation officers and federal U.S. Fish and Wildlife Service agents issued 23 tickets and warnings during a waterfowl-hunting investigation at Swan Lake. There had been a growing number of complaints about hunting violations at Swan Lake.

NOVEMBER

• Pat Smith, sheriff of Le Sueur County, was cited by federal agents for hunting game birds near a baited area.

DECEMBER

• Two men were charged in the shooting of one of the trophy deer killed in Bloomington in late 1994. At the time the men were charged, conservation officers still were looking for another trophy deer they believed also may have been poached.

1996 — The FBI arrested Ted Kaczynski, better known as the Unabomber. His bombs killed three people and injured 23.

• About 30 million people in the U.S. used the Internet; 44 percent of households owned a computer.

• President Bill Clinton nominated Madeleine Albright as secretary of state. She became the first female to hold the position.

• An outbreak of Mad Cow Disease caused alarm in the United Kingdom.

• Airplane crashes in the Florida Everglades and off Long Island, N.Y., claimed the lives of all people aboard, which totalled 340.

JANUARY

• The snowmobile death toll was on a record pace. From December through the first week of January, 17 people had died as a result of snowmobile accidents. "I can't comprehend how it could get this bad this quickly," said Mike Grupa, DNR administrative enforcement officer. Part of the reason: large amounts of snow.

• Outdoor News launched Operation Stay In Touch, which offered free subscriptions to those soldiers stationed overseas supporting the United Nation's peace-keeping effort in Bosnia.

• Deer groups in Roseau and Thief River Falls began to distribute eight tons of feed to 14 deer yards in the northwestern part of the state to help the animals survive the challenging winter.

• The DNR announced plans to begin emergency deer feeding measures in the northwestern part of the state in February. Deer in five counties were hit hard by deep snow and a blizzard in mid-January.

FEBRUARY

• DNR deer experts predicted 30 to 40 percent of the state's northern forest deer herd could perish due to the severe winter. For deer in some parts of the state, it was the toughest winter in decades.

• A DNR aerial survey confirmed there were nearly 600 deer within Minnetonka city limits. The city had a deer-control program, which a group – Minnetonkans

15-POUND WALLEYE. Tom Locnikar caught this 15-pound 33-inch walleye Jan 2 while fishing on an Avon area lake. Locnikar used a jig to catch the lunker. *Photo courtesy Avon True Value*

An avid hunter, Bud Grant bagged this dandy buck during a trip to the South. He also enjoys waterfowling, pheasant hunting, trout fishing and just about any other activity that will get him outdoors.

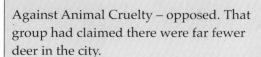

Against Animal Cruelty – opposed. That group had claimed there were far fewer deer in the city.

• A Minnesota House committee endorsed a bill allocating $1 million to an emergency deer feeding program. Another committee approved an "ethanol bill" that would exempt premium gasoline from a state law requiring a minimum oxygen content of 2.7 percent. And other lawmakers spent time debating changes to the state Wetland Conservation Act, which was passed in 1991.

• Handguns became legal throughout the state for deer hunting. Previously, they only could be used in the state's rifle zone.

MARCH

• Three animal rights activists were arrested in Minnetonka for interferring with a trap used in the city's deer management program.

• The DNR began feeding deer in the northern portion of the state using $750,000 from the Game and Fish Fund. The money allowed the DNR to distribute 4,000 tons of food pellets at 44 sites over four weeks.

• The Minnesota chapter of the Make-A-Wish Foundation granted Erik Ness his dream – to hunt an Alaskan brown bear. Ness, a 17-year-old, had discovered the previous year he had a brain tumor. Anti-hunters quickly pressured the foundation to reverse its decision.

• The state Senate passed a bill that would allow voters to decide if the state constitution should include the right to hunt, fish, and trap.

• The Legislature approved creation of a $5 turkey stamp.

• Darrin Stream set a new state record archery kill for black bear in Minnesota with a bruin he arrowed Sept. 2, 1995 in Pine County. It weighed 435 pounds field dressed, and the skull scored 21$\frac{15}{16}$. The bear was the third-largest ever taken in the state.

Les Kouba and Bud Grant put the final touches on a Turn In Poachers fundraiser painting.

JIM PETERSON, founder and former editor of Outdoor News celebrated his 43rd consecutive bass opener at Lake Geneva. See story on page 16. Photo by Jim Peterson

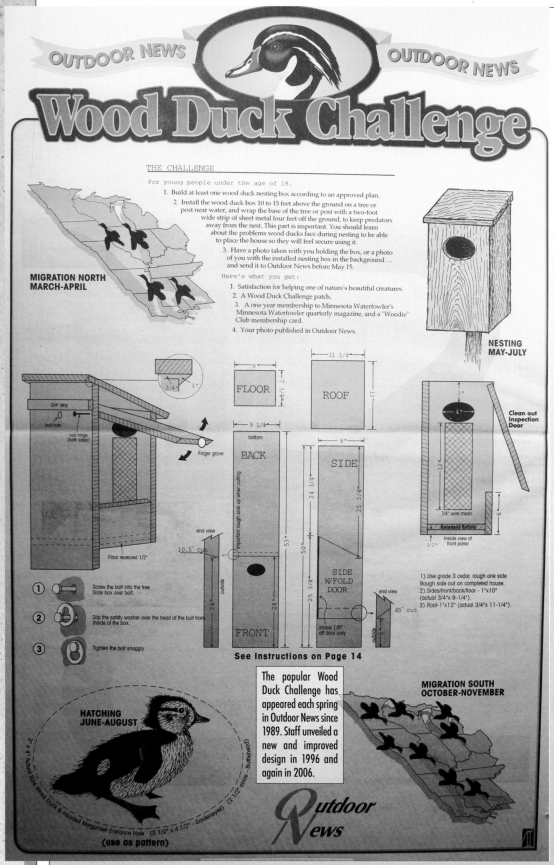

• A state conservation officer supervisor was disciplined and reassigned for illegally searching several unlocked hunting cabins in the Mille Lacs area.

• After a legislative mandate to eliminate the name "squaw" from state geographic features, a committee was formed to come up with a new name for Itasca County's Squaw Lake.

APRIL

• During the legislative session, lawmakers "approved weakening the state's 1991 Wetland Conservation Act;" changed trespassing laws; and repealed the "second chance" muzzleloader hunt that was approved in 1995, among others.

MAY

• John Kvasnicka announced he was resigning as executive director of the Minnesota Deer Hunters Association. Kvasnicka, who'd been at the helm for seven years, cited personal and career goals he wished to achieve.

JUNE

• Three state-record fish were caught earlier in 1996. They were: a 10-pound, 7-ounce splake from Tofte Lake; a 2-pound, 14.9-ounce white

crappie from Lake Mary; and a 10-pound, 3-ounce river redhorse from the Kettle River.
• Vandals caused more than $2,000 in damage to Wayzata Bait and Tackle. Evidence suggested it was the work of an animal rights group called the Animal Liberation Front.

July
• Erik Ness didn't shoot an Alaskan brown bear, but had positive memories and good things to say about his Make-A-Wish trip to "the last wild place."
• Itasca State Park officials were concerned about a growing bark beetle population that threatened the park's pine trees.
• The Animal Liberation Front took credit for cutting through a fence at a mink ranch and attempting to release 1,000 mink. About 900 of the animals refused to leave. By July of 1996, 14 attacks on Minnesota businesses had been attributed to the Animal Liberation Front.

August
• Joe Wood was appointed the new executive director of the Minnesota Deer Hunters Association. One of his goals: Reduce friction within the group related to winter deer feeding.
• A botulism outbreak killed 82,000 ducks on Whitewater Lake in Manitoba.

October
• After Erik Ness failed to shoot an Alaska brown bear during his Make-A-Wish trip, the Safari Club

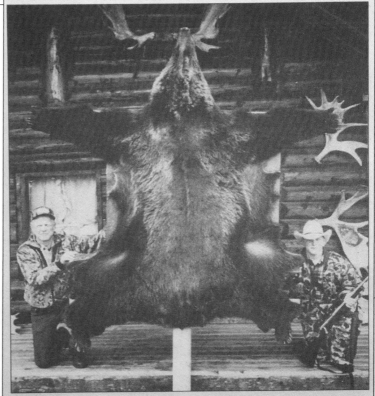

Erik (right) and his father, Brock, pose with the hide of the bear. The bear will be converted into a full-body mount, with the work being donated by a local taxidermist.

donated a second hunt to him. Ness connected the second time, killing a 7-foot, 9-inch bear that weighed between 650 and 700 pounds.
• A 19-year-old confessed to shooting an 18-point buck that was a family's pet.
• Jim's Bait, an institution in Duluth since the 1950s, closed at the end of the month. Jim Keuten, who operated the shop, passed away the previous winter.

November
• Galyan's opened a new 100,000-square-foot outdoor retail store in Minnetonka.
• The Sierra Club called upon federal and state officials to ban boat travel between the Mississippi and St. Croix rivers, hoping to prevent the spread of zebra mussels into the St. Croix.

December
• The DNR announced plans to convert its licensing system to an electronic format. It became known as the Electronic Licensing System (ELS).

Robert Wenker of White Bear Lake, Minn., caught this new Wisconsin-record brown trout Aug. 14 off the coast of Algoma. It weighed 35.11 pounds and had a 29¼-inch girth. Photo by Kevin Naze

1997 — Oklahoma City bomber Timothy McVeigh was sentenced to death for his role in the bombing of the federal building in that city.

• O.J. Simpson was found guilty in a civil suit in the death of Nicole Brown Simpson and Ronald Goldman, and ordered to make financial reparations.

• The movie Titanic hit theaters. At a cost of as much as $300 million to film and market, it was the most expensive movie to date.

• Princess Diana Spencer, a member of the British Royal Family, died at the age of 36 in a car accident in Paris.

• A team of British scientists created Dolly, a genetically engineered lamb that had a human gene in each cell of its body.

• The median household income in the U.S. rose above $37,000, while the unemployment rate dropped below 5 percent.

• The U.S. population neared $268 million; the world population was 5.8 billion.

☞ JANUARY

• In the wake of the growing popularity of snowmobiles, thefts were on the rise, too. At one point, the property room at the Isanti County sheriff's office had 50 snowmobile engines, and the same number were waiting to be inventoried.

• The moose population at Agassiz National Wildlife Refuge – a microcosm for the entire northwestern part of the state – continued to plummet, and researchers were baffled. The moose population on the refuge was 270 in 1993; 115 in 1995; and 71 in 1997. A study into the decline was set to begin.

• Deep snow and severe weather took a toll on pheasants.

• Sportsmen gathered at the State Capitol for Outdoor Heritage Day. The reason: "We just want to let (lawmakers) know that we are here," said Jim Klatt, an executive board member of the Outdoor Heritage Alliance.

• An ex-DNR employee was arrested after allegedly making verbal threats to other DNR employees. As a result of the bomb scare, officials closed DNR offices in St. Paul and the southeastern part of the state.

DNR Slices Game and Fish Fund

How the DNR Wildlife spends its share of the Game and Fish Fund (** includes planning and evaluation, facility management, program direction, continuing education, division administration, aminal damage, treaty assessment, and funds rollign forward to the next fiscal year.):

How DNR Wildlife spends its share of the Game & Fish

- Coordination & Technical Assistance 5.25%
- Habitat Management 15.04%
- Resource Protection & Acquisition 7.83%
- Information Managment 4.85%
- Private Land Habitat 2.08%
- Operations 22.21%
- Populations & Inventory 14.49%
- Deer Feeding 12.12%
- Leave 9.01%
- Other** 12.12%

In the late 1990s, Outdoor News began devoting more space to scrutinizing DNR expenditures.

Erik Ness, who made headlines for his Make-A-Wish bear hunting request, joined the Outdoor News crew for a fine lake trout trip in 1997. Ness passed away in 1999 at age 21.

TROUT—THE BEST MEDICINE. One year after finding himself center stage in a national debate on hunting, Erik Ness attends college and spends as much time as possible outdoors. He caught these lake trout last weekend in Ontario with his dad, Brock, and the *Outdoor News* crew. Photo by Rob Drieslein

FEBRUARY

• A federal judge ruled the Mille Lacs Band of Ojibwe had the authority to begin exercising their treaty rights on land inside the ceded territory. The judge ruled the band's conservation code and management plans would not present a public health or public safety problem.

• Lawmakers were considering provisions that, in total, would allocate $1 million for winter deer feeding in northern Minnesota.

MARCH

• The DNR set a 15-inch minimum size limit for walleyes on Lake Mille Lacs. The limit remained six fish, though only one could be longer than 20 inches. DNR biologists said the reduction would reduce harvest, necessary to maintain quality fishing as tribal harvest was set to begin.

• The eight Chippewa bands announced plans to net and spear in Lake Mille Lacs and 28 other lakes. The DNR set about evaluating if it needed to make any changes to its regulations to prevent damage to the fisheries. "Quite frankly, I'm surprised at the magnitude of the harvest being proposed for small lakes," DNR Commissioner Ron Sando said.

APRIL

• A conservation officer was under investigation for writing a letter to Sen. Bob Lessard. The officer's letter had to do with his concern about the 4 p.m. duck-hunting closure.

• Publisher Glenn Meyer hired Rob Drieslein as editor of Outdoor News. A hunter and angler who'd grown up around U.S. Fish and Wildlife Service refuges, Drieslein majored in science-

GREAT WHITE FAWN. Pat Reeve spotted this still-wet albino fawn while turkey hunting in this spring. Albino deer usually survive to adulthood in areas with few natural predators. Photo by Pat Reeve

Forrest Woods (l), Irwin Jacobs, and Gov. Arne Carlson unveiled plans for a $1 million Lake Minnetonka bass tournament during a Mall of America press conference on Monday. Photo by Ron Hustvedt

Minnesota deer hunters won't see the buck that sported this Boone-and-Crockett rack afield when deer hunting opens next weekend, because a poacher shot it in August.

Photo courtesy of Dan Book

While fishing Lake Michigan on Saturday, July 26, Debbie Morrison tied into this state record rainbow trout. The fish measured 42½ inches and weighed 27.11 pounds.

Photo by Kevin Naze

writing journalism in college and had spent two years as the outdoors editor at the Winona Daily News, followed by three years as associate editor of Bowhunting World magazine in the Twin Cities.

• Helicopter crews captured 70 moose in the northwest and equipped them with radio collars.

MAY

• The Mille Lacs Band of Ojibwe began harvesting fish from Lake Mille Lacs.

• Responding to legislative proposals to shorten or cancel the deer hunting season, the DNR agreed to hold public hearings to receive input on the upcoming deer season.

• The DNR announced cancellation of the moose hunt in the northwestern part of the state.

• A year after Erik Ness ruffled the feathers of the animal rights movement, he went fishing with the *Outdoor News* crew in Ontario. He was feeling good, attending Lake Vermilion Junior College in Ely, and spending lots of time outdoors.

• The Legislature added $2 to the cost of Minnesota fishing licenses.

SEPTEMBER

• The DNR captured a 2.5-year-old albino bear near Orr. The agency planned to hold it in captivity during the 1997 season so it wouldn't be killed during the bear-hunting season. DNR officials said their counterparts in British Columbia were studying white bears, and asked the DNR to protect it.

• Outdoor News announced that Joe Fellegy would begin writing a regular column called Rocking the Boat.

OCTOBER

• Off-duty CO Gary Westby was killed in a car crash with a Paynesville police officer who was chasing an unlicensed motorist suspect. Westby, who covered the New London/Spicer area, was a 22-year DNR veteran. He was 51. In a commentary in the following paper, Westby was remembered as an officer who "never wrote a ticket that he didn't feel bad about."

NOVEMBER

• The DNR announced two meetings to determine whether the spearing ban on Cass Lake – in place since 1988 – would remain in place.
• A federal appeals court refused to reconsider a ruling that allowed eight Chippewa bands in Minnesota and Wisconsin to hunt and fish in the ceded area without state regulation. The state had asked the appeals

High water flooded the Red River Valley and other portions of western Minnesota during the spring of 1997.

RECOGNIZE THIS PLACE? Kerry Christoffer, manager of Lac qui Parle State Park, stands in a place familiar to many goose hunters, the county highway bridge crossing the Lac qui Parle outlet. The flood-swollen Minnesota River inundated the highway crossing.

YUCK! Yes, those are flooded outhouses behind Kerry Christoffer at a Lac qui Parle public access. The high waters are flushing enormous amounts of human and animal wastes downstream. Look out New Orleans!

court for a hearing, but it declined. The state announced it would ask the U.S. Supreme Court for a hearing.

DECEMBER

• Tim Bremicker, wildlife chief for the DNR since 1991, was reassigned as assistant director of operations in the Division of Waters. Larry Nelson, regional administrator in Rochester, succeeded him. Commissioner Rod Sando said the temporary reassignments would allow both to "develop new skills and bring a different perspective to their jobs."
• Proponents of dove hunting in the state announced plans to have another dove-hunting bill introduced at the Legislature.

WOOD DUCK CHALLENGE '97. Shulstad brothers Nathan, age 9, and Eric, age 6, of Pelican Rapids, rose to the challenge this year and constructed two wood duck houses. Great job.

1998 — Iranian President Mohammed Khatami retracts a fatwa against Satanic Verses author Salman Rushdie that was in force since 1989.

• The Unabomber Ted Kaczynski was sentenced to four life terms for the string of bombings for which he was responsible.

• The wreck of the aircraft carrier U.S.S. Yorktown, sunk during the Battle of Midway in 1942, is found near Midway Atoll by a team led by former U.S. Navy officer Robert D. Ballard.

• The movie Titanic grossed more than $580 million in the U.S., becoming the highest grossing film of all-time. The film won a record 11 Academy Awards.

• Europeans agreed to make the euro their official currency and began minting the first coins.

• About 76 million people watched the final episode of Seinfeld.

• The national unemployment rate dropped to 4.5 percent.

JANUARY

• Fears of poor, unsafe ice conditions were hurting business on Lake Mille Lacs. Linda Eno, of Twin Pines Resort, called the reports "sensationalistic," but guessed one-quarter of the resort's customers stayed home. "I don't know how many times I've heard from guys that their wives won't let them come up because of bad ice," she said.

• Sen. LeRoy Stumpf, DFL-Thief River Falls, announced plans to introduce a bill to give the DNR the authority to manage the state's wolf population. One idea on the table: hunting and trapping. Stumpf said the goal was to manage the state's wolves at an acceptable level.

• Ontario changed fishing rules for Lake of the Woods; American anglers based in American resorts were unable to keep walleyes and sauger caught in Ontario waters. Resort owners at the Northwest Angle were especially hurt.

FEBRUARY

• State Sen. Bob Lessard sought to establish a committee of state anglers to review underwater video cameras. The question he wanted answered: Should anglers be allowed to use new cam-

Big gobbler taken near Lake City is state's heaviest ever

By Rob Drieslein
Editor

A Lake City hunter has bagged what appears to be the heaviest turkey ever taken in Minnesota. Hunting south of Lake City in Zone 342 on Sunday, May 3, Clem Nardinger, age 53, called in and shot a 29½-pound gobbler at about 9:30 a.m.

And in one of those twists that always seems to accompany trophy hunting stories—it was his first time turkey hunting.

"I got picked once about 15 years ago but decided it wasn't for me, then this year I thought 'Heck, I'll try it,'" he said. "I'm getting old, but maybe that was an old turkey."

Nardinger had the bird weighed and witnessed on three scales—two state certified—and it weighed 29.46, 29.47 and 29.5 pounds respectively on the different scales. The previous state record entering the 1998 spring season weighed 28½ pounds, according to Kevin Lines of the DNR Section of Wildlife in St. Paul. There were reports in the Zumbrota area of a 29-pounder earlier this season.

The Lake City bird sported a 12¼-inch beard and 33 mm spurs, according to John Mauer at Mauer Brothers Tavern in Elba, one of the three locations where Nardinger weighed the bird.

Nardinger said he has already hired a taxidermist to mount the bird.

"Between all the turkey calls and getting it mounted, I guess I'll spend a lot of money on this bird," he said. "But it's worth it."

The state of Minnesota doesn't maintain any official records of trophy turkeys and their weights; however, the National Wild Turkey Federation is encouraging people to register their large birds with its organization.

Minnesota hunters should contact Tom Glines, NWTF regional director NWTF at (612) 767-2717 if they're interested in registering such a bird. There is a $10 application fee.

A lot of deer with bizarre antlers have appeared in Outdoor News over the years. Mike Diemer of Nisswa took this 8-pointer in Crow Wing County. The rack on the deer had broken loose in a fight with another buck.

eras that allow them to see what's going on underwater as they fish?

• Gov. Arne Carlson signed into law a bill extending the ice-fishing season by two weeks – to March 1. The season typically closes on the third Sunday in February, but resorters and others said unseasonably warm weather hurt business. The DNR wasn't thrilled with the extension.

• DNR Commissioner Rod Sando asked lawmakers to consider limiting the use of underwater cameras by fishermen.

• The state formally asked the U.S. Supreme Court to overturn a ruling granting the Chippewa bands the right to hunt and fish on ceded land without state regulation.

MARCH

• The right to hunt and fish bill cleared a big hurdle when the Senate Judiciary Committee passed it. The bill sought to allow voters to alter the state constitution to recognize Minnesota's hunting and fishing heritage.

• The Minnesota Senate voted to prohibit allowing fishermen to use underwater cameras for the taking of fish.

• Former Vikings coach Bud Grant was one of six men cited in Nebraska for hunting snow geese in a field baited with corn.

• In-Fisherman magazine signed an intent to sell with New York-based publishing giant Primedia.

• Holiday Sports and Gander Mountain merged.

APRIL

• State and tribal officials announced they planned to limit harvest of Red Lake walleyes. The band was to totally end harvest, while the state was to reduce the limit to two walleyes per day.

• Bud Grant paid a $250 fine for hunt-

Joe Alexander 1923-1998

Joseph Alexander, 75, Minnesota's Commissioner of Natural Resources from 1978 through 1990, died late Saturday from complications following surgery at Rochester Methodist Hospital.

Alexander had the distinction of having the longest tenure of any DNR commissioner and also had the honor of serving in this capacity under both political parties. He was first appointed by Governor Rudy Perpich in 1978 and reappointed in 1979 by Governor Al Quie.

Alexander's career began at the Department of Conservation in September of 1957 when he was hired as a game warden. In February of 1966 he was promoted to regional enforcement

Joe Alexander

Chemical Dependency Unit at Abbott-Northwestern Hospital in Minneapolis.

SMILING BOB. Nearly 200 people turned out Monday night at the Northland Inn in Brooklyn Park to raise funds for the Preserve Hunting and Fishing Heritage amendment drive and to roast Sen. Bob Lessard, DFL-International Falls. Lessard took the good-natured ribbing in stride, then roasted the roasters during his closing comments. Photo by Ron Hustvedt

Though this fish counted as registered in Michigan, anglers who fish from Minnesota waters might find it compelling, too.
Lucas Lanczy (r) is the lucky angler holding the 61-pound, 8-ounce lake trout taken from Lake Superior, Mich., on August 17, 1997. His brother, Bela, Jr., (l) assists while Alan Price looks on. The fish was recently recognized as a 17-pound line class world record by the National Fresh water Fishing Hall of Fame in Hayward, Wis., the largest lake trout ever registered in Michigan, and is unofficially the largest laker caught in the United States.   Photo courtesy of Freshwater Fishing Hall of Fame

DNR fisheries personnel had to see it to believe it when they heard reports of a monster sturgeon in Lake Harriet. The behemoth weighed 105.4 pounds and measured over 6 feet.

ing over a baited field in Nebraska. He maintained his innocence, but said, in part, "the liability for being in that field lies with me, as the federal waterfowl baiting regulations clearly state."

• The U.S. Fish and Wildlife Service authorized fish farmers in Minnesota and 12 southern states to kill cormorants without a federal permit if the birds are preying on fish stocks.

• Cabela's opened its first store in Minnesota. The store covered 150,000 square feet.

• The Legislature passed the right to hunt and fish bill, which resulted in voters being asked if they wanted the following added to the state constitution: "Hunting, fishing and the taking of game and fish are a valued part of our heritage that shall be forever preserved for the people and shall be managed by law and regulation for the public good."

MAY

• A Staples man accused of shooting at a deer and instead hitting a 13-year-old girl practicing her clarinet in her living room was charged with felony reckless discharge of a firearm. The man had been hunting the previous November, and was 3,900 feet (three-fourths of a mile) from the house when he shot.

• Fishing with "Tackle" Terry Tuma, Gov. Arne Carlson finally caught a fish – a Mississippi River sauger – during his last governor's fishing opener.

• Cuffs and Collars, a weekly compilation of reports from state conservation officers, debuted.

JULY

• Interior Secretary Bruce Babbitt announced the U.S. Fish and Wildlife Service would propose removing some timber wolf populations – including in Minnesota – from the endangered species list.

• A new law set for November would subject anyone buying a

firearm from a federally licensed dealer to a background check.

AUGUST

• A cougar was confirmed to be the culprit in a fatal attack on a cow and calf north of Isle.

SEPTEMBER

• Wildlife artist Les Kouba passed away in his sleep on Sept. 13.
• Lake Mille Lacs became the 91st body of water in the state to be infested with Eurasian watermilfoil.

OCTOBER

• Outdoor News announced its 1998 Youth Writing Contest, which included prizes up to $300.
• Former DNR Commissioner Joe Alexander, the longest-serving commissioner (12 years) died after complications from surgery. He was 75 years old. Alexander first was hired as a game warden by the DNR in 1957.
• Loral I Delaney for the third consecutive year won the women's World Flyer Championship.

NOVEMBER

• On the same night they elected Jesse Ventura governor, voters approved of constitutionally guaranteeing the right, trap and fish in Minnesota. Seventy-seven percent of voters voted in favor of Amendment 2.

CUFFS & COLLARS

The following information was provided by the DNR Division of Enforcement and contains recent reports from conservation officers around the state. *Outdoor News* begins publishing it this week in a new department called *Cuffs and Collars*.

DISTRICT 1
Success on Lake of the Woods was good to excellent depending on the area. Lake of the Woods officers wrote about 10 citations for violations including: no fishing licenses, boat registration, and no lights after sunset. 15 warnings were issued for PFDs, fire extinguishers, and boat registration, and no license in possession.

Sunday morning Officer Jeff Birchem assisted local law enforcement in a 60-mile pursuit of stolen vehicle (suspect had just been released from prison) Suspect was arrested without incident.

Officer Birchem responded to call of sinking boat and fire on Lake of the Woods, fire was out and officers towed in boat.

DISTRICT 3
Fishing on Leech and Winnie was very good to excellent with angler numbers as high as ever. Rest of district fair to good. Officers wrote about 50 contacts for common fishing and boating violations.

DISTRICT 6
Grand Marais area action very slow. People count and fish count down, probably due to fire ban. District wide—three closed season arrests, two over limits and few no PFDs

DISTRICT 7
Officers worked a variety of situations including: two intoxicated ATV operators in the Otter Tail City area, one on a stolen ATV which was recovered. Charges pending on the DWI, possession of stolen property, with additional charges possible.

Four young men, two without fishing license, three with closed season bass, and all in possession of marijuana. Marijuana case turned over to Hubbard County Sheriff's office.

A deer jumped into a basement of a home under construction in the Lake George area. Roping skills tested.

Citations—fishing opener as follows:
Two ATV DWI pending. Possess stolen property—pending, two ATV registrations, seven boat Registrations. one careless boating.

Five boating violations, five closed season bass, two extra lines, three fish license.

DISTRICT 8
The fishing opener varied from fair to good. In the Alexandria area, anglers averaged two walleyes per boat. Lake Osakis saw a few limits of walleyes. Northerns were biting very well in most areas. No real enforcement problems, just a few registration and PFD citations and a couple of no license violations.

Officers expressed some concern of possible over limits or double trips as walleyes and northern pike are being caught so easily.

Last week, arson fires were reported in the Minnesota River bottoms, including the burning of a state wildlife management area.

Compliance was excellent, with citations written for overlimits (one), fishing in posted fish management area (two), No PFDs (four). Warnings included No License in Possession (seven), unattended lines (two).

DISTRICT 11
The fishing opener was fairly good throughout the district. All District COs reported at least one lake in their areas that the fish were hitting on. There was some rain over the weekend that slowed the anglers down—but most braved the rain.

Officers wrote several arrests and warnings for fishing and boating violations.

DISTRICT 12
Above average number of anglers. Arrests and warnings also seem up. Many "no license" citations. Four arrests for closed season fish, either early walleye (Friday), or taking bass. Approximately 40 citation/warnings for fishing related violations; 40 citations/warnings for boating; 10 other citation/warning violations, including alcohol, drugs, ATVs, and one warrant arrest.

DISTRICT 13
The opening weekend went well even though the fishing success wasn't particularly good. In the Brainerd area, Gull Lake was probably the best with some nice-sized walleyes being taken. Some of the smaller lakes in the area had fair northern success.

Arrests for the weekend were mainly watercraft related with a number of license, closed area, early bass, and several ATV tickets, also.

DISTRICT 15
Excellent opener - Mille Lacs very busy.

15 tickets. 37 warnings. nine civil citations trespass, one body recovered—Knife Lake, May 9 (drowning victim from May 3)

DISTRICT 16
Overall fishing pressure in District 16 was heavy, fish harvest was fair to good (plenty of panfish caught) on most lakes. We had a very high regulation compliance. Jim Konrad reported that the boating activity became so busy by 2 p.m. on the opener that the smaller boats gave way to the larger boating traffic.

Tickets: 11 fishing without a license, one take bass during closed season, two boat/failure to display registration. Warnings: eight fishing related, seven boating related.

The first-ever Cuffs and Collars appeared on Page 4 of the May 15, 1998 edition. Actual field reports from state conservation officers, it now fills an entire page.

DECEMBER

• The photo of a huge buck taken in Michigan by Mitch Rompola became the highest traffic story in the history of the *Detroit Free Press* website. There was strong skepticism about whether the world-record sized buck was, in fact, real.

Here's the year-by-year tally of payments made by Minnesota to the tribal government of the Leech Lake Band of Chippewa since 1975:

Year	Amount	Year	Amount
1974	$62,288;	1988	$1,375,575;
1975	$240,576;	1989	$1,532,380;
1976	$260,356;	1990	$1,593,162;
1977	$186,906;	1991	$1,593,906;
1978	$290,918;	1992	$1,735,893;
1979	$431,083;	1993	$1,753,816;
1980	$230,743;	1994	$1,822,436;
1981	$585,683;	1995	$1,811,544;
1982	$708,250;	1996	$1,787,490;
1983	$1,243,897;	1997	$1,795,821;
1984	$1,087,368;	1998 (estimate)	$1,886,577.
1985	$1,158,719;	Total:	$27,638,848
1986	$1,194,716;		...and growing.
1987	$1,226,457;		

This graph provided some background for a Jan. 23, 1998 Joe Fellegy column.

1999 — The so-called Y2K bug was the topic of many conversations, with some people believing the computer problem would lead to Armageddon. The actual results were negligible.

• An earthquake that measured 7.1 struck Turkey, killing nearly 16,000 people and leaving another 600,000 without homes.

• The Columbine massacre left 12 students and a teacher dead at Columbine High School in Littleton, Colo. The gunmen – Eric Harris and Dylan Klebold – killed themselves after attacking the school.

• The U.S. Senate opened impeachment hearings against President Bill Clinton. The Senate acquitted him, and rejected an attempt to censure him.

• Louisville, Ky., doctors perform the first hand transplant ever in the U.S.

• The national unemployment rate dropped to 4.2 percent.

JANUARY

• Gov. Jesse Ventura selected Bloomington businessman Alan Horner to be DNR commissioner. About a week after Ventura announced the selection, Horner resigned on his first official day on the job. He'd come under fire when it became public he'd been cited for fishing violations.

• Gary Clancy's new column, Strictly Whitetails, began. The column was to be devoted entirely to white-tailed deer.

• Two men caught state-record splake on the opening day of the winter trout season outside the Boundary Waters. One angler caught the new record – 11 pounds, 3 ounces – on Larson Lake. Another angler fishing Tofte Lake near Ely caught an 11-pound, 3.36-ounce splake the same day.

FEBRUARY

• Gov. Jesse Ventura appointed Allen Garber, the Champlin Police chief and former FBI agent, to lead the DNR as commissioner. Garber, 56, was neither a hunter nor a fishermen, which Ventura cited as an asset.

• A bill introduced in the state House sought to legalize big-game shooting preserves in Minnesota. The Minnesota Conservation Federation came out in opposition to the bill.

• Six people were charged with gross misdemeanors in Martin County for their roles in the poaching of four deer in October of 1998.

Dalton Humphrey, of Bloomington, caught this 4-pound, 18-inch piranha on Prior Lake. Dalton's dad, Jon, is holding the fish. DNR believes it was probably dumped from an aquarium.

Outdoor News launched its annual Man of the Year Award in 1999, and named Pheasants Forever's Joe Duggan its inaugural recipient. The story accompanying the announcement noted that Duggan had played a crucial role in the passage of the Heritage Hunting and Fishing Amendment in 1998.

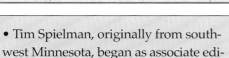
• Tim Spielman, originally from southwest Minnesota, began as associate editor of Outdoor News.

• Snowmobile deaths were on a decline in 1997 and 1998 – after peaking at 32 during the winter of 1996-'97 – but officials figured it had to do with a lack of snow.

MARCH

• St. Cloud Times outdoors contributor Glen Schmitt joined the Outdoor News advertising department.

APRIL

• The U.S. Supreme Court, in a 5-4 decision, upheld the Chippewas' right to hunt and fish on 13 million acres of public land in central Minnesota, free of state regulation. "After an examination of the historical record, we conclude that the Chippewa retain the … rights guaranteed to them under the 1837 Treaty," Justice Sandra Day O'Connor wrote for the court.

• Minnesota anglers set six state records in 1998.

• The state and the Red Lake Band signed a memorandum of understanding to implement the Red Lake Walleye Recovery Plan. Stocking was set to begin in the spring. A key aspect of the plan was a walleye-harvest moratorium.

• A semi hit a timber wolf near Rochester. It was struck on Highway 52, and DNR officials said it was a male that likely was wandering.

MAY

• Three Twin Cities men were charged with illegally taking 630 rainbow trout. Officers suspected the fish were netted at a hatchery in Iowa.

JUNE

• A state conservation officer (Grant

SWEARING IN. Minnesota DNR Enforcement Chief Bill Bernhjelm formally swears in new enforcement officer candidate Vuthy Pril on Monday in the State Capitol rotunda. Pril is the first of four COs of Southeast Asian descent who will serve Minnesota. See complete story, right. Image courtesy of DNR

RECORD BREAKER. On March 15, Almer D. Pederson, of Nashwauk, hooked the third state record splake caught in 1999.

This photo of a massive Manitoba northern pike—a potential world record—turned up in the *Outdoor News* office last week by way of Twin Cities resident Bill Keating. Photo courtesy of Bill Keating.

Coyour) and a graduate student (Eric Cox) studying moose in northwestern Minnesota were killed when their plane crashed in the Red Lake Wildlife Management Area.

JULY
• Jeff Finden, who'd headed Pheasants Forever for 17 years, announced plans to step down June 30, 2000.
• Geese Unlimited ended its 15-year run in the state. Officials said the group had accomplished its mission of expanding geese in the state.
• Seven people were confirmed to have died on state waters during the Fourth of July weekend, making it one of the deadliest on record.
• About 250,000 acres of the Boundary Waters were affected by a severe windstorm. At least 19 people with serious injuries were evacuated.
• Willard Munger, known as Mr.

Clancy's quick-and-easy squirrel recipe

Cut the squirrels into pieces. (Front legs, back and hind legs). Wash each piece and then dip in plain flour seasoned with salt and pepper. Brown in medium hot oil. Put the squirrels, the drippings from the fry pan, and one can of cream of chicken or cream of mushroom soup into a crockpot. Set the crockpot on low and let it simmer all day. Even the toughest old bushytail will be melt-in-your-mouth tender.

Food and wild game cooking has had a growing presence in Outdoor News over the years. Gary Clancy often offers cooking tips.

Environment and the oldest lawmaker in state history, died at 88. Munger was a DFLer from Duluth who was in his 43rd year in the state House of Representatives.
• A fisherman caught a 34-pound,

National Wild Turkey Federation Minnesota wild turkey records

Heaviest gobblers taken in Minnesota
1) 29.46 pounds, by Clem Nardinger of Lake City, 1998.
2) 27.4375 pounds, by Gary Detjen of Prior Lake, 1991.
3) 27.00 pounds, by Frank LaNasa, Jr. of Roseville, 1981.
4) 26.0625 pounds, by Carlyn Doely of Spring Grove, 1991.
5) 25.50 pounds, by Thomas Ryan of Roseville, 1988.
6) 25.25 pounds, by Jeffrey Bunke of Rushford, 1983.
7) 25.00 pounds, by Robert Bunke of Rushford, 1995.
8) 24.93 pounds, by William Urbaniak of Hugo, 1993.
9) 24.75 pounds, by Jay Bunke of Rochester, 1982.
10) 24.5 pounds, by Daniel Dexter of Duluth, 1985.

Longest spurs on a Minnesota gobbler
1) 1.6875 inches, by Carlyn Doely of Spring Grove, 1991.
2) 1.50 inches, by Paul Vitse of Mabel, 1991.
3) -tie- 1.4375 inches, by Don Busse of Austin, 1992.
   Gary Detjen of Prior Lake, 1991.
5) -tie- 1.375 inches, by Thomas Ryan of Roseville, 1988.
   Richard Kirby of Orchard Park, NY, 1996.
   Jeff Fuchs of Blue Earth, 1998.
8) -tie- 1.3125 inches, by Harry Kuefler of Forest Lake, 1995; Clem Nardinger of Lake City, 1998;
10) -tie- 1.25 inches, by Lane Grant of Rochester, 1986; Gene Barlage of Wheaton, 1986; Ted Roberton of Rushford, 1997; John Bolanda of Coon Rapids, 1992.

Longest beard on a Minnesota gobbler
1) 12.25 inches , by Clem Nardinger of Lake City, 1998.
2) 11.75 inches, by Richard Alford of Mound, 1997.
3) 11.625 inches, by Don Busse of Austin, 1992.
4) -tie- 11.50 inches, by Jeff Bunke of Rushford, 1983.
   James Bennett of Minnetonka, 1995.
6) 11.375 inches, by William Urbaniak of Hugo, 1993.
7) 11.25 inches, by Paul Vitse of Mabel, 1991.
8) 11.065 inches, by Robert Johnson of Farmington, 1994.
9) -tie- 11.00 inches, by Frank LaNasa, Jr. or Roseville, 1981; Thomas Ryan of Roseville, 1988; Carlyn Doely of Spring Grove, 1991; Harry Kuefler of Forest Lake, 1995.

Overall typical score
(Combination of spurs, weight, and beard)
1) 81.812, by Carlyn Doely of Spring Grove, 1991.
2) 80.22, by Clem Nardinger of Lake City, 1998.
3) 76.55, by Gary Detjen of Prior Lake, 1991.
4) 74.312, by Paul Vitse of Mabel, 1991.
5) 73.80, by Thomas Ryan of Roseville, 1988.
6) 72.18, by Don Busse of Austin, 1992.
7) 71.875, by Harry Kuefler of Forest Lake, 1995.
8) 71.50, by Frank LaNasa, Jr. of Roseville, 1981.
9) 70.75, by Jeff Bunke of Rushford, 1983.
10) 67.88, by Lane Grant of Rochester, 1986.

12-ounce tiger muskie from Lake Elmo in the east metro. It beat the state record by a pound.

AUGUST

• Erik Ness died at his home of a brain tumor. He was 16 when he found out he had cancer, and died at 21.

• A northern pike that apparently was 70 pounds was caught by an aboriginal fisherman in Manitoba. While it would have been a world record, the man, who caught it in a net in Cedar Lake, photographed the fish and ate it.

• Shawn Perich flew over the Boundary Waters and described the damage from the windstorm.

• An $8 million marina – the Silver Bay Safe Harbor – opened on the North Shore of Lake Superior.

SEPTEMBER

• A group opposed to stocking muskies in Lake Miltona formed. The Lake Miltona Property Owners Association sought to end muskie stocking in the lake.

• A North Dakota man paid $3,725 in fines after being caught with 560 fillets of fish caught in Otter Tail Lake.

• Gov. Jesse Ventura angered hunters when, on his radio show, he told a DNR wildlife manager that he couldn't hunt "Bambi." Ventura's spokesman said he meant the comments to not be taken seriously.

OCTOBER

• A headline – Friend or Foe – appeared in Outdoor News over a photo of Gov. Jesse Ventura. Asked about the right to bear arms, he told "Playboy" magazine, in part: "It's not in there to make sure I can go hunting on weekends. I don't deer hunt, by the way. That's not really hunting. I prefer when the opposition can shoot back – then you're hunting."

• Vuthy Pril was sworn in as the state's first Southeast Asian conservation officer candidate.

=BEST BUCK WEEKLY WINNER=

Nationally know outdoors television personality Tiffany Lakosky appeared in Outdoor News reader shots during the early days of her hunting career.

WEEKLY WINNER. Tiffany Profant, of Columbia Heights, bagged her first buck with her first shot at a deer while bowhunting in Washington County. She downed this 6-pointer with her PSE compound bow.

NOVEMBER

• Ontario conservation officers busted a number of anglers – primarily Minnesotans – who were fishing the Canadian side of the Rainy River.

• Minnesota and Ontario resolved their border fishing dispute, promising to work together on conservation and management of fish in border waters.

• A Grand Rapids area man killed a 24-point, 277-pound buck on opening day of the firearms deer opener after the wounded deer charged him. The hunter had to wrestle the deer and dispatch it with a knife.

DECEMBER

• A federal judge ruled the state had to pay $4 million in legal fees to seven of the eight Ojibwe bands that battled with the DNR over treaty rights.

• Outdoor News interviewed retiring DNR Fish and Wildlife Division Director Roger Holmes.

Decoy use pays off for CO

Northome, Minn.—Area Conservation Officer Tony Cornish and Delbert the Decoy Deer No. 3 had another productive season targeting poachers. Delbert No. 1 and 2 had to be retired according to Cornish because "they were full of holes."

Many state COs deploy deer decoys to catch people who would shine and shoot deer from roads. Officer Tony Cornish and "Delbert" confiscated these firearms from such violators.

2000 — The closest presidential election in decades tipped in favor of George W. Bush, who defeated Al Gore. The election occurred in early November; the U.S. Supreme Court gave Bush the victory about a month later.

• The national unemployment rate hit 4 percent.

• A suicide attack against the U.S.S. Cole, a U.S. Navy ship in the Yemen port of Aden, killed 17 and injured 39 American sailors. The terrorist group al-Qaeda claimed responsibility.

• Stocks plunged, signaling the begining of the end of the so-called dot-com boom of Internet stocks.

• Vicente Fox was elected president of Mexico, as candidate of the rightist PAN (National Action Party), ending 71 years of PRI (Institutional Revolutionary Party) rule.

• The world population topped 6 billion.

Actor and National Rifle Association President Charlton Heston visited the Twin Cities during election season 2000 to stump for U.S. Sen. Rod Grams. He sat down with Outdoor News to discuss the upcoming election and gun politics.

JANUARY

• Grand Rapids area conservation officer Dale Honer died of cancer at the age of 43. Honer was the third officer to die in 1999.

• Michigan bowhunter Mitch Rompola, who claimed to have shot a whitetail buck that scored 218⅝ and would be a world record, agreed not to claim world record status. Rompola had refused to identify the scorers who measured his deer.

FEBRUARY

• The Bluffland Whitetails Association became an official organization. Its mission: "The Bluffland Whitetails Association promotes continuous improvement in white-tailed deer management, knowledge, and research so as to ensure a healthy and balanced deer herd today and in the future through providing education to its members, the wildlife management community, and the public."

• State Sen. Bob Lessard and Rep. Mark Holsten introduced a bill to dedicate 1/8 of one percent of the state sales tax to the Minnesota DNR for fish and wildlife management and enforcement. The bill was modeled after similar legislation in Missouri. Outdoor News began a series of articles looking at how the funding mechanism worked in Missouri, and whether it could work in Minnesota.

• The DNR initiated a study in southeastern Minnesota to deter-

MAN OF THE YEAR. Harvey Nelson (l) recently accepted the *Outdoor News* Man of the Year award from Editor Rob Drieslein. For the full story on Nelson's lifetime of achievements for waterfowl and conservation, see Page 12. **Staff Photo**

mine seasonal survival rates and causes of mortality of deer. Animals were radio-collared as part of the effort.

MARCH

• Hunting and fishing license vendors across the state began using an electronic licensing system, which did away with hand-written licenses.

• A full-page feature outlined how 5.8 percent of every $1 lottery ticket sold went into the Environment and Natural Resources Trust Fund, and how 15.3 percent went into the state's General Fund. State Sen. Bob Lessard and Rep. Mark Holsten introduced legislation that would have resulted in the portion going to the General Fund going instead to the Game and Fish Fund, and to state and metro parks.

• The DNR tracked down a deer-poaching suspect who appeared in a graphic home video in which he took credit for an apparently untagged deer. Eight deer appeared in the video.

• The U.S. Fish and Wildlife Service listed the Canada lynx as threatened under the Endangered Species Act.

• CO Grant Coyour, who was killed in a plane crash while taking part in a moose study in 1999, was posthumously named conservation officer of the year for 1999.

APRIL

• In response to increased demand, the Minnesota DNR expanded its channel catfish stocking efforts in Twin Cities lakes.

• Gov. Jesse Ventura signed legislation creating a variety of lifetime fishing and hunting licenses.

MAY

• The Minnesota DNR confirmed major progress in the recovery of the

FILL 'ER UP! Three Canadian CL-215s, specialized firefighting aircraft, have landed in Minnesota in recent weeks to help the Minnesota DNR and U.S. Forest Service during the fire season. This one is based in Brainerd. See Page 13. Photo by Rob Drieslein

REMEMBERING

This buck was shot in 1950 by an unknown hunter in Kittson County. The rack had barbed wire twisted around its antlers. Look closely, and you will see another set of antlers that were pulled from the skull of a second buck that was also tangled in the barbed wire. Photo courtesy of Bruce Becker

Share Your Memories

*Got a hunting or fishing photo from **before 1960**? Send it to Remembering, c/o Outdoor News, 3410 Winnetka Ave. No., New Hope, MN 55427. Please identify all persons in photo if possible and the year photo was taken. Outdoor News will return all REMEMBERING photos submitted.*

FIGHTIN' THE ELEMENTS. Don Dittberner (l-r), Tim Spielman, Ron Nelson, and Rob Drieslein ride the three- and four-foot rollers on Lake Mille Lacs last week.

From Jim Peterson's era to the present, Outdoor News staffers have a long history of enjoying Minnesota's natural resources.

Red Lake walleye population. Spring surveys showed young walleyes stocked in 1999 survived the winter in good shape.

• A 63-year-old Edina man was arrested in connection with the theft of about $25,000 in merchandise from Cabela's in Owatonna and Ahlman's Custom Gun Shop in Morristown.

JUNE

• Spring turkey hunters killed 6,154 birds, smashing the previous record kill.

• DNR Commissioner Allen Garber decided not to fill the Fish and Wildlife Division director position vacated by Roger Holmes. Instead, he announced a realignment that resulted in three new sections in what had been the Fish and Wildlife Division. Those sections were Ecological Services, Fisheries, and Wildlife, and the section managers who used to report to Holmes would report instead to Garber.

JULY

• Lake Mille Lacs launch captain caught a monster muskie while fishing for walleyes on the lake's mud flats – it weighed 50 pounds and measured 52 inches in length. The fish, which he caught and released, was hooked just ahead of its tail fin.

• A new feature – From the Backyard – appeared in Outdoor News. The feature was aimed at readers who enjoy watching wildlife, and to answer questions about nature in general.

• State Sen. Bob Lessard left the DFL party, which he'd been a part for 24 years. He said he would seek

ONE OF THOSE DAYS. The highpoint of Clancy's Iowa hunt? This heifer, while searching for salt, found itself "stuck behind the wheel." After a fair amount of grunting and pulling, the group removed the persistent bovine without injury to beast nor vehicle.

Photos courtesy of Gary Clancy

Minnesota State Sen. Bob Lessard received the State Legislator of the Year Award at the Safari Club International Convention held in Reno earlier this month. Sen. Lessard has accomplished much for sportsmen and women during his 24 years as a state senator. He is credited with being the main motivator behind the legislation allowing the voters of Minnesota to vote on the Constitutional Amendment to preserve the hunting and fishing rights for all Minnesotans. Sen. Lessard is pictured with his daughter, Kelly, at the Reno Convention.

re-election as an independent. "The liberal wing of the DFL has turned its back on the people I represent," Lessard, of International Falls, said.

SEPTEMBER

• After Star Tribune Outdoor Editor Dennis Anderson wrote a column suggesting the DNR stayed mum on the possibility of studying lower fish bag limits until the Legislature approved funding for the agency, DNR Commissioner Allen Garber directed agency personnel to deny interviews to Anderson unless he allowed them to read his articles before publication. Garber's directive led to a firestorm of criticism, including from Outdoor News contributor Tony Dean, who on his website called on Garber to resign.

Duane Lafki, of Baudette, caught this 76-pound, 69-inch sturgeon with a jig and minnow while fishing the Rainy River on April 7. The fish took an 1½ hours to land.

• Charlton Heston, a Hollywood actor and president of the National Rifle Association, was in Minneapolis to support Rod Grams' re-election to the U.S. Senate.

OCTOBER

• Outdoor News unveiled its first website via a full page in the newspaper.
• A fire that began on private property swept over the Carlos Avery Wildlife Management Area, burning 6,500 acres.

NOVEMBER

• A 45-year-old man was killed when a captive eight-point buck – one of seven pet deer the man's family owned – gored him to death in the animals' pen.

DECEMBER

• Canadian health officials worked to eradicate more than 1,600 game farm elk in Saskatchewan in an effort to wipe out an outbreak of chronic wasting disease in the province.

After years of issuing hunting and fishing licenses by hand, license vendors in 2000 implemented the DNR's electronic licensing system.

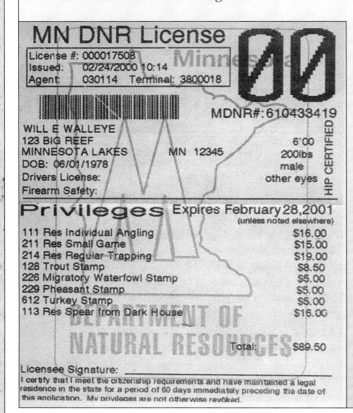

MN DNR License 00

License #: 000017508
Issued: 02/24/2000 10:14
Agent 030114 Terminal: 3800018

MDNR#: 610433419

WILL E WALLEYE
123 BIG REEF
MINNESOTA LAKES   MN   12345
DOB: 06/01/1978
Drivers License:
Firearm Safety:

6'00
200lbs
male
other eyes

HIP CERTIFIED

Privileges Expires February 28, 2001
(unless noted elsewhere)

111 Res Individual Angling	$16.00
211 Res Small Game	$15.00
214 Res Regular Trapping	$19.00
128 Trout Stamp	$8.50
226 Migratory Waterfowl Stamp	$5.00
229 Pheasant Stamp	$5.00
612 Turkey Stamp	$5.00
113 Res Spear from Dark House	$16.00
Total:	$89.50

DEPARTMENT OF NATURAL RESOURCES

Licensee Signature: _____
I certify that I meet the citizenship requirements and have maintained a legal residence in the state for a period of 60 days immediately preceding the date of this application. My privileges are not otherwise revoked.

2001 — *George W. Bush was sworn in as the 43rd president of the U.S.*

• *Terrorists hijacked four commercial airliners in the U.S., crashing two into the two towers of the World Trade Center, one into the Pentagon, and another into a field in Pennsylvania. Thousands of Americans perished; al-Qaeda claimed responsibility for the attacks. U.S. and British forces soon launched attacks in Afghanistan.*

• *FBI agent Robert Hanssen was charged with spying for Russia.*

• *President Bush signed a law that cut taxes by the highest level in two decades.*

• *Timothy McVeigh was executed.*

• *The U.S. unemployment rate rose to 4.8 percent.*

• *The National Academy of Sciences reported global warming on the rise.*

• *Noted racecar driver Dale Earnhardt died in a crash at the Daytona 500.*

• *Enron's Chapter 11 bankruptcy becomes the largest in U.S. history.*

JANUARY

• DNR officials at the Wildlife Roundtable asked hunters if the state should consider a walk-in access program whereby private landowners would receive payment in exchange for allowing hunters to access their land. The conversation was the result of increased interest from hunters.

• Al Farmes received a Meritorious Service Award from DNR Commissioner Allen Garber for a lifetime spent creating and protecting wildlife management areas.

• The Supreme Court of the United States ruled that Section 404 of the Clean Water Act – the key part of federal law for wetlands protection – doesn't apply to isolated wetlands. Rather, it said the law applies only to those connected to navigable waters. Conservationists said the ruling dealt a serious blow to wetland conservation.

• Pheasants Forever, with guidance from the DNR, released 30 pheasants from South Dakota into southwestern Otter Tail County. The release was intended to supplement birds in an area where the population had been decimated in part by harsh winters.

FEBRUARY

• The DNR planned to spend $6 million to buy two amphibious air-

Resort owner and writer Justine Kerfoot is shown in an undated photo. Kerfoot, known for her work in the BWCAW, died last Wednesday afternoon, May 30, 2001, in Grand Marais. **AP Photo/Duluth News Tribune**

Pfeifer-Hamilton Publishers

In a story lamenting the declining quality of duck hunting, writer Bill Klein cited the concerns of veteran waterfowlers like Bud Grant.

NFL Hall of Famer and ex-Minnesota Vikings coach Bud Grant with the late Jimmy Robinson, legendary duck camp operator and guide. Grant, Robinson and Grant's lab, Molly, took these ducks on the Delta Marsh near Winnipeg.

planes that it had been leasing to help fight potential forest fires in the northeastern part of the state.

• Scientists said Minnesota wildlife populations were shifting in response to a warming climate, and that some flora and fauna may disappear from the northern part of the state as a result of warming. DNR scientist Bill Berg said the warmth may favor deer at the expense of moose.

MARCH

• The DNR cancelled a plan to use ice divers to study the extent of illegal spear fishing in the Bemidji area. The plan was to look for speared walleyes and muskies, but was abandoned when it became clear divers could not survey a sufficiently large area.

• The DNR announced it was conducting an internal investigation after a conservation officer killed two dogs in the Brookston area. The officer was responding to a call of dogs chasing deer, but the two dogs he shot were neither chasing deer nor on deer tracks when they were killed.

• Sen. Bob Lessard again introduced a bill to dedicate 3/16 of one percent of the general state sales tax to fish and wildlife habitat and other causes. The bill also included a citizen/legislator council that would determine spending.

• The DNR said it supported the basic concept of the 3/16 proposal, but opposed the formation of a council to oversee how the money is spent.

• A lawmaker introduced a bill that would allow county boards to offer coyote bounties. The DNR opposed, saying bounties aren't effective.

APRIL

• Outdoor News unveiled a full-page "From the Backyard" feature, which featured a variety of nature-related tidbits, and columns by Val Cunningham and Stan Tekiela.

• Gov. Jesse Ventura angered hunters

HUNTING HISTORY DATES

1858: First big game laws are established.
1887: Deer hunting season limited to November.
1895: Deer limit increased to five deer per person.
1899: Big game license is established (.25¢-resident, $25-nonresidents)
1901: Deer limit reduced to three deer per person.
1903: Resident big game license increases to $1.
1905: Deer limit reduced to two deer
1911: On-site deer tagging begins
1915: Deer limit is reduced to one
1919: All big game hunters required to buy license
1921: Resident big game license increases to $2
1923: Deer hunting season open only on even years
1931: Department of Conservation is established
1951: Nine-day deer season established. That runs through 1969.
1971: Deer season closes due to harsh winters and overharvest of does.
1976: Antlerless permit system starts. Deer biologists use doe harvest to regulate herds.
1992: Firearms deer hunters harvest a record 243,000 whitetails.

An Oct. 26, 2001, story by Tori McCormick took a look at 150 years of big-game laws and deer hunting in Minnesota.

MILLE LACS GIANT. Mike Beltz, of St. Paul, caught and released this 52-inch muskie while trolling a crankbait with Duell guide Service on Mille Lacs on Sept. 15. The fish had a 31-inch girth.

when, during an "interview" with Star Tribune Outdoors Editor Dennis Anderson, he said, in part, "... Until you've hunted man, you haven't hunted yet. Because you really need to hunt something that can shoot back at you to really classify yourself as a hunter. You need to understand the feeling of what it's like to go into the field and know that your opposition can take you out. Not just go out there and shoot Bambi."

• DNR conservation officer Frank Rezac was suspended five days without pay for shooting and killing two dogs in February. An internal investigation found Rezac had no malicious intent, but that he misunderstood the state statute giving COs the authority to destroy dogs to protect big-game animals.

MAY

• A bill that would have applied harsher penalties in excessive overbagging cases was defeated on the floor of the state House of Representatives.

JUNE

• Al Lindner announced he was leaving In-Fisherman. The split was amicable, and Lindner said he and his brother Ron planned to start a new fishing show with a Christian message.

WHERE'S WALDO? Or in this case, Jason Ross, who — with a 4.82-pound northern — won first place last weekend at the 19th Annual Golden Rainbow Ice Fishing Contest, sponsored by the Hopkins Jaycees. Thousands of fishermen gathered on Forest Lake Sunday afternoon, Feb. 4, 2001, for the event. Prizes worth over $125,000 were awarded. AP Photo/Star Tribune, Brian Peterson

WATERBOMBER. A CL-215 aircraft dwarfs officials in a Minnesota Air National Guard hangar in Minneapolis as DNR Commissioner Allen Garber (l) and Tom Appleton, president of Bombardier Aerospace, shake hands after transferring ownership of two planes on Monday. AP Photo/Jim Mone

Rick Parent (above) and his hunting party took this bull near Grand Marais. Not pictured are party members Robert and Jeralyn Parent. The rack is the second largest ever taken in Minnesota, and it had a 68⅜-inch spread.

Photos by Eric Meyer

69th Annual
Northwest
SPORTSHOW

Hours: Friday, March 16 - 5 to 10 p.m.; Saturdays, March 17 & March 24 - 10 a.m. to 9 p.m.; Sundays, March 18 & March 25 - 10 a.m. to 6 p.m.; Monday through Friday, March 19 to 23 - 2 to 10 p.m.; **Admission:** Adults-$8; children 5 to 11-$4; children under 5-free.

MAN OF THE YEAR. Frank Schneider, Jr., is the *Outdoor News* 2001 Man of the Year. For the full story on Schneider's achievements, see Page 24, Section A.

Photo by Rob Drieslein

• The DNR announced anglers would be able to keep one trophy walleye longer than 30 inches from Lake Mille Lacs. The agency added the trophy walleye piece to the existing slot that allows anglers to keep only walleyes between 16 and 18 inches in length.

JULY

• The DNR spent nearly $300,000 in preparation for a state government shutdown.

• Steven Williams, secretary of Kansas Wildlife and Parks, was tapped by President George Bush to lead the U.S. Fish and Wildlife Service.

SEPTEMBER

• Two public unions that were poised to strike later in September included 2,239 of the DNR's total staff of 3,321.

• The DNR warned archery deer hunters to be aware of anthrax, which had killed two deer, two horses, and 73 cattle in the state in 2001.

• There were conversations about cancelling the annual deer hunts at the Camp Ripley Military Reserve as a result of the Sept. 11 terrorist attacks.

• Before the Sept. 11 attacks, conservationists were optimistic that conservation funding would be a priority in the farm bill. But after the attacks? "It's clear budget priorities have shifted," said Jim Mosher, of the Izaak Walton League.

• Tom Meyers, a board member of the Minnesota Conservation Federation and an inaugural inductee into the Muskies, Inc. Hall of Fame, passed away. He was 60

years old.

• A picture making the email rounds appeared to show two northern pike joined at the head. An Iowa angler allegedly caught the fish in the Mississippi River. Most fisheries officials believed the photo was a prank.

OCTOBER

• A shakeup in the DNR commissioners office resulted in Kim Bonde and Kurt Ulrich taking on new responsibilities.

• An appeals court ruling appeared to allow ice fishermen in fish houses the same privacy they would be afforded if they were in their own homes. DNR enforcement officials weren't pleased by the outcome, but said they had additional options to protect natural resources.

• DNR Commissioner Allen Garber suspended negotiations about cooperative natural resources management with the White Earth Band of Chippewa.

NOVEMBER

• Outdoor News started Operation Stay in Touch once again. The program gave free subscriptions to men and women serving overseas.

• Shawn Perich examined green terrorism, and reported it had continued domestically after the Sept. 11 attacks.

2002 — *In his first State of the Union Address, President George Bush says he'll expand the war on terrorism, and calls Iran, Iraq, and North Korea an "Axis of Evil."*

• President Bush addressed the United Nations and called for regime change in Iraq; two months later, the UN Security Council passed a unanimous resolution calling on Iraq to disarm or face serious consequences.

• Snipers targeted people in the greater Washington, D.C., area, killing 10 and injuring others in a spree that lasted nearly a month. Two men later were arrested and charged.

• French scientists reported finding a skull of a human ancestor estimated at 7 million years old in Chad.

• Terrorists detonated a bomb in Bali, killing hundreds of people.

• The national unemployment rate rose to 5.8 percent, while the U.S. population hit 290 million.

JANUARY

• Outdoor News celebrated its 35th anniversary, in part, with a multi-paged feature that included readers', writers', and sources' thoughts about the paper. Said TV personality and former Star Tribune outdoors writer Ron Schara: "I know the writers for both daily newspapers will check the Outdoor News to see what's going on." Said Brad Moore, assistant DNR commissioner for operations: "The paper does a really good job of getting opinions of the public and keeps the agency grounded in what's going on."
• Gov. Jesse Ventura's proposed budget for the DNR would slash $15 million from the agency's operating budget.

FEBRUARY

• A Fridley fisherman caught a 12-pound, 15-ounce rainbow trout. The angler didn't reveal the lake, but it likely came from 30-acre Cenaiko Lake in Anoka County, which was one of seven metro lakes stocked with trout.
• Scottish lawmakers outlawed fox hunting with dogs. Similar legislation also was a hot topic in the rest of the United Kingdom.

MARCH

• In a column, Publisher Glenn Meyer angrily criticized many of the outdoor hunting and fishing television shows, calling many of them nothing more than 30-minute commercials. "Don't expect an 'Outdoor News Fishing Show' in the near future," he wrote.
• Outdoor News ran a full-page ad for Gary Clancy's "Strictly Whitetails" book, which included many of Clancy's most popular columns, as well as previously unpublished material.

METRO RAINBOW. Kevin Klemz, of Fridley, caught this 12-pound, 15-ounce rainbow trout on a metro lake. The fish hit a red and yellow Hellgamite Spoon.

METRO COUGAR. Using a motion-sensitive camera, Kerry Kammann photographed this mountain lion feeding on a deer carcass in the Minnesota River bottoms in Savage. See story, Page 3.

• Justin Fuhrer, of Pine River, paid $4,000 to get his airplane back from the Red Lake Band. Fuhrer inadvertently landed his plane on Lower Red Lake in February. The process of getting it back took six weeks.

• Both the House and Senate passed a bill to increase fines for gross overlimits. The same bill failed to pass the House in 2001.

MAY

• The plan to dedicate 3/16 of one percent of the state sales tax gained new life, when Rep. Mark Holsten's bill was set for a committee hearing.

• Tom Donovan caught a 3-pound, 6-ounce white crappie that exceeded the

LIVELY DEBATE. U.S. Sen. Paul Wellstone (r) and Republican challenger Norm Coleman (second from right) sparred frequently during a candidate debate on outdoor issues Saturday at Game Fair. Also shown are Green Party candidate Ed McGaa (l) and *Outdoor News* Editor Rob Drieslein. Photo by Eric Meyer

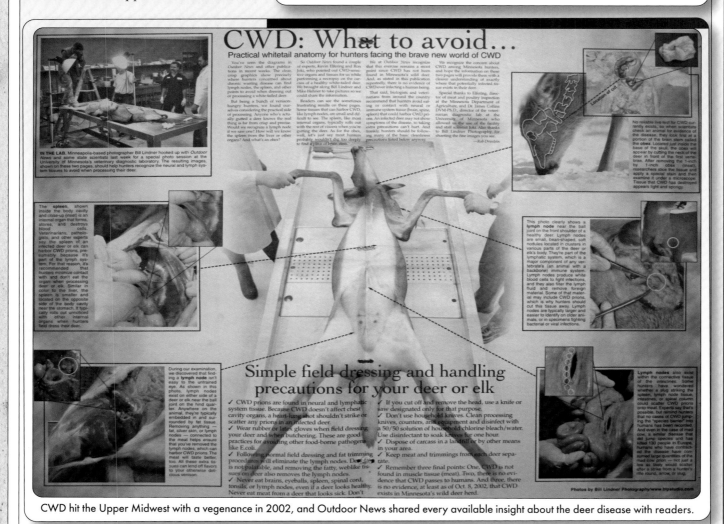

CWD: What to avoid...
Practical whitetail anatomy for hunters facing the brave new world of CWD

Simple field dressing and handling precautions for your deer or elk

CWD hit the Upper Midwest with a vegeance in 2002, and Outdoor News shared every available insight about the deer disease with readers.

prior state record, which was 3 pounds, 4 ounces. He was fishing Whaletail Lake.

• Terry Gfeller caught a 5-pound, 12-ounce tullibee in St. Louis County's Little Long Lake. The new state-record fish beat the previous record of 4 pounds, 5 ounces.

• Two wild deer had tested positive in Saskatchewan for CWD (one in 2000, another in 2002), and the province said it had spent $33 million in an effort to eradicate the disease from wild and captive animals.

• St. Joseph resident Jack Brickweg caught a 8-pound, 4-ounce redhorse in the Sauk River, beating the old state record of 7 pounds, 9 ounces.

JUNE

• The Fish and Wildlife Legislative Alliance, an umbrella group for several fishing and hunting groups, ceased to exist. Lack of participation, especially in the forms of funds, was cited by the group's executive director, Gary Botzek, as the reason.

• The DNR offered the highest number of antlerless permits ever – 363,765. The DNR said hunters needed to harvest a record, or near-record, number of deer that fall to keep the state's deer population in check.

MOOSE ANTLERS
a spring 'hunting' opportunity
in the northeast

Terry Englund, of Grand Marias, found this matching set of sheds in northeast Minnesota.

SEE THE STATE RECORD EELPOUT AT THE *OUTDOOR NEWS* BOOTH

John Galles, of South St. Paul, was recognized at the Northwest Sportshow at the Minneapolis Convention Center last weekend for his catch of the new state record eelpout. Galles caught the record fish on Lake of the Woods on Feb. 17, 2001, using a jig on 12-pound-test line. The 19.16-pound fish measured 38 inches and had a 24-inch girth. Sportsmen and women can see a mount of the fish at the *Outdoor News* booth at the Northwest Sportshow, booth No. 44-45. DNR Assistant Commissioner for Operations Brad Moore presented the award to Galles.

BWCAW BURNING. A fire burns off the Gunflint Trail near Grand Marais on Monday, Sept. 16, 2002, as the U.S. Forest Service works on a control burn in the Boundary Waters Canoe Area Wilderness. For the full story on the USFS's prescribed burning efforts last week in the BWCAW, see story, Page 7.

JULY

• Curt Kalk, natural resources commissioner for the Mille Lacs Band, wrote a letter to the DNR, voicing concerns about the state's continuation of walleye regulations on Mille Lacs, even though state anglers had exceeded their quota.

• The Minnesota Court of Appeals ruled that conservation officers couldn't search boats without consent or probable cause. Enforcement officials said they were in a wait and see mode.

AUGUST

• The deaths of three outdoorsmen from brain-destroying illnesses prompted an investigation of whether chronic wasting disease had crossed from animals into humans. The men knew each other and had eaten deer and elk meat together. All died in the 1990s.

SEPTEMBER

• Health officials in Minneapolis announced the first two cases of West Nile virus in humans. Two men – aged 35 and 29 – from the metro area were hospitalized and released.

• The DNR began an intense surveillance effort after a captive elk in Aitkin County was discovered to have chronic wasting disease. The first 10 wild deer killed as part of the surveillance tested negative for the disease.

OCTOBER

• Federal officials hoped funding would become available to step up lynx monitoring and research efforts in the state. There had been numerous lynx sightings in northeastern Minnesota the past two years. The animals had rarely been seen in the state

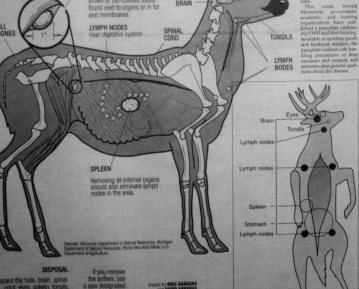

Concerned about CWD? Follow these tips for butchering and processing your deer

Chronic wasting disease is a fatal neurodegenerative illness of deer and elk. It is characterized by accumulations of abnormal prions – forms of protein – that differ in shape from normal prions, which occur naturally in the brains of deer and elk. The abnormal prions are very difficult to destroy; they can survive many traditional sterilization techniques, including gamma and ultraviolet radiation. While they don't have DNA nor RNA, they are able to transform normal proteins to their own image, creating spongelike holes in the brain. Because of their long incubation periods, prion diseases have been mistaken for "slow viruses."

According to the World Health Organization, **there is no evidence that the disease passes to humans**. To reduce the risk of exposure the Wisconsin Department of Agriculture, Trade and Consumer Protection recommends the following guidelines for removing prions from venison.

FIELD DRESSING
■ Wear rubber or latex gloves.
■ Do not use household knives or utensils.
■ Remove all internal organs and minimize contact with them.
■ Clean knives, counters and equipment of residue and disinfect with a 50/50 solution of household chlorine bleach and water and dry.
■ Use disinfectant to soak knives for one hour.

CUTTING AND PROCESSING
(Follow field-dressing guidelines as well)
■ Do not cut into or through bones.
■ Do not cut through the spinal column, except to remove the head. Use a knife designated only for that purpose.
■ Bone out the meat and remove all fat and connective tissue (the weblike membranes attached to the meat).

CONSUMPTION
■ Never eat a deer's brain, eyeballs, spinal cord, spleen or lymph nodes.

ORGANS TO BE AVOIDED AND DISCARDED

LYMPH NODES — Lumps of slimy gray, yellowish-brown or tan-colored tissue found next to organs or in fat and membranes.
ALL BONES
LYMPH NODES near digestive system
BRAIN
EYES
SPINAL CORD
TONSILS
LYMPH NODES
SPLEEN — Removing all internal organs should also eliminate lymph nodes in the area.

Eyes
Brain
Tonsils
Lymph nodes
Lymph nodes
Spleen
Stomach
Lymph nodes

DISPOSAL — Discard the hide, brain, spinal cord, eyes, spleen, tonsils, bones and head in a landfill or by other means available in your area.
If you remove the antlers, use a saw designated for that purpose only, and dispose of the blade.

Sources: Wisconsin Department of Natural Resources, Michigan Department of Natural Resources, Rocky Mountain News, U.S. Department of Agriculture.

Graphic by RIKA KARAOKA and DAVID ARBANAS, Journal Sentinel

Field dressing tips for venison

Staff Report

State officials from the Minnesota and Wisconsin DNRs have provided venison processing tips and suggestions for hunters who may be concerned about chronic wasting disease. The accompanying graphic was developed by the Milwaukee Journal-Sentinel (MJS). Outdoor News bought secondary publishing rights for this diagram from the MJS.

Keep in mind, no chronic wasting disease has been found in wild deer in Minnesota, and biologists and meat scientists long have recommended wearing rubber gloves and similar sanitary precautions for processing any wild game.

CWD experts like Dr. Terry Kreeger (see Page 15) believe people have been hunting and even consuming CWD-infected deer for decades out west without a single example of it affecting humans. CWD is an illness that affects the neural tissue of cervidae, not the muscle or other meat tissues.

This week, several Minnesota government, academic, and hunting organizations have published a pamphlet addressing CWD and deer hunting. Available at sporting goods and hardware retailers, the pamphlet outlines safe handling procedures of deer carcasses and venison, and answers other general questions about the disease.

Prior to the 2002 firearms deer season, Outdoor News created a four-page special section devoted to investigating chronic wasting disease and explaining what it meant to Minnesota hunters.

the previous two decades.

NOVEMBER

• Outdoor News and Cabela's announced the 118-seat Outdoor News Theatre at the Cabela's Outlet Mall near Owatonna. The venue was to host a variety of seminars. The first: venison processing.

• The DNR paid $70,000 to acquire an incinerator to burn the carcasses of deer taken as part of the chronic wasting disease surveillance effort in Aitkin County.

• Outdoor News printed an article about bighead carp, which potentially was the first the publication carried about the invasive fish.

Matt Yernatich, of Duluth, took this bull moose with a 59-inch spread while hunting the Wrangle Mountains in Alaska. Matt and Jim Mustonen (left) then took time to read *Outdoor News*.

2003 — In President Bush's second State of the Union Address, he said he'd attack Iraq with or without a mandate from the United Nations. Shortly thereafter, Secretary of State Colin Powell laid out to the U.N. the Bush administration's rationale for attacking. The U.S. and Britain launched war against Iraq on March 20. Baghdad fell on April 10.

• U.S. troops captured Saddam Hussein in December.

• The space shuttle Columbia exploded, killing all 10 astronauts on board. A follow-up investigation showed organizational problems at NASA.

• Actor Arnold Schwarzenegger was elected governor of California after the incumbent governer was recalled.

• A number of notable people died, including: Johnny Cash, Fred Rogers, Strom Thurmond, and John Ritter.

• The cost of a first-class stamp was 37 cents.

JANUARY

• Among the news stories covered in 2003, according to an *Outdoor News* review of 2002: A new commissioner of the DNR; a Legislature facing a $4.5 billion budget deficit; and potential changes to deer management in Zone 3 in southeastern Minnesota.

• State Sens. Yvonne Prettner Solon, DFL-Duluth, and Tom Bakk, DFL-Cook, would have banned the use of lead fishing sinkers less than 1 ounce in weight. Prettner Solon noted the loons are being killed by lead poisoning.

• A "black hole" in North Long Lake near Brainerd appeared for the second consecutive year, baffling citizens and scientists alike. The hole stayed open until January, then froze during an unseasonably warm day. The hole opened, then froze again on a night the temperature reached 10 degrees below zero, and then re-opened when the temperature was 12 degrees below zero.

• Republican Gov. Tim Pawlenty named Gene Merriam, a former DFL state senator from Coon Rapids, as the commissioner of the DNR. Merriam served in the Legislature from 1974 to 1996, and was the chair of the Agricultural and Natural Resources Committee for six years. He chaired the Senate Finance Committee for a decade.

In 2003, Jane Krentz became the first woman to win the Outdoor News Person of the Year.

Jane Krentz's legislative accomplishments and continuing commitment to conservation garnered her the *Outdoor News* Woman of the Year Award.

Outdoor News Associate Editor Tim Spielman took this Northwest Territories caribou on the fifth day of the hunt. It was the second of two bulls he killed with his .270. Photos by Tim Spielman

MARCH

• DNR officials announced plans to treat 4,000-acre Lake Christina, one of the state's top waterfowl lakes, with a chemical intended to kill the lake's fish. It previously had been treated with rotenone in 1987, and the water quality improved thereafter.

• The state Supreme Court heard the case of a man – John Colosimo – who wouldn't let a game warden inspect his boat on a portage between two lakes. He was convicted for refusing the inspection, but the conviction was overturned by the state Court of Appeals. The St. Louis County attorney prosecuting the case argued wardens would be hamstrung if they needed to establish probable cause before conducting "limited inspections" of boats. The case was similar to a previously-decided case in which the state Supreme Court ruled conservation officers needed permission

WHITE ROOSTER. Preston Eitland bagged this white rooster pheasant while hunting in Iowa in November. He is pictured with a friend's dog, Gunner.

Scott Thorpe (above) stopped by the *Outdoor News* office last week with the mount of the 16-pound, 6-ounce steelhead he caught in northeast Minnesota in 1980. Below, Thorpe at age 29 in Grand Marais with the fish the day after he caught it.

WOODBURY BEAR. The Woodbury Police Department, including officer Brian Cline, responded to a call of a black bear in the east metro suburb on Monday. After monitoring and watching the 100-pound animal, officers determined that it wasn't a threat or causing problems beyond tipping over bird feeders and bird baths. On Tuesday afternoon, Woodbury PD Sgt. Brian Salo said he hadn't heard any more complaints about the animal. The DNR said the bear likely was a yearling recently given its walking papers by its mother. Photo by Officer Vickie Braman, Woodbury Police Department

or a warrant before entering fish houses.

• A U.S. Fish and Wildlife Service proposal would allow state fish and wildlife agencies in 24 states, including Minnesota, greater flexibility in managing double-crested cormorants through lethal and non-lethal methods.

• The DNR cut off financial ties with the Minnesota Waterfowl Association after the state auditor found the group had improperly administered state grants. Shortly thereafter, the MWA board voted to keep Executive Director Mike McGinty, but removed some financial aspects from his control.

• The DNR Commissioner's Office directed the Wildlife Division to support legislation to authorize hunting bears with hounds, when the bill is introduced.

Jerry Lundquist caught this new state record silver redhorse sucker on April 24 on the Rainy River. The fish weighed 9.145 pounds, besting the previous record by more than half a pound.
Photo courtesy of Minnesota DNR

APRIL

• Hunters and anglers were required to give their social security numbers when buying hunting and fishing licenses. The federal government mandated collection, saying it was necessary to help find people who failed to pay child support.

OWAA AWARD. Bill Monroe (l), chairman of the Outdoor Writers Association of America board, congratulates Rob Drieslein, *Outdoor News* editor, Sunday night at the organization's convention in Columbia, Mo. The group awarded Drieslein its President's Award for the top newspaper entry of 2002. See Outdoor Notes, Page 3.

MAY

• Gov. Tim Pawlenty signed concealed carry legislation that required sheriffs to give handgun permits to most law-abiding adults who seek them.

• A Minnesota Department of Agriculture spokesman said it was unlikely there was a link between Mad Cow Disease and chronic wasting disease. "From a scientific standpoint, there is no evidence of transmissibility of CWD to domestic cattle," said Kevin Elfering, director of dairy, food and meat inspection for Minnesota.

JUNE

• The Outdoor Writers Association of America presented Editor Rob Drieslein with its President's Award for the top newspaper entry of 2002. His entry was a four-page spread entitled: "CWD: An expert's opinion. What we know, and don't know, about chronic wasting disease."

JULY

• State officials were monitoring federal legislation to ban bear baiting and feeding on federal land. At the time, hunting bears with bait was legal in Minnesota (remains legal) and eight other states.

AUGUST
• As of Aug. 1, Minnesota banned the import of whole deer carcasses. The rule, meant to minimize the risk of spreading CWD, also applied to carcasses being moved through the state.

SEPTEMBER
• The board of the Minnesota Waterfowl Associa-

tion dismissed the group's executive director, Mike McGinty, who had led the nonprofit for nine years. "This is starting a new chapter in the MWA," said MWA President Jim Cox. The reasons for McGinty's dismissal, according to Cox: "poor fiscal management, the inability to keep working relationships with our conservation partners, and forgery."
• Minnesota Gov. Tim Pawlenty and North Dakota Gov. John Hoeven agreed to meet in Fargo to discuss new laws in North Dakota that, in part, gave North Dakota residents a week's headstart over nonresidents in many hunting seasons.

OCTOBER
• The Minnesota Supreme Court ruled conservation officers could search boats without consent of the owners or probable cause to suspect illegal activity. DNR Enforcement chief Mike Hamm called the ruling "a great thing."

Stearns County gobbler sets new state record

By Rob Drieslein
Editor

Richmond, Minn. — A Stearns County gobbler has set new records in two categories for Minnesota wild turkeys.

On Saturday, May 17, John Kuhl, of Richmond, Minn., shot a gobbler that officially regis-tered as the top typical wild turkey ever taken in Minnesota under the National Wild Turkey Federation's overall scoring system. It also occupies the top spot for spur length.

The NWTF divides its scoring into typical (birds with one

(See **Record Turkey** Page 30)

John Kuhl killed this new state record wild turkey in May while hunting in Stearns County.

Photo courtesy of John Kuhl

Sgt. Dustin Benoit and Sgt. Josh Behrens pose with their copies of *Outdoor News* while stationed in Iraq. They say they look forward to every issue, and that it's a great morale booster.

• A helicopter the DNR had contracted to apply rotenone in Lake Christina crashed into the lake. The helicopter was one of three working on the project. The pilot was OK and treatment continued.
• A group of "old duck hunters" including Art Hawkins and Duluth's Dave Nomsen convened for the first time to discuss growing concerns with the status of North American waterfowl populations.

'He hunted them down is what he did'

Sixth person dies from Wisconsin shootings

By Dean Bortz
Staff Writer

Chai Soua Vang

Hayward, Wis. — One of three hunters wounded in the Nov. 21 Sawyer County massacre died on Tuesday, Nov. 23, bringing the death toll to six people in the case.

The suspect, Chai Soua Vang, 36, of St. Paul, Minn., remained in custody in Sawyer County Jail as of Tuesday, Nov. 23.

Doug Drew, 55, of Rice Lake, died on Tuesday from wounds suffered during the shooting. The five hunters who died at the scene were Robert Crotteau, 42; his son Joe Crotteau, 20; Al Laski, 43; Mark Roidt, 28; and Jessica Willers, 27. All are from the Rice Lake area. Willers is the daughter of Terry Willers, who was wounded. Also wounded was Lauren Hesebeck.

Vang was apprehended at about 5:20 p.m. on Sunday, Nov. 21 when he came out of the woods riding on the back of an ATV driven by a hunter who did not know that Vang was a suspect in a shooting spree that initially killed five hunters and wounded three others earlier that day. Vang allegedly fired upon mostly unarmed hunters who approached Vang when they found him sitting in a deer stand on private property.

(See **WI Murders** Page 6)

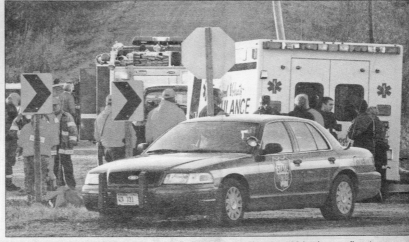

Emergency personnel gather near the scene, on Sunday, Nov. 21, 2004, where a dispute among deer hunters over a treestand in northwestern Wisconsin erupted in a series of shootings that left six people dead and two injured, near Hayward, Wis. The suspected gunman, Chai Soua Vang, 36, of St. Paul, (shown in booking photo, above left) was later arrested at the Rusk and Sawyer county line, according to Sawyer County sheriff's officials.

AP Photo/Terrell Boettcher

Wisconsin bigmouth buffalo a world record

Associated Press

Janesville, Wis. — It only took 45 minutes for Dave Tilton to set an unofficial world record. He caught a 73-pound, 1 ounce bigmouth buffalo — 3 pounds, 1 ounce more than the world record.

"I knew it was a big one," he said. "It feels pretty good ... I wish it could have been a muskie or a walleye, but I'll take it."

Tilton, an avid fisherman from Janesville, was wading along

(See **Bigmouth Buffalo** Page 28)

Dave Tilton shows off his 73.1-pound bigmouth buffalo fish he caught in Lake Koshkonong while walleye fishing on Monday, March 22, in Janesville, Wis. Although not yet verified, the fish is expected to be a world record catch, eclipsing the previous mark by 3 pounds.

AP Photo/The Janesville Gazette, Al Hoc...

☞ **JANUARY**

• Outdoor News founder and longtime publisher Jim Peterson passed away in his sleep on Jan. 17. He was 83 years old.
• Nearly 12,000 fishermen participated in the 14th annual Brainerd Jaycees Ice Fishing Extravaganza on Gull Lake.

FEBRUARY

• In legislation aimed at North Dakota, Sen. Pat Pariseau, R-Farmington, introduced a bill that would have prohibited nonresidents from fishing the first 14 days of the Minnesota fishing season if their state or province excludes nonresidents from parts of fishing and small-game seasons.

MARCH

• Minnesota sued North Dakota over its nonresident hunting restrictions. Said Minnesota Gov. Tim

2004 — *Domestic diva Martha Stewart was sentenced to five months in prison after she was found guilty in a case that began with her selling shares of a biotech stock.*

• *Terrorist attacks killed more than 200 people in Spain. Al-Qaeda claimed responsibility.*

• *Palestinian leader Yasir Arafat died in Paris.*

• *More than 200,000 people were killed when a tsunami hit Asia.*

• *John Kerry was nominated as the Democratic candidate for president. Republican incumbent George Bush defeated him in the election.*

• *An investigation found no weapons of mass destruction in Iraq. Their believed presence was one of the U.S.'s reasons for attacking.*

• *The Google search engine company went public, making its founders billionaires.*

Pawlenty: "Limiting out-of-state hunters – even if they own land in North Dakota – from hunting during the legal season sets an alarming precedent for interaction between the states. There is a maze of issues involved: property rights, who owns migratory birds, not to mention fundamental fairness."

APRIL

• The DNR made changes in the way it conducted its annual winter aerial moose count in northeastern Minnesota. Among the changes: using a helicopter rather than a fixed-wing aircraft. As a result, the agency estimated there were 8,500 to 11,000 moose in the northeast. Since 1997,

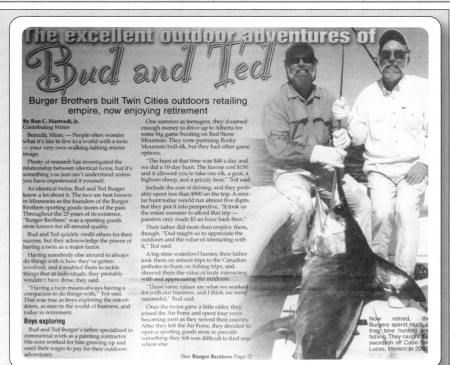

The excellent outdoor adventures of Bud and Ted

Burger Brothers built Twin Cities outdoors retailing empire, now enjoying retirement

By Ron C. Hustvedt, Jr.
Contributing Writer

Bemidji, Minn. — People often wonder what it's like to live in a world with a twin — your very own walking-talking mirror image.

Plenty of research has investigated the relationship between identical twins, but it's something you just can't understand unless you have experienced it yourself.

As identical twins, Bud and Ted Burger know a lot about it. The two are best known in Minnesota as the founders of the Burger Brothers sporting goods stores of the past. Throughout the 25 years of its existence, "Burger Brothers" was a sporting goods store known for all-around quality.

Bud and Ted quickly credit others for their success, but they acknowledge the power of having a twin as a major factor.

Having somebody else around to always do things with is how they've gotten involved, and it enabled them to tackle things that as individuals, they probably wouldn't have done, they said.

"Having a twin means always having a companion to do things with," Ted said. That was true as boys exploring the out-of-doors, as men in the world of business, and today in retirement.

Boys exploring

Bud and Ted Burger's father specialized in commercial work as a painting contractor. His sons worked for him growing up and used their wages to pay for their outdoors adventures.

One summer as teenagers, they'd earned enough money to drive up to Alberta for some big game hunting on Red Stone Mountain. They were pursuing Rocky Mountain bull elk, but they had other game options.

"The hunt at that time was $48 a day and we did a 10-day hunt. The license cost $150 and it allowed you to take one elk, a goat, a bighorn sheep, and a grizzly bear," Ted said.

Include the cost of driving, and they probably spent less than $900 on the trip. A similar hunt today would run almost five digits, but they put it into perspective, "It took us the entire summer to afford that trip — painters only made $3 an hour back then."

Their father did more than employ them, though. "Dad taught us to appreciate the outdoors and the value of interacting with it," Ted said.

A big-time waterfowl hunter, their father took them on annual trips to the Canadian potholes to hunt, on fishing trips, and showed them the value of truly interacting with and appreciating the outdoors.

"Those same values are what we worked for with our business, and I think we were successful," Bud said.

Once the twins grew a little older, they joined the Air Force and spent four years becoming men as they served their country. After they left the Air Force, they decided to open a sporting goods store to provide something they felt was difficult to find anywhere else.

Now retired, the Burgers spend much of their time hunting and fishing. They caught this swordfish off Cabo San Lucas, Mexico, in 2003.

(See Burger Brothers Page 2)

Sheds from potential record moose found

By Shawn Perich
Field Editor

Somewhere in Minnesota's northwoods walks a monstrous moose. Earlier this year, Jim Ceglar, of Aurora, found two massive antlers at an undisclosed location; they should set the world record for recovered moose sheds.

Moose calling expert Mark Braaten of Duluth, who visited Ceglar and photographed the antlers, reports the right one weighs 31 pounds and scores 86, while the left one weighs 30 pounds and scores 85. The gross score was 171, with a net of 163⅜. Each antler has 17 points. The current record moose shed antlers score 150

and were found in Nova Scotia.

If and when someone legally kills the moose, it likely would be a Minnesota state record for harvest, Braaten said. Larger live record moose have been taken elsewhere, he said.

Ceglar found the left antler in February and the right one in April, says Braaten. He will not reveal the location of the find, but it is within a zone open to moose hunting. Ceglar also has the right antler from the previous year, which weighed 23 pounds, as well as partially decomposed antler.

Braaten says he hopes to display the antlers in his booth at Game Fair in August.

MEGA SHEDS. Jim Ceglar, of Aurora, found these massive moose sheds in St. Louis County earlier this year. A pair of Minnesota-based Boone and Crockett scorers measured them as the potential new world record sheds.

14.1-pound walleye landed on Mississippi

By Tim Spielman
Associate Editor

Red Wing, Minn. — Glen Lundt still gets "the shakes" when he recounts the battle with the giant Mississippi River walleye — even though more than a week has passed since he landed the 14-pounder.

"I'm still pretty excited about it," he said this week.

How he came to fish the Lower Mississippi on April 5 is nearly as unlikely as the fish he caught.

Lundt, 26, of Eden Prairie, is

(See Big Walleye Page 22)

14-POUND MISSISSIPPEYE. Glen Lundt, of Eden Prairie, caught this 14-pound-plus walleye while fishing the Mississippi River on April 5.   Photo courtesy James Holst

officials estimated there were 4,000 moose. "This does not mean we have more moose," said Tom Rusch, DNR area wildlife manager in Tower.

• DNR Fish and Wildlife Division director John Guenther announced changes in management of the division. Rather than section chiefs, assistant operations managers, research managers, and education managers, he opted for a "team management" approach that reduced the number of managers from eight to six. Guenther named Larry Nelson, a former DNR staffer working in Colorado, as his assistant.

• Lake Superior's Knife Island became the first site of state efforts to control double-crested cormorants. Early efforts included destroying cormorant nests and using noise-makers to drive away the birds.

GULL LAKE SPRAWL. Nearly 12,000 anglers participated in the 14th annual Brainerd Jaycees Ice Fishing Extravaganza on Gull Lake last Saturday. Prizes worth more than $150,000 were awarded. Proceeds from the charity tournament benefit the nearby Camp Confidence. For complete details about the event and the story behind the big winners, including the 4.46-pound walleye that took top prize, see Ron Hustvedt's report on Page 6.

RECORD BOOK BULL. This bull moose with antlers measuring 61 inches wide and scoring 189% was taken by Mike Withers, of Plainview, and Mike Mauer, of Elba (not pictured), on Sept. 30, while hunting near Grand Marais. The antlers were the largest measured at the 2004 Minnesota Deer Classic. See Page 27 for all the winners. *Photo by Eric Meyer*

MAY

• A headline in Outdoor News: "Wanted: Moose hunters." DNR officials lamented the apparent decline in the number of moose hunters, but also that moose hunters as a whole were getting older. "Our talent pool is being drained, and moose hunters are getting older," said Tom Rusch, DNR area wildlife manager in Tower. "We just don't have 21-year-old hunters biting at the bit to get a moose tag."

• Gov. Tim Pawlenty signed legislation to create the state's first mourning dove hunting season since 1946. DNR officials expected between 30,000 and 50,000 hunters to participate.

JUNE

• Spring turkey hunters, for the 10th consecutive year, killed a record number of wild turkeys. The total take was 8,300.

JULY

• The Build A Wildlife Area effort, led by Pheas-

BUILD A SUCCESS! Multiple resource agencies, conservation groups, and private businesses joined forces last year to raise money for the first-ever Build A Wildlife Area campaign in Minnesota. The effort culminated on Friday, June 25, with a ceremony at the Morrison County property. Sponsors from around the state and local area posed in front of the signs dedicating the property. At right, DNR Commissioner Gene Merriam and Pheasants Forever's Joe Duggan.   Staff photos

Build A Wildlife Area effort pays off

ants Forever, and co-sponsored by Outdoor News resulted in the dedication of a 318-acre addition to the Mud Lake Wildlife Management Area near Little Falls. The effort raised more than $50,000.

Men caught with 117 walleyes

Home search finds 305 sunfish

Lino Lakes, Minn. — A routine traffic stop in which an officer smelled something fishy led to the discovery of 117 walleyes in a car trunk, authorities said last Friday.

"The vehicle had been stopped for speeding when the officer noticed the strong odor of fish," said Anoka Conservation Officer Travis Muyres. "We later counted 117 walleye in the trunk."

The Lino Lakes police officer called the DNR after pulling over the car along Interstate 35W. The men told authorities they caught the walleyes in the St. Louis River in Duluth.

Charged with gross misdemeanor overlimits in Anoka County were Bunchan Srey, 51; Dymong Chhoun, 20; Bunsean Lieng, 19; Samnang Pich, 19; and a juvenile, all from Minneapolis.

The men should have had no more than 10 St. Louis River walleyes in the vehicle, police said.

Officers then obtained a search warrant for the home of three of

(See **Fish Bust** Page 26)

A TRULY 'GROSS' OVERLIMIT. State Conservation Officer Travis Muyres sizes up more than 100 walleyes that he and other law enforcement personnel confiscated last week from a group of Minneapolis men. The smell of fish during a routine traffic stop alerted a Lino Lakes officer to the alleged crime. For complete state conservation officer reports, check out Cuffs and Collars, on Page 35.   Photo courtesy of Minnesota DNR

• The Minnesota DNR was in the second year of a study looking at hooking mortality of walleyes in Lake Mille Lacs. The study was in response to complaints of dead walleyes floating in the lake in 2002.

• Outdoor News ran a feature about Salt Lake WMA in Lac qui Parle County. Due to alkaline soils and the lack of an outlet, the lake had a salt content about one-third of that found in the ocean. A variety of birds typically not common in Minnesota, like the American avocet – a western species – often appeared at the lake.

SEPTEMBER

• The first dove hunt in the state in nearly 60 years kicked off Sept. 1. Officials warned hunters to target the birds early, noting they were among the first species to migrate south.

NOVEMBER

• The top headline in the Nov. 26 issue of Outdoor News: "He hunted them down is what he did." The headline and accompanying story detailed a shooting in Wisconsin that began as a dispute among deer hunters. The shooter, Chai Soua Vang, of St. Paul, Minn., was apprehended. The incident, near Hayward, Wis., left six dead and two injured.

THE DOVE SQUAD. Key Minnesota conservation leaders who helped pass the mourning dove legislation last week include (l-r) Mark LaBarbera, Lance Ness, Mark Herwig, Mike Sidders, Kevin Ausland, Hugh Price, John Schroers, Gordy Meyer, and Gary Botzek. For more complete kudos to everyone who helped make the season a reality, see the Opinion section, Page 3.   Photo by Rob Drieslein

JANUARY

• Declines in the population of lesser scaup seemed to be connected to a reduction in available food on their journey to their Canadian breeding grounds, according to ongoing research. Researchers documented a decline in amphipods, which are the primary food of scaup. "Our preliminary results suggest that females currently are arriving on many northern breeding areas in poor body condition or perhaps arrive late or not at all," Louisiana State University graduate student Mike Anteau wrote. He was working with Dr. Al Afton, a researcher at the Louisiana State University Cooperative Wildlife Unit.

FEBRUARY

• A variety of interests, ranging from hunters to those more associated with an environmental agenda, gathered in Bloomington, Minn., to begin working together on a conservation agenda. The group appointed Dave Zentner, a past president of the Izaak Walton League, coordinator of a rally the group set for the steps of the state capitol on April 2. One of the coalition's main goals: Pressure the Legislature to pass a dedicated funding bill that had been floundering in St. Paul.

APRIL

• The Rally for Ducks, Wetlands and Clean Water drew 5,000 sportsmen to the state Capitol. Organizers were satisfied with the turnout. Among the speakers were Senate Majority

WHAT A BEAST. Longtime bass chaser Mark Raveling, of Spring Park, caught this massive 8-pound, 15-ounce largemouth bass Monday morning in Lake Auburn near Victoria. It tops the previous Minnesota state record largemouth, caught in 1994, by more than two ounces.
Photo by Tim Lesmeister

2005 — Hurricane Katrina struck the Gulf Coast; the storm came ashore in Louisiana. An extraordinarily powerful hurricane, Katrina killed nearly 2,000 people and left hundreds of thousands more without homes. Many accused the government of being ill-prepared for dealing with such a catastrophe.

• President George Bush was sworn in for his second term.

• Terrorists struck trains in London, killing 52 and wounding about 700 people. It marked the worst attack in Great Britain since World War II.

• An earthquake in the Kashmir region between Pakistan and India measured 7.6, killed more than 80,000 people, and left several million homeless.

• Pope John Paul II, who was pope for 26 years, died. Pope Benedict XVI was chosen to replace him.

• Noted journalist and ABC World News Tonight anchor Peter Jennings died.

WORLD RECORD BLUE. An Illinois man, Tim Pruitt, hauled this new world record blue catfish from the Mississippi River near Alton, Ill., last week. See details in Beyond Minnesota on Page 10.

Leader Dean Johnson, retired Vikings coach Bud Grant, and Gov. Tim Pawlenty, who said attendees shared a common goal: "… to make Minnesota the best place in America to be a duck."

• A plan to dedicate funds to natural resources was tabled in a Senate committee. The Environment and Natural Resources Committee chair, Sen. John Marty, DFL-Roseville, said he had the hearing as a courtesy and would fully consider the bill in 2005.

MAY

• Federal sharpshooters began shooting cormorants on Leech Lake's Little Pelican Island. Their plan was to reduce adult cormorant numbers by 80 percent – from 5,000 to 1,000. DNR Fisheries Chief Ron Payer said killing cormorants "gives us the best chance

CANADIAN BIGHORN. Steve Bruggeman, of Shoreview, harvested this Rocky Mountain bighorn sheep last November while muzzleloading in southern British Columbia. The ram is a new muzzleloader world record, with an official B&C score of 197⅞.

Game warden testifies in Vang trial

Terry Willers answers a question while holding a rifle during his testimony in the Chai Soua Vang murder trial, Monday, Sept. 12, 2005, in Hayward, Wis. Willers testified that he was shot by Vang in the Nov. 21, 2004 shootings, which left six hunters dead, in the isolated woods in Sawyer County, Wis.   (AP Photo/Jeffrey Phelps, pool)

By Robert Imrie
Associated Press

Hayward, Wis. (AP) — A man in a blaze orange jacket frantically waved to the first law enforcement officers to arrive at the scene where six deer hunters were fatally shot last fall, a state conservation warden testified Monday in the trial of a Minnesota man accused in the Wisconsin killings.

The man told the officers his relatives were shot over a trespassing issue, and five already were dead, said Brian Knepper of the Wisconsin DNR. A sixth died later at the hospital.

Knepper did not identify the man who met them near a driveway leading to the Sawyer County deer camp where 15 people had gathered Nov. 21.

As the murder trial of Chai Soua Vang resumed Monday, Sawyer County Circuit Judge Norman Yackel agreed to allow two photographers into the courtroom as long as they made less noise and took fewer photos.

He imposed the ban on still photographers Saturday after Vang's attorneys complained about the camera noise.

The trial opened Saturday with attorneys' opening statements and four law enforcement

(See **Vang Trial** Page 34)

Rogers Cabela's to open Oct. 14

By Joe Albert
Staff Writer

Rogers, Minn. — Metro area hunters and anglers have a new, giant option for getting their bullets, guns, rods, and reels.

Cabela's in Rogers, a 188,000-square-foot store that cost $50 million to build, is set to open Oct. 14. The Sidney, Neb.-based business has other stores in Owatonna and East Grand Forks, but company officials expect the Rogers store to draw metro-area hunters and anglers on a regular basis.

"We cater to the whole family, but I would say for percentage of hard-core hunting and fishing, firearms, rods, and reels, we're in the ballpark of 50 to 60 percent of our store," said Shane Etzwiler, the store's manager.

In addition to such equipment, there's camouflage clothing, casual clothing, footwear, a gift shop, and an art gallery. The store caters to the spouses of today's hard-

Including its Owatonna and East Grand Forks stores, the Rogers location is Cabela's third in Minnesota.   Photo by Rob Drieslein

core hunter, too.

Etzwiler expects the store, located along Interstate 94 near the intersection with Highway 101, to attract more than 4 million shoppers each year.

Some of those will buy live bait on their way to the lake – there's a bait shop that will open before the rest of the store, likely every day during the fishing season, weekends the rest of the year – while others will shop for a boat in the

store's showroom.

The Rogers store will have many of the same features as the Owatonna location, but will include some new things, like a simulated, computerized lazer shooting range.

"You've got animals that are moving, animals that are falling over…" Etzwiler said.

The store has a selection of basic hunting and fishing goods, too, for those fishing locally, or "If you have someone going on an elk trip

of restoring that walleye fishery." Indeed, the walleye fishery at Leech had been on the decline, and officials believed cormorants were at least part of the problem.

• One provision in a larger game and fish bill that passed the state House would have made it illegal to hunt ducks in Minnesota while using motorized decoys.

• Freeport angler Robin Schmitz caught a 12-pound, 22.5-ounce greater redhorse in the Sauk River. The fish was a state record, and a world record. The fish hit a jig and nightcrawler.

• Authorities were investigating the discovery of a 200-foot net in Lake Vermilion. The net contained an estimated 75 to 100 fish – primarily walleyes. It had been in the water for about three weeks.

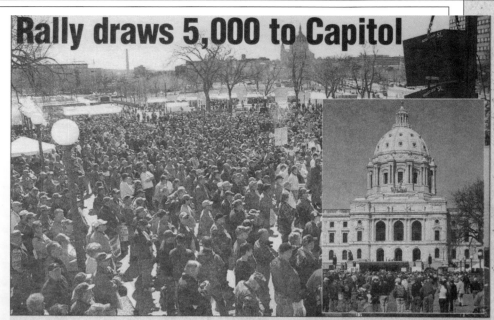

Rally draws 5,000 to Capitol

RALLYING FOR HABITAT. Between 4,000 and 5,000 state sportsmen and women, along with birders and environmentalists, rendezvoused on Saturday for the Ducks, Wetlands, and Clean Water Rally on the lawn of the State Capitol. For the full story on the rally, see below. For comments from Ducks Unlimited's Don Young, who attended the rally, see Page 7.

Photos by Joe Albert

JUNE

• The DNR announced a wide variety of changes to the state's deer season. Among the big changes were the creation of an early antlerless season in eight permit areas, and special regulations – earn-a-buck and antler-point restrictions – in seven state parks.

JULY

• The Clean Water Legacy Act appeared dead for the year, having never gained traction in the state House. The act, put forward by farm, business and environmental interests, was designed to clean the state's lakes and rivers. Proponents said it would cost $80 million per year.

In this photo released by World Wildlife Fund-National Geographic Society, two Thai fishermen show a 293-kilogram (646-pound) giant catfish they caught from the Mekong River in Chiang Khong district of Chiang Rai province, northern Thailand on May 1. It's believed to be the world's heaviest living freshwater fish, though it died and was eaten after environmentalists and officials negotiated for its release to allow it to spawn.

AP Photo/Suthep Kritsanavarin, HO

• According to figures from the U.S. Fish and Wildlife Service, about 14,000 hunters targeted doves in Minnesota in 2004, the state's first season in nearly 60 years. The DNR had estimated as many as 50,000 hunters might participate. The hunters who did participate killed 107,000 doves, according to the U.S. Fish and Wildlife Service.

• The Minnesota Waterfowl Association raised the $150,000 it needed to stay afloat. The board then voted to keep the 39-year-old conservation group running.

MANITOBA PIKE. Austin Dewanz, age 11, of Alexandria, caught and released this 42-inch northern pike while fishing Cedar Lake in Manitoba in July. The fish had very unique color and markings.

CANADA BULL. Mark Almgren, of Watkins, bagged this bull moose while hunting in the Yukon last September. The bull had a 71-inch spread, and scored 221⅝.

AUGUST

• Frank Schneider Jr., the 2001 Outdoor News Man of the Year, passed away. Schneider was active in many fishing causes in the state, and helped organize groups such as Muskies, Inc., and the Minnesota Outdoor Heritage Alliance.

• Two zebra mussels were found in Lake Mille Lacs. They were found on the lake's northwest side on rocks in 11 to 12 feet of water. Divers searched more than 20 additional sites in the lake and didn't find more zebra mussels.

SEPTEMBER

• After three hours of deliberations, jurors in Wisconsin found St. Paul hunter Chai Soua Vang guilty of first-degree murder in the shooting deaths of six deer hunters in Wisconsin. The jury also found him guilty of three counts of attempted murder. In convicting him, the jury rejected Vang's claim that he acted in self-defense.

OCTOBER

• Veteran Minnesota tournament angler Mark Raveling caught an 8-pound, 15-ounce bass from Auburn Lake near Victoria. It beat the previous state-record bass by more than 2 ounces.

NOVEMBER

• A judge sentenced Chai Soua Vang to life in prison without the possibility of parole. Vang didn't apologize, but said in court: "I understand your anger, your frustration, your grief."

Guide Bob Christianson (l) poses with Mike O'Callaghan, (c), and Jack O'Donnell, who bagged the 630½-pound bear on opening day of the season.

JANUARY

• Gas in Canada topped $3 per gallon ($1 per liter). According to columnist Gord Ellis, "it was the most serious increase in gas prices in Canada since the oil crisis of the late 1970s."

• Canadian Prime Minister Paul Martin announced that, if re-elected, he would ban all handguns in Canada.

• Despite a challenge from the World Record Muskie Alliance, the National Fresh Water Fishing Hall of Fame's board of directors decided to uphold Louis Spray's world record muskie, which weighed 69 pounds, 11 ounces.

FEBRUARY

• Thanks to the U.S. Intelligence Reform and Terrorism Prevention Act, by Jan. 1, 2008, all people traveling by land to Canada must have a passport to re-enter the United States. Those going by air or sea must have a passport by Jan. 1, 2007.

• Vice President Dick Cheney accidentally shot his hunting partner, Harry Whittington, while the two were quail hunting together in Texas. Whittington, struck in the face, neck and chest, was admitted to the hospital and later released.

MARCH

• Art Hawkins, a longtime wildlife biologist for the U.S. Fish and Wildlife Service, passed away at the age of 92. Hawkins studied under Aldo Leopold at the University of Wisconsin. "He was a legend among us … one of the real pioneers to come on the scene," said Harvey Nelson, who worked as a wildlife biologist

2006 — An Iraqi court convicted deposed President Saddam Hussein of crimes against humanity. He was hanged in Baghdad.

• *The U.S. House of Representatives, which looked into the aftermath of Hurricane Katrina, found failures at all levels of government.*

• *During the midterm elections, Democrats gained control of both the U.S. House and Senate.*

• *A federal study that lasted eight years and cost $415 million left many in the medical community bewildered, as it found a low-fat diet doesn't decrease cancer, heart disease, or stroke risks.*

• *The U.S. population hit 300 million people.*

• *Television personality and conservationist Steve Irwin, known as the Crocodile Hunter, was killed after he was stung in the chest by a stringray.*

• *President Bush renewed the controversial Patriot Act.*

BEST BUCK WEEKLY WINNER. Deb Luzinski, of Woodbury, took this 24-point nontypical buck in Ramsey County on Oct. 27. The rack had a 20⅝-inch inside spread, and it green scored 227⅞. For contest details see Page 20

William Somphanthabansouk, 9, of Worthington (l), holds a piranha he pulled out of shallow water at Buss Field on Monday, while his friend, Jay Syhavong, 11, of Worthington, props open the fish's mouth to reveal the teeth. The youths and three other friends discovered the fish while looking for a good fishing spot on Lake Okabena. Photo courtesy of Worthington Daily Globe

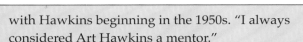

with Hawkins beginning in the 1950s. "I always considered Art Hawkins a mentor."

• A captive white-tailed deer on a farm in western Minnesota's Lac qui Parle County tested positive for chronic wasting disease. It was the first deer in the state to test positive for the disease. Previous to the discovery, only elk at farms in Aitkin and Stearns counties had tested positive.

MAY

• Plans to dedicate funding for natural resources passed both the state House and Senate, but the two versions were different in that the House plan dedicated existing taxes, while the Senate plan would have increased taxes.

• For the first time, invasive New Zealand mud-snails were found in the Duluth-Superior Harbor of Lake Superior.

JUNE

• Members of a House and Senate conference committee failed to reach agreement on a bill to dedicate funds to natural resources. The Senate, led by then Senate Majority Leader Dean Johnson, decided not to offer a counter-proposal to the House, which had moved off its position and offered a bill that would have raised taxes to dedicate to habitat and clean water. Said John Schroers, president of the Minnesota Outdoor Heritage Alliance: "When it comes to Minnesota's habitat and natural resource needs, a clear win was snatched from the jaws of victory by election-year politics."

Holsten named new DNR commissioner

By Joe Albert
Staff Writer

St. Paul — The announcement earlier this month that DNR Commissioner Gene Merriam was stepping down took most observers of state government by surprise.

In days following, few names were dropped consistently as potential successors, except for two: Mark Holsten, the DNR deputy commissioner, and Brad Moore, acting commissioner of the Pollution Control Agency and formerly a DNR assistant commissioner.

Mark Holsten

WESTERN MONARCH. Rick Arend, of Rochester, harvested this 9x10 mule deer buck while hunting on Santa Rosa Island, California in November. The rack gross green scored 227⅞.

Outdoor News field staffer Eric Meyer took first place in the muzzleloader typical division for 2005. The antlers rank third overall in the Minnesota Record Book in that division.   Photos by Eric Meyer

• Ely outdoorsman and humorist "Jackpine" Bob Cary passed away at the age of 84. Cary once ran for president on the fictitious Independent Fisherman's Party ticket.

• As of June 20, federal sharpshooters had killed 2,864 adult cormorants at Leech Lake. The take was similar in 2005.

JULY

• The DNR announced it would try intensively managing eight fields totalling 57 acres for dove hunting. State officials took their cues from Southern states, where dove fields had been successful at attracting and holding doves.

• Tennessee native Thurman Tucker announced he was starting the state's first Quail Forever chapter, in southeastern Minnesota's Houston County. "I realize Minnesota is on the northern border of bobwhite range, but their numbers could be higher with better habitat," Tucker said.

AUGUST

• Troy Lee Gentry, one half of the country music duo

OPENER ON UPPER RED. After nearly seven years of a ban on Red Lake walleye fishing, anglers plied the waters of newly opened Upper Red last Sunday. Despite unseasonably low temperatures and high winds across much of the state, anglers reported good walleye fishing on Red Lake, Mille Lacs, and other waterways around Minnesota. For complete reports, see Joe Albert's story, this page, Cuffs and Collars on Page 26, and the weekly fishing report on Page 27. Photo by Joe Albert

Montgomery Gentry, was charged in federal court with shooting a tame black bear, and then tagging it as though he had killed it in the wild. Authorities alleged Gentry purchased the bear, and then killed it in an enclosed pen in 2004. Gentry, in a plea agreement, eventually pleaded guilty. He was fined $15,000 and ordered to not hunt in Minnesota for five years.

Latest invader found in Superior

New Zealand mudsnail

MINNESOTA MOOSE. Jeff Holmin, of St. Peter, harvested this bull moose off the Gunflint Trail on Oct. 4. The rack had a spread of 50 inches.

NOVEMBER

• Changes made by the U.S. Department of Agriculture due to the deadly fish dis-

'Fang deer' discovered in Fillmore County

By Tim Spielman
Associate Editor

Fountain, Minn. — Kevin Eickhoff thought little more than he had a pretty nice 8-point buck when he took the animal to Smitty's Taxidermy to have the skull "boiled" for a European-style mount. After all, he already had a fine 10-point specimen at Smitty's that was harvested last year. There wasn't anything particularly unique about this year's buck.

So the 50-year-old man from Fountain was a bit surprised when he received a call from Travis Smith, operator of the taxidermy shop, to tell him he'd better come down and check out the deer.

"It has fang teeth," Eickhoff was told by Smith.

"This was really weird, because when I had talked to (Smith) earlier this fall, he was telling me about deer that sometimes grow fang teeth," Eickhoff said. "He said we should check the deer we shoot to see if they...

This southeastern Minnesota deer featured two prominent canine teeth (front of skull) that a taxidermist noticed while creating a skull mount. Such teeth, extremely rare in whitetails, apparently are an evolutionary "echo."
Photo courtesy of Kevin Eickhoff

ease VHS resulted in an importation ban on several fish species from a number of Great Lakes. It affected aquaculture farmers and led to changes in the way the state screens for VHS.

DECEMBER

• The DNR banned recreational deer feeding across a 4,000-square-mile part of northwestern Minnesota as

Rochester resident Michelle Leqve became the first woman to take a polar bear via bow last month while hunting in northern Nunavut.   Photo courtesy of Michele Leqve

Randy Tetrick, of Lakeville, and his brothers bought the mount from Morales in December 2005 and presented it at the 2006 Minnesota Deer Classic where it placed second in the whitetail firearms typical historical division.
Photo by Eric Meyer

MINNESOTA BULL. Gunnar Smith, of Litchfield (pictured), and Brent Reiner, of Hutchinson, called in and shot this bull elk near Grygla on Sept. 16. A 30-yard shot downed the animal. See Page 7 for the picture of Brent Reiner. For more on Minnesota elk, see the story on Page 29.

part of an effort to reduce the risk of spreading bovine tuberculosis, which was found in wild deer in the northwest in 2005.

• Gene Merriam, who led the DNR for four years, stepped down. It was a move that caught many people by surprise. Gov. Tim Pawlenty appointed Merriam's deputy, Mark Holsten, to fill the position. In addition to his time at DNR, Holsten, 41, of Stillwater, also was a Republican state rep for 10 years.

☞ JANUARY
• The DNR announced that hunters in 2006 bought nearly 130,000 pheasant stamps, which was a record high. During the 2006 season, hunters killed 587,580 pheasants, which marked the second year in a row the ring-neck kill exceeded 500,000.
• The DNR announced it would convene a group to explore the possibility of simplifying the state's deer-hunting regulations.

FEBRUARY
• The U.S. Fish and Wildlife Service said it would remove timber wolves from the endangered species list in Minnesota, Wisconsin and Michigan. Officials said they expected legal challenges.
• The Red Lake Band planned to begin selling walleyes caught in its waters of Red Lake. But officials

2007 — Though the U.S. declared an official end to combat operations in Iraq in May of 2003, President Bush approved of a surge of 30,000 U.S. troops into Iraq in an attempt to curtail what had become an increasingly dangerous situation marked by bombings and other attacks by insurgent groups.
• *Democrats were in control of both houses of Congress for the first time in more than a decade. Nancy Pelosi, a Democrat from California, became the first woman to serve as Speaker of the House.*
• *President Bush signed an energy bill that required a 40-percent increase in the fuel economy standards of passenger vehicles by 2020.*
• *The Intergovernmental Panel on Climate Change found human activity likely was causing global warming.*

said the fishery initially would be totally hook-and-line, and that band members were in favor of strict rules and regulations.
• The DNR released wild turkeys in Martin and Jackson counties in southwestern Minnesota. Officials said there were isolated blocks of habitat for turkeys in that part of the state, but that they could become better established.
• At a meeting in

northwestern Minnesota, the DNR outlined plans to combat bovine tuberculosis, which had been found in seven cattle herds and seven wild deer. The gist of the agency's plans: Reduce deer numbers in the area via hunters and federal sharpshooters.

2007 MAN OF THE YEAR. To honor John Schroers' lifetime of dedication to conservation and educating kids in the ways of waterfowling, *Outdoor News* proudly has named him its 2007 Man of the Year. See a full description of Schroers' work on Page 32.

Hunting with his muzzleloader, 23-year-old Ben Knisley, of Paynesville, took this impressive central Minnesota buck on Nov. 4, 2006. The 9-pointer scored 184⅞ net Boone and Crockett and had an inside spread of 25⅞ inches. It likely ranks in the top 10 in the world ever taken via muzzleloader. Photos courtesy of Ben Knisley

MARCH

• Senate Majority Leader Larry Pogemiller took over the dedicated funding bill in that body. His bill would raise the state sales tax by 3/8 of 1 percent, and split the proceeds between fish and wildlife habitat (34 percent); parks, trails and zoos (22 percent); clean water (22 percent); and arts and humanities (22 percent).

• State Sen. Dallas Sams, DFL-Staples, passed away at age 54. He had been a champion of dedicated funding and other outdoors measures.

• Ashby, Minn.-based wildlife artist John House became the first artist to win all four of Minnesota's stamp contests when he won the wild turkey stamp contest.

• On March 12, the DNR took over management responsibility for wolves in the state. Dave Schad, Fish and Wildlife Division director, called their recovery "a remarkable success story."

APRIL

• DNR conservation officers in 2006 issued 118 citations and warnings for baiting deer. It marked the highest number ever recorded, though the number had been on the rise for years.

MAY

• The assessment of the walleye-fishing opener: "Best in many years."

• For the second year in a row, the Senate passed a dedicated funding bill. The House also passed a

Tom Schlough, of St. Cloud, landed this 30-pound jack crevalle off the Pacific coast of Costa Rica in mid-February.

Tony Licence, age 11, of Frazee, caught this 44½-inch, 30-pound northern pike while fishing Lake Sakakawea.

Patti Keding, of Maple Plain, caught this 60-pound King salmon while fishing the Kenai River in Alaska last July. It took her a half hour to land the fish.

Andrew Zimmern of the Travel Channel's Bizarre Foods joined columnist Shawn Perich (r) and friends for some wild game cooking in 2007.

bill – as did a House-Senate conference committee – but it never made it off the House floor before the session wrapped up.

JUNE
• Gordie Meyer, a longtime conservationist and president of the Minnesota Conservation Federation, passed away at 73.

JULY
• After 40 years on the list of endangered and threatened species, the U.S. Fish and Wildlife Service removed the bald eagle from the list.

• DNR Commissioner Mark Holsten stood along the shores of Lake Vermilion and announced the DNR's desire to create on the lake the first's state park in nearly 30 years. The land had been set to be developed.

AUGUST
• Severe flooding hit the southeastern part of the state after 10 to 20 inches of rain fell in less than a day. Conservation officers were called to rescue peo-

SCENE OF DESTRUCTION. DNR personnel played an important role during the flooding that occurred in southeastern Minnesota last weekend. Below, Tim Spielman describes how state conservation officers assisted area citizens and, on Page 8, Mike Kallok outlines some of the impacts the flood may have on southeast fisheries on waterways like the Middle Branch of the Whitewater River near Elba (above) and other natural resources. *Photo courtesy of Minnesota DNR*

ple stranded in trees. At least six fatalities resulted from the flooding.

• A Texas Tech University professor who took over the northwestern Minnesota moose research project (after the CO pilot and graduate student died in a plane crash while collecting data) predicted moose would be extinct from the northwest by 2058.

• South Dakota pheasant counts hit record highs, and officials predicted a 2-million bird harvest.

Tim Adams, of Wabasha, Minn., holds the 39.4-inch, 28.7-pound bighead carp caught last week on Lake Pepin near Frontenac.

Joe Kiritschenko, of Woodbury, caught this massive Mille Lacs muskie in late October.
Photo courtesy of Mille Lacs Messenger

Canadian rainbow could be record

Konrad with his potential world record rainbow trout.

Photo courtesy of trophytroutguide.com

Saskatoon Sask. — The world rainbow trout record, which has stood since 1970, may fall after a 43.6-pound monster was hauled in by Adam Konrad, age 26, of Saskatoon, Sask.

The fish was caught on June 5 on Lake Diefenbaker, a man-made

Minnesota's heaviest rainbow trout, a 33-inch, 16-pound 6-ounce fish was caught on April 27, 1980 in the Devil Track River.

— Mike Kallok

RAINY RIVER GIANT. Jeff Gardas, of Bethel, caught and released this 71-inch sturgeon while fishing the Rainy River on April 12. It took about an hour to land the fish.

BEST BUCK ENTRY. Bob Derr, of Ely, shot this 13-point St. Louis County buck on Nov. 3. The 240-pound buck had a 14-inch inside spread.

SEPTEMBER

• Sportsmen, led by Garry Leaf, of Bloomington, began discussions of a council that eventually would oversee spending from the Outdoor Heritage Fund.

• The Red Lake Band began taking fish for commercial sale from Red Lake.

NOVEMBER

• Reports from Lake Winnibigoshish indicated a scaup die-off was due to trematodes, small intestinal parasites that also had been responsible for killing thousands of ducks on the Mississippi River.

The Minnesota Fishing Hall of Fame announced three new inductees last weekend at the Northwest Sportshow, including Dick "The Griz" Grzywinski. For the full story, see Page 8.

2008 — Early signs of the financial crisis that went on to engulf the U.S. emerged. Among them: The Federal Reserve created a $200 billion loan to help the country's largest banks stave off collapse. JP Morgan Chase used a $30 billion government loan to buy the failing Bear Stearns.

• The California Supreme Court ruled 4-3 that homosexuals have a constitutional right to marry.

• Barack Obama, a Democratic senator from Illinois won the presidential election, defeating John McCain and becoming the first African American to serve as president of the United States.

• Polar bears gained protection under the Endangered Species Act.

• Cuban President Fidel Castro stepped down. He'd been in power for nearly 50 years.

JANUARY

• Despite opposition from some quarters, the DNR said it wouldn't cancel a 16-day late season hunt (set to begin Dec. 29) in Permit Area 101 in the northwestern part of the state. The hunt was part of an effort to fight bovine tuberculosis.

• During the first year of a program that allowed hunters to donate their deer to food shelves for free, they donated nearly 2,000.

FEBRUARY

• An angler fishing the south shore of Lake of the Woods caught a 23-pound lake trout. Officials speculate the fish traveled 40 miles from Canadian waters. "It's basically unheard of around here," said Gary Moeller, of Ballards Resort.

• Two days into the legislative session, both the House and Senate approved a dedicated funding bill to increase the state sales tax by 3/8 of 1 percent and split the proceeds between fish and wildlife habitat; clean water; parks and trails; and arts and culture. Supporters celebrated at the State Capitol when the measure finally passed, and then set to work on creating a council to oversee the habitat portion of the fund.

MARCH

• DNR officials announced they were exploring the possibility of a season for sandhill cranes in the north-

CREAM-COLORED COYOTE. Larame Kuhlmann, of Oronoco, shot this uniquely colored coyote while hunting in Olmsted County on Jan. 21.

Outdoor News cited Jim Klatt's work on Amendment 2 in 1998 in naming him Man of the Year. Klatt passed away in 2013.

2008 MAN OF THE YEAR. To honor Jim Klatt's lifetime of dedication to conservation and the political issues affecting the outdoors in Minnesota, *Outdoor News* has named him its 2008 Man of the Year. See a full description of Klatt's work on Page 32.

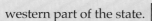

western part of the state.

• John Velin, who served as director of the commission that recommended funding from the lottery-funded Environment and Natural Resources Trust Fund beginning in 1988, retired.

APRIL

• After venison at food pantries in North Dakota tested positive for lead, state officials asked food shelves that distribut hunter-harvested venison to halt the practice. Follow-up tests found lead in the meat Minnesota hunters had donated, and the state told food shelves to throw away any venson they hadn't

This massive Ontario moose, which Fred Hilliard of Thunder Bay killed on Nov. 15, just might be a new provincial record. The rack had a total spread of 64 inches and it net green scored nearly 229 inches. The current Ontario record is 220. Photo courtesy of Gord Ellis

distributed. The state also advised people who had picked up venison from food shelves to throw it away. Hunter reaction to the discovery of lead varied.

• A Belle Plaine man accidentally shot and killed his 8-

Mark Nodo, of Rice, caught and released this bigmouth buffalo while fishing Little Rock Lake for walleyes near his home. The fish accidentally was snagged in the tail with a crankbait.

Duane Mathews, of Oronoco, shot this 9½-foot Kodiak brown bear last October on Kodiak Island, Alaska.

year-old son after mistaking him for a wild turkey.

MAY
• DNR Enforcement chief Mike Hamm, and his wife, Capt. Cathy Hamm, were placed on administrative leave as investigation into a state-supported conservation officer conference began.
• For the first time ever, the spring turkey kill in the state topped 10,000 birds.
• The DNR announced a suite of simplified deer regulations, including doing away with Zone 4 and creating a nine-day season in the former area.
• The Legislature created the Lessard-Sams Outdoor Heritage Council to advise the Legislature on spending from the Outdoor Heritage Fund.

JUNE
• The DNR announced it would offer 23 permits to elk hunters in the northwestern part of the state. That was a record number of permits.

Legislators applaud original dedicated funding author Bob Lessard (now retired from the state Legislature) after the bill's passage. At right, Sportsmen for Change members outside the Capitol parking lot reminded legislators of the pending vote when the session kicked off last Tuesday. Above photo by Joe Albert; photo at right courtesy of Kevin Ausland

JULY
• The DNR conducted a study of bullet-fragmentation patterns as part of an attempt to help hunters worried about lead in venison determine which bullets to use.

AUGUST
• Al Farmes, a longtime conservationist and one of the founders of the Fish and Wildlife Legislative Alliance, passed away at age 93.
• A St. Michael man won $1 million in a fantasy fishing league started by Irwin Jacobs.

SEPTEMBER
• The state legislative auditor found the DNR misspent nearly $300,000 in state money, and didn't follow state or agency policy, when it put on a conference for conservation officers. DNR Enforcement direc-

Best Buck WEEKLY WINNER

WEEKLY WINNER. Kelly Gustafson, of Welch, harvested this 20-point nontypical buck near her home on Nov. 8. The rack green scored 202% gross nontypical.

Mora man boats 74-inch Rainy sturgeon

By Tim Spielman
Associate Editor

Baudette, Minn. — Jake Grabowski likes to fish for a little of this, a little of that, but most of his acquaintances might refer to the Mora man as a "muskie guy."

But move over muskellunge; a fish the 27-year-old construction salesman caught Saturday probably ranks right up there with his most memorable muskie catches.

Maybe higher.

On his spring journey to the Rainy River, Grabowski got to see the big one – a 74-inch lake sturgeon estimated to weigh about 125 pounds.

"Every year we hook a fish that we never see," Grabowski said, referring to the proverbial "ones that got away."

This year, Grabowski was fishing the Rainy River's catch-and-release sturgeon season where the river dumps into Lake of the Woods, with friends Patrick Finn, of Burnsville, and Rick Youngquist, of Stacy. Neither had fished for Rainy sturgeon in the past. It's likely they will in the future; Grabowski said the trio boated four sturgeon over 50 pounds during the April 18-19

(See Sturgeon Page 20)

Patrick Finn (l) assists Jake Grabowski in hoisting Grabowski's 74-inch, estimated 125-pound Rainy River sturgeon Saturday.

tor Mike Hamm, who maintained the conference was a good thing for conservation officers and the state, retired after a four-month administrative leave. Hamm said he "was not given any options" and retired after a meeting with DNR Commissioner Mark Holsten. (Hamm's wife, Cathy, was fired; she says she retired.)

OCTOBER
• Famed outdoors broadcaster Tony Dean died at age 67. He died from complications of having his appendix removed.

Hog on the loose was probably a pet pot-belly

Detroit Lakes, Minn. (AP) — State wildlife officials are now saying the wild hog that was spotted near Detroit Lakes was actually a pot-bellied pig that likely escaped.

NOVEMBER
• State voters approved the Clean Water, Land and Legacy Amendment. Fifty-six percent of voters voted for the amendment. The passage marked the culmination of nearly a decade of work. "We got a great victory," said Garry Leaf, of Sportsmen for Change.

DECEMBER
• Roger Holmes, who worked for the DNR for 41 years, and spent a decade as director of the Fish and Wildlife Division, passed away at 72 from complications from prostate cancer. He retired from the DNR in 2000, but remained active in state and national conservation issues.

WRIGHT COUNTY GIANT. Joe Maurer, of South Haven, shot this 22-point buck in Wright County on Nov. 11. The rack had a 21-inch inside spread and green scored 220 nontypical.

Outdoors broadcaster Tony Dean dies

Pierre, S.D. (AP) — Tony Dean, a nationally known outdoor enthusiast who promoted South Dakota with his radio and television shows, has died.

Dean died Sunday morning. He was 67.

Dean, whose real name was Anthony DeChandt, returned to his Pierre home last week after being hospitalized for complica-

(See **Tony Dean** Page 6)

Remembering

Eldert Menth, of New Germany, caught this 18-inch, 3-pound, 3½-ounce crappie on Yaeger's Lake near Winsted in 1964. Photo courtesy of Donna Menth

2009 — The nation's financial crisis deepened, with insurance giant American International Group reporting a more than $60 billion quarterly loss at the end of 2008. The company received about $170 billion from the federal government, and came under withering criticism when the company announced it would pay more than $165 million in bonuses to top executives.

• The national unemployment rate hit 8.1 percent, the highest since 1983.

• Wildfires in Australia killed 181 people.

• President Obama signed a $787 billion economic stimulus package in hopes it would provide jobs.

• Auto company giants Chrysler and General Motors filed for bankruptcy protection.

• Sen. Edward Kennedy died at 77 years old. He'd been a senator for 46 years.

JANUARY

• The DNR, for the first time in about 30 years, didn't trap wild turkeys in one part of the state and transport them to other parts of the state. "Now it's going to be up to the turkeys to decide how far they expand in Minnesota," said Eric Dunton, DNR wild turkey research biologist.

• An elk on a farm north of Rochester tested positive for chronic wasting disease. The find was the first since 2006, and occurred on a farm with hundreds of animals, likely the largest in the state.

FEBRUARY

• The DNR proposed liberalizing the fall turkey hunting season, including creating a continuous 30-day season and allowing turkey hunters to use dogs. The latter proposal was not put into place.

• Don "The Duckman" Helmeke passed away at the age of 62. Helmeke, of Maple Grove, authored the instructions that accompany Outdoor News' Wood Duck Challenge, and was involved in a variety of other aspects of waterfowling, including making calls and camo. In addition, he was an active member of the group that pushed for passage of Min-

Paul Allison, of Blooming Prairie, caught this 150-inch, 671-pound blue marlin while charter fishing near Honolulu, Hawaii, on Jan. 8.

LOTW PIKE. Merle Hoverson, age 10, of East Grand Forks, caught this 46½-inch, 28-pound, 12-ounce northern pike while fishing near Rocky Point on Lake of the Woods recently. The fish hit a sucker minnow on a tip-up.

nesota's Clean Water, Land and Legacy Amendment.

MARCH

• A 26-year DNR veteran, Jim Konrad, was chosen to replace former Enforcement Division chief Mike Hamm, who retired after the fallout over his role in a controversial conservation officers conference. One of Konrad's main priorities? "We have to restore people's faith in us," he said.

• For the second consecutive year, sharpshooters in airplanes killed deer in the bovine tuberculosis area of northwestern Minnesota.

Car hits, kills cougar on south side of Bemidji

By Joe Albert
Associate Editor

Bemidji, Minn. — State wildlife officials haven't determined if an animal hit and killed by a vehicle in Bemidji last Friday was wild or not, but one thing is clear: It was a mountain lion.

The cougar, a male that weighed about 110 pounds, was struck and killed about 10:40 p.m. on a bridge that crosses the Schoolcraft River on the south side of town.

"To my knowledge, it's the first (road-killed cougar) that we have ever had," said John Erb, a furbearer biologist for the DNR.

Beltrami County Sheriff's Deputy Lee Anderson hoists a mountain lion that an automobile struck and killed last Friday night on Carr Lake Road near Bemidji.
Photo courtesy of Beltrami County Sheriff's Office

MAY

• The Legislature, as part of the Game and Fish Bill, approved of allowing hunters to transport uncased firearms and bows, so long as the weapons aren't loaded and are being transported at a shooting range, or between hunting locations. Pistols were excluded.

JUNE

• The DNR and the Blandin Paper Company signed an agreement to create a conservation easement on the company's 187,000 acres in north-central Minnesota. The perpetual easement cost $45 million – of which

Young Girl, Enormous Moose

Kelly Holmin, age 12, of Nicollet, harvested this 58-inch bull moose Oct. 13. **See Page 7**

At left, Matt Stans with two pairs of sheds from the Cannon Falls Buck. Above, Red Wing-area CO Tyler Quandt with the buck's rack, which will be on display this weekend. *Photos courtesy Hugh Price*

$36 million came from the newly created Outdoor Heritage Fund – and guaranteed public access in perpetuity. Many considered the project the early signature accomplishment of the Clean Water, Land and Legacy Amendment.

JULY

• The Game and Fish Fund Budgetary Oversight Committee recommended the DNR begin looking at increasing the costs of hunting and fishing licenses as a way to keep the Game and Fish Fund from going into the red.

• After a few years of extremely slow fishing that had the DNR working hard to bring it back, Leech Lake was among the hottest walleye lakes during the early part of the season.

SEPTEMBER

• A vehicle struck and killed a wild mountain lion near Bemidji. It was the first time one of the cats ever had been killed in Minnesota.

• Steve Kufrin passed away at the age of 66. A one-time journalist, Kufrin spent much of his career with the U.S. Fish and Wildlife Service helping private landowners preserve wetlands. "… He could sell conservation," said his USFWS colleague, Greg Brown. He was the 2005 Outdoor News Man of the Year.

Eric Madson, of Elk River, took this 1,500-pound moose while hunting near Tofte on Oct. 8. The antlers had a 60-inch spread.

WORLD-RECORD ELK. Denny Austad, of Ammon, Idaho, used a self-designed rifle to kill this world-record American elk bull in Utah on Sept. 30, 2008. The final score of the elk was 478%

Photo courtesy of Denny Austad

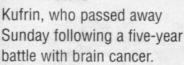

▶ A Legend Passes

State conservationists this week mourned the loss of dedicated waterfowler and public servant Steve Kufrin, who passed away Sunday following a five-year battle with brain cancer.

WHITE ROOSTER. Scott Riley, of Medford, shot this white rooster pheasant near his hometown on Dec. 17. The bird had a 23-inch tail.

Garry Leaf: 2009 *ON* Man of the Year

NOVEMBER
• The DNR seized the record-breaking 8-point rack from a man who allegedly poached the deer near Cannon Falls. Charges also were filed against Troy Alan Reinke. The taxidermist working on the deer called the rack "breathtaking."

WEEKLY WINNER. Bryan King, of Rochester, arrowed this 22-point non-typical buck in Olmsted County on Oct. 5. The rack had a 19⅜-inch inside spread and green scored 183⅞ gross non-typical.

OUTDOOR INSIGHTS

Rob Drieslein
Editor

Long-time supporter of the state outdoors scene, Ken "Burgie" Burgland, passed away Dec. 9 at the VA Hospital in Minneapolis. Burgie, age 84, lived his final years in Savage but spent 42 in Minnetonka. Following full military honors at Ft. Snelling, his memorial service was on Monday at All-Saints Lutheran Church in Minnetonka. Burgie was an American hero who served his country during World War II as a Marine in the Pacific; he was first-wave Okinawa and saw fierce action in the Marshall Islands. Shell-shock from WWII damaged Burgie's hearing, which deteriorated later in his life. But that disability never slowed him down. He had a great career in sales and volunteered countless hours for conservation groups like Turn In Poachers.

Burgie was my connection to the old guard of Minnesota's outdoors scene. He'd hunted the Delta Marsh with Jimmy Robinson, and spent many days with his friend Les Kouba. He knew *Outdoor News* founder Jim Petersen well, and – while fishing with Burgie in Canada – I heard many stories about their hunting and fishing glory days. He outlived them all. Many sportsmen met Burgie at the Black Hills Turkey Track Camp, which he attended for 30-plus years, including spring 2009.

The staffers here send our condolences to Audrey, Burgie's wife of 63 years, as well as their entire family.

Ken "Burgie" Burgland

Remembering

Gene Nothnagel poses with a northern pike speared by Andy Nothnagel of Litchfield on Lake Koronis in 1952.

Photo courtesy of Perry Pehl

2010 — President Obama signed his signature piece of legislation, the Patient Protection and Affordable Care act, also known as Obamacare.

• The Supreme Court ruled 5-4 that the Second Amendment applies to state and local gun control laws.

• The national unemployment rate dropped from 10 percent at the end of 2009 to 9.7 percent.

• The BP oil spill leaked 5 million gallons of oil into the Gulf of Mexico, making the spill the largest ever.

• A Picasso painting, painted in one day, sold at auction for $106.5 million, a record amount.

• More than two months after they first became trapped, 33 Chilean miners were rescued from a mine a half-mile underground.

cials weren't surprised by the decline, given years of efforts to reduce deer densities in the state.

• DNR Commissioner Mark Holsten announced the agency would begin a third leg of its duck-management strategy: The use of moist-soil units to provide feeding and resting areas for ducks.

• A University of Michigan study linked government incentives for corn-based ethanol to declines in grassland birds in four states of the Prairie Pothole Region, including Minnesota.

JANUARY

• Deer hunters in the state killed fewer than 200,000 deer in 2009. That marked the first time since 1999 that harvest had dropped below the 200,000 threshold. DNR offi-

FEBRUARY

• Harvey Nelson, a 42-year veteran of the U.S. Fish and Wildlife Service, passed away at the age of 85. Nelson held a number of jobs with the Service, and ended his career as head of the North American Waterfowl Management Plan. He remained active in conservation in retirement. "He ranks way up there with people like Art Hawkins, Frank

Harvey Nelson had an amazing retirement, remaining extremely active with the Minnesota Waterfowl Association.

ONTARIO LAKER. Dennis Warner, of Grand Rapids, caught and released this 40-inch, 29-pound, 9-ounce lake trout while fishing Clearwater West Lake near Atikokan, Ontario on Jan. 3. The fish had a 24-inch girth.

Tim Bradach, age 51, of Gilbert, found these two massive bull moose dead and with locked antlers while he was searching for sheds in Lake County.
Photo courtesy of Tim Bradach

Bellrose, and Al Hochbaum – the people who have led us in learning what we know about waterfowl," said Steve Wilds, the retired regional migratory bird chief who worked with Nelson in various capacities over a 40-year period.

MARCH

• A legislative audit found the DNR lacked the resources to manage and maintain the 5.6 million acres of land it owned.

• Troy Alan Reinke, the Cannon Falls man accused of poaching a world-record class 8-point buck, pleaded guilty to one gross misdemeanor and two misdemeanor charges. He was sentenced to a year in jail, fined $583, and ordered to pay $1,500 in restitution.

MAY

• Five members of the Leech Lake and White Earth bands of Chippewa set gill nets along the shores of Lake Bemidji, the latest chapter in treaty disputes between the state and Indian bands. DNR conservation officers seized the nets.

• Turkey hunters killed more than 13,100 birds during the spring season, marking the fourth year in a row of a record spring harvest.

JUNE

• The state and U.S. Steel closed the deal for the state to buy 3,000 acres on the eastern shore of Lake

Manabu Kurita and his 22-pound, 4-ounce largemouth bass caught last summer in Japan's Lake Biwa. The big fish tied the IGFA world record. Photo courtesy of IGFA

Jim Rowe, of Jackson, shot this black coyote while hunting near his home on Jan. 30.

Clint C. Corrow, of Marcell, shot this 10-foot, 6-inch brown bear near Cold Bay, Alaska, on May 19. The skull green-scored 29%₁₆ inches.

WELL DESERVED. Associate Editor Joe Albert won the Minnesota Waterfowl Association's Media Award in 2010.

Vermilion. The land, which cost $18 million, was set to become the state's newest state park.

• The DNR announced deer hunters in the southeastern part of the state would have to abide by restrictions that mandated they not shoot antlered bucks unless they had at least four antler points on one side.

Retired U.S. Army Gen. Norman Schwarzkopf presented Lessard with SCI's state legislator of the year award in 1999.

JULY

• The DNR announced it would hold a season for sandhill cranes in the northwestern part of the state.

AUGUST

• Despite aggressive efforts aimed at preventing the spread of zebra mussels were confirmed in Lake Minnetonka.
• Newcastle disease was blamed for the death of hundreds of double-crested cormorants nesting on Marsh Lake in Big Stone County.

Big buck

Cannon Falls man gets jail time, fines, more for illegally killing record-book 8-pointer.

DEER CLASSIC BUCK. Kenneth Kalien, of Red Wing, shot this 17-point buck on Nov. 7 while hunting on the family farm. The antlers scored 228 net nontypical. The inside spread measured 23% with 30-inch main beams and 13½-inch G2s. See complete Minnesota Deer Classic results on Page 10.   Photo by Eric Meye

John Hoeschen, of Sauk Rapids, shot this unique rooster while hunting near Lake Henry on Nov. 14. The tail feathers were completely white.

SEPTEMBER

• A 7-pound, 4.5-ounce quillback carp-sucker that Tyler Brasel caught on Upper Red Lake be-came the new state record, beating the

BOWFISHING GAR. Tammie Schreiber, of Fergus Falls, arrowed this 47-inch long-nose gar while bowfishing an area lake in June.

Tyler Brasel with his new state record quillback carpsucker.
Photo courtesy of Tyler Brasel

previous record by serveral ounces.

• Construction began at Lake Christina to install a pump to allow the DNR to manipulate the lake's water levels and keep it from careening back and forth between the clear- and turbid-water state.

DECEMBER

• Editor Rob Drieslein announced that after an extensive search, he had found two new colum-nists to write about hunting and fishing issues in the Dakotas. Pat Stockdill of Garrison, N.D., came on board with "North Dakota News and Notes," and John Pollman of Dell Rapids, S.D., began writing the "The South Dakota Report." Long-time "View from the Dakotas" columnist Curt Wells had announced earlier that he had accepted the position of editor of *Bowhunter* magazine.

Columnist Shawn Perich examined the history of woodland caribou in northeastern Minnesota and included an image from the 1980s.

In the early 1980s, a few woodland caribou wandered into extreme north-east Minnesota from Ontario. Bill Peterson, DNR Grand Marais area wildlife manager at the time, snapped these photos.
Images courtesy of Bill Peterson

A large crowd attended a gubernatorial debate that Outdoor News sponsored during Game Fair 2010. The candidates included: (l-r) DFLer Mark Dayton, the Resource Party's Linda Eno, Republican Tom Emmer, and Tom Horner, Independence Party.

2011 — For years, al-Qaeda leader Osama bin Laden had been public enemy No. 1. In May 2011, U.S. troops and CIA personnel raided a Pakistani compound where they found and killed him.

• As part of the unfolding Arab Spring across the Middle East, Egyptian President Hosni Mubarak resigns.

• At least 140 were killed when a tornado struck Joplin, Miss. All told, it was one of the deadliest tornado seasons in the nation's history.

JANUARY

• Tom Landwehr, a 55-year-old with experience that included time at the DNR, Ducks Unlimited, and The Nature Conservancy, was named by Gov. Mark Dayton to lead the DNR as commissioner.

• The DNR announced that a bowhunter hunting near Pine Island in southeastern Minnesota killed a deer that tested positive for chronic wasting disease. While CWD had been found in captive animals in the state, it marked the first time the disease was found in the wild. The discovery set off a massive surveillance effort aimed at reducing the deer population in the area and trying to ascertain the ex-

Over the years, Outdoor News has heard from many readers who have saved every issue of the weekly newspaper.

Steven Kuhl, 68, of Blaine collected and stored every edition of *Outdoor News* going back to its first year of publishing in 1968.

Photos by Rob Drieslein

Ryan and Josie Muirhead, of Roseau, display the massive rack of a bull elk in East Grand Forks. Ryan was hunting deer with a muzzleloader in Kittson County in northern Minnesota on Dec. 12 when he and a couple of buddies came across the bull lying on its back with its antlers mired in the mud after tripping while crossing a fence. Muirhead and seven others freed the elk, but it died two days later. The rack was green-scored at 456½ inches. If the score holds after the mandatory 60-day drying period, it will become the No. 5-ranked elk rack in the world. AP Photo/Grand Forks Herald, Brad Dokken

▶ 2011 Man of the Year: Gary Botzek

tent of the disease on the landscape.

MARCH

• Outdoor News stories documented concerns DNR wildlife managers had about the facility in Pine Island where a captive elk tested positive for CWD in 2009. Their concerns centered around the fact that deer apparently had been able to get inside the fenced facility. The wild deer that tested positive for CWD was killed about three miles from the facility.

• Gov. Mark Dayton and the DNR announced plans to push legislation aimed at slowing the spread of aquatic invasive species in the state. DNR Commissioner Tom Landwehr called aquatic invasives a "silent plague," while Dayton said "the clock is ticking."

DAKOTA TUNDRA SWAN. *Outdoor News* contributing photographer Joshua Baklund, of Hutchinson, shot this tundra swan while hunting in North Dakota on Oct. 29.

APRIL

• The DNR convened a waterfowl focus group, which it planned to use as part of its waterfowl regulation decision-making process.

• Outdoor News printed the first story of an in-depth series about Asian carp. The series included background information about Asian carp, as well as in-state reporting on how the fish had altered the fish community in the Illinois River.

MAY

• DNA testing of a cougar killed on the road near Bemidji in 2009 showed the animal likely had come from North Dakota. DNR officials said the cat was a

Many factors contribute to muskie mortality, including other muskies, as the author discovered last summer on Baby Lake near Longville.

To mark their 30th year of Game Fair, Outdoor News profiled Chuck and Loral I Delaney in the August 12, 2011, edition.

Loral I and Chuck will mark 51 years of marriage in 2011.

Joe's win makes it 10 for Hautman brothers

Joe Hautman

By Tim Spielman
Associate Editor

Washington — An image of a single wood duck by Minnesota artist Joe Hautman won top honors in the 2011 Federal Duck Stamp Art Contest. The image will appear on the 2012-2013 duck stamp.

It was Hautman's fourth

(See **Joe Hautman** Page 29)

Plymouth resident Jim Hautman last weekend won the federal Duck Stamp contest for the fourth time with this wood duck painting. The image will appear on the 2012-13 duck stamp. Image courtesy of USFWS

young male, and it fit the profile of an animal dispersing in an attempt to set up its own territory.

Hunter takes rare piebald deer

In this Nov. 5 cell phone photo, Joshua Winchell, 33, of Oakdale, Minn., poses with a rare piebald, or spotted, deer on public land near Outing on the opening day of the state's deer firearms season. It was only Winchel's second time deer hunting and his first kill.

AP Photo/Joshua Winchell via The St. Paul Pioneer Press, Pat Maranda

OPENING DAY TROUT. Josh Kral, of Rochester, landed this 12-pound, 4-ounce male brown trout on April 16 while fishing the Root River near Lanesboro. He caught the 30.5-inch fish on 4-pound-test line tipped with a small nightcrawler. DNR Fisheries officials in Lanesboro say it's the largest brown trout ever caught in the area by an angler, and it was not a brood stock fish. The state record brown trout, a 16-pound, 12-ouncer, was caught on Lake Superior in St. Louis County. Photo by Lisa Kral

• DNR officials reported little evidence of negative effects on loons as a result of the oil spill in the Gulf of Mexico in 2010.
• The legislative session ended without lawmakers passing the $450 million Legacy bill. Gov. Mark Dayton also vetoed a number of budget bills, as he and

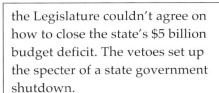

the Legislature couldn't agree on how to close the state's $5 billion budget deficit. The vetoes set up the specter of a state government shutdown.

JULY

• Jeff Foiles, a professional waterfowl-hunting guide and call maker from Illinois, pleaded guilty to two charges related to regularly exceeding bag limits on hunts in which he participated. Foiles was sentenced to 13 months in prison.

• The state government shutdown left state parks closed and many DNR employees out of work, but the state's conservation officers remained on the job. Some people didn't get the message that COs would still be on the job, and one group of 11 was arrested after trying to burglarize Afton State Park.

• Bill Stevens, an "icon" in the firearms industry, passed away at the age of 72. He worked at Federal Ammunition for more than 40 years. His priorities were youth, conservation, and shooting sports.

AUGUST

• Zebra mussel numbers exploded in Lake Mille Lacs. In some spots, mussel density was as high as 3,000 per square foot. The average was 1,000 zebes per square foot.

SEPTEMBER

• Noted Minnesota wildlife artist James Meger passed away at the age of 69. He won a variety of state wildlife art contests and was selected six times as the Print of the Year artist for Pheasants Forever, more than any other artist.

• A wildfire in the Boundary Wa-

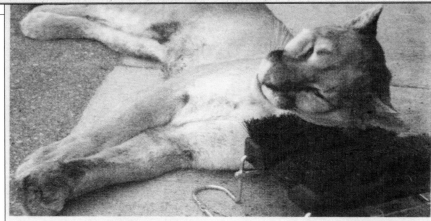

The DNR last week said the cougar killed in southwestern Minnesota last month likely is the first one shot by a citizen in the state's modern history. Photo courtesy of the DNR

ters Canoe Area Wilderness, pushed by high winds, intensified by hot air, and supported by low humidity, grew to more than 60,000 acres, and continued to expand.

NOVEMBER

• Minnesota artist Joe Hautman painted an image of a wood duck that won the federal duck stamp contest. It was his fourth victory in the federal contest, and marked the tenth time one of the three Hautman brothers had won.

DECEMBER

• Susan Thornton, executive director of the Legislative-Citizen Commission on Minnesota Resources, was told by the Legislative Coordinating Commission that she was out of a job. Those responsible – House Speaker Kurt Zellers, R-Maple Grove, and LCC director Greg Hubinger – wouldn't comment. Thornton eventually was reinstated.

Road-killed cougar near Bemidji likely came from North Dakota

By Joe Albert
Associate Editor

Grand Rapids, Minn. — DNA tests of a mountain lion killed by a car near Bemidji in September 2009 show the cat is genetically consistent with animals in North Dakota.

While DNR officials say the test results don't show the path the cougar took to get to the northern part of the state, they do show that North and South Dakota have genetically distinct populations.

The results also don't prove the cat had spent its entire life living in the wild. But all indications are the cat was a wild one, said John Erb, DNR furbearer biologist.

The state recovered this cougar near Bemidji in September 2009, but it took 18 months to get thorough results back from a lab in Missoula, Mont. Photo courtesy Beltrami County Sheriff's Office

2012 — James Holmes killed 12 and wounded 58 people when he opened fire at a movie theater near Denver. Adam Lanza walked into an elementary school in Newtown, Conn., and killed 26 people, including 20 students ages 6 and 7.

• *The world population for the first time topped 7 billion people.*

• *President Obama defeated Republican challenger Mitt Romney.*

• *American swimmer Michael Phelps won his 19th gold medal at the Olympics in London, becoming the winningest Olympian of all time.*

 JANUARY

• The firing of LCCMR director Susan Thornton was "suspended," and Republicans called it a personnel matter and refused to comment further.

• The DNR outlined how it would manage the state's first wolf hunting and trapping season. The agency proposed to give out 6,000 licenses to hunters and trappers, and to allow them to take up to a quota of 400 wolves. The agency wanted the season to run Nov. 24 through Jan. 5, 2013. The Legislature, however, altered the season so there was an early season that coincided with the firearms deer season.

FIRST WOLF HUNT. Garrett Mikrut, of Circle Pines, shot this timber wolf while deer hunting north of Duluth in St. Louis County on Saturday morning. The male animal weighed about 80 pounds.

Remembering

Adolph Raduenz, of Giese, Minn., shot this sow black bear and her three cubs in the late 1940s. Photo courtesy of Doris Hicks

MARCH

• A Bemidji man named Aaron Guthrie caught a 19.54-pound eelpout while fishing Lake of the Woods. The fish beat the old state record, which was 19 pounds, 3 ounces.

• A silver carp caught in a commercial net near Winona, Minn., marked the northernmost find of the jumping variety of Asian carp. "Here they come," said Tim Adams, the commercial fisherman who netted the fish.

APRIL

• Legislative proposals emerged to open the walleye-fishing season a week earlier, given the warm spring. Lawmakers said the early opener would apply only in 2012; the DNR opposed the proposal.

• Don McMillan, president of the Minnesota Outdoor Heritage Alliance and a longtime conservation advocate, died at the age of 74. He was heavily involved in lobbying for conservation at the Legislature, and both the state House and Senate observed moments of silence for McMillan. "Don was a good man and a good leader," said Gary Botzek, executive director of the Minnesota Conservation Federation.

Don McMillan

JUNE

• A captive red deer at a farm in North Oaks in the north metro tested positive for chronic wasting disease. It marked the fifth time the disease had been found in a farmed facility in the state, and the first time a red deer was found to have the disease.

• Ray Ostrom, one of the two men responsible for bringing Rapala to the United States, passed away at the age of

12-year-old Motley lad takes 27-point buck

By Matt Erickson
Brainerd Dispatch

Motley, Minn. — That this year's deer hunt might be the hunt of a lifetime for 12-year-old Dylan Beach-Bittner, of Motley, might be an understatement.

About a half hour after Dylan and his stepdad, Wilbur Verbeck, got into their treestand on Saturday morning, Nov. 3, Dylan noticed a deer walk out of the woods about 100 yards away.

He said he knew it was a big deer while it slowly made its way toward the deer stand. He just didn't know how big.

"I was shaking a little," Dylan said of the moments before he fired his .270-caliber rifle.

At about 50 yards, the deer turned broadside and Dylan fired a round into its front shoulder. The deer dropped immediately, got up a few seconds later, and walked a few feet before finally falling for the last time.

Above, Dylan Beach-Bittner took an incredible buck on Nov. 3 of the 2012 firearms deer season near Sebeka. The largest antlers entered at the 2013 Minnesota Deer Classic, the 27-pointer took first place in the nontypical firearms youth division, scoring 243 net nontypical.

TOP MINNESOTA TOM. Trevor Meister, of Montgomery, shot this 30-pound gobbler while hunting in Le Sueur County on April 28. The bird had an 11-inch beard, 1¼-inch spurs, and was the heaviest recorded in the state by weight. It ranks fifth based on the NWTF's overall measurement formula. See full story, Page 15.

While ice fishing two weeks ago, Lon Peterson and his daughter Chloe pulled these old elk antlers from a lake in the Fergus Falls area of Otter Tail County.
Photo courtesy of Lon Peterson

GIANT COMMON CARP. Justin Mueller, of Watkins, shot this 54-pound carp while bowfishing an area lake on May 12. In comparison, the state record carp by hook and line is 55.5 pounds.

Ostrom (r) is pictured here with Ron Weber in 1975. The two men were responsible for Rapala lures first being available in the United States.

85. Ostrom is a National Fresh Water Fishing Hall of Fame "legendary angler" and a member of the Minnesota Fishing Hall of Fame.

JULY

• The continental breeding waterfowl population jumped to a record high, according to the U.S. Fish and Wildlife Service. The estimate: 48.6 million ducks, which was 7 percent higher than 2011. The counts were the highest since the survey began in 1955.

AUGUST

• A conservation officer in the Ely area killed a collared bear

Daniel Williams, age 12, and his father, Dennis, of Eyota, pose with a rare white gobbler Daniel shot on April 22 in southeast Minnesota. The bird weighed 20 poinds and had a 7-inch beard.

Brad Standke, of Morristown, caught this 18-inch, 3½-pound crappie while fishing a lake near Faribault on May 3.

that entered a property and refused to leave. The bear wasn't one that bear researcher Lynn Rogers had been studying as part of his larger study, but he had a collar on it and had interacted with it. He speculated the bear was raised by humans and released into the wild.

SEPTEMBER

• On the heels of continual declines in the moose population in the northeastern part of the state, the DNR issued 76 licenses – the lowest number ever.

OCTOBER

• "Tackle" Terry Tuma, an Outdoor News employee for more than 25 years and a man who had spent more than 40 years in the fishing industry, was inducted into the 2013 class of the Hayward, Wis.-based National Freshwater Fishing Hall of Fame. In Tuma's biography, the Hall wrote, "While Terry may have decided early on he would focus on the Upper Midwest and southern Canada, today's unlimited range of web-based media and his frequent appearances on national television programs has projected his influence far beyond these boundaries. Tuma has been, and still is, a pioneer in outdoor communications. He has introduced numerous programs to the public that never existed until he brought them to the forefront."

NOVEMBER

• Fall turkey hunters killed a record number of birds – 1,715.

Commercial fishermen (l-r): George Richtman, Tim Adams, and Bob Davis hold three species of Asian carp caught in the same seine haul in Mississippi River Pool 6, near Winona, Minn., in March. From left to right are a grass carp, silver carp, and bighead carp. The silver represents the most upstream occurrence of that species.   *Photo by Nick Schlesser*

Outdoor News Person of the Year: Elizabeth Wilkins

Big burbot looks like probable state record

By Joe Albert
Associate Editor

Bemidji, Minn. — Aaron Guthrie had no idea catching a big fish would be like this.

"It's been kind of a whirlwind the past few days," the 35-year-old Bemidji resident said. "Radio shows, newspaper interviews – it's been a lot of fun. We're pretty proud of our burbot in Bemidji, so it's definitely a good thing."

The "it" he refers to?

(See **Big Burbot** Page 31)

RECORD BURBOT. Aaron Guthrie, of Bemidji, caught this 19.54-pound eelpout at 4:30 a.m. while fishing Lake of the Woods.   *Photo courtesy of Aaron Guthrie*

2013 — *Three women who had been missing for a decade were found alive in a Cleveland home. They'd been held captive since their kidnappings.*

• *Two bombs exploded near the finish line of the Boston Marathon, killing three people and wounding about 264 others. Two Chechen brothers were suspected of the bombing; one died in a shootout, the other was found after an intense manhunt.*

• *A typhoon struck the Philippines in November bringing with it 195-mph winds and a 20-foot storm surge. More than 6,000 people died.*

• *Barack Obama was inaugurated for a second term as U.S. president.*

• *Nelson Mandela, anti-apartheid leader and first black president of South Africa, died at age 95.*

• *American Edward Snowden disclosed U.S. government mass surveillance program operations to news publications and fled the country.*

Trail Crossings

This flying squirrel was captured on trail camera in Kittson County last October by Donald Mathrowetz, of Springfield.

JANUARY

• The Minnesota legislative auditor announced he'd investigate a data privacy breach at the DNR, in which an Enforcement employee – John Hunt – was accused of accessing motor vehicle records of about 5,000 people. Hunt, who had been the division's data practices designee, ultimately was fired from the agency.

FEBRUARY

• The safe harvest level at Lake Mille Lacs dropped from 357,500 pounds in 2012, to 250,000 pounds in 2013. The state's allocation of that was 178,750 pounds.
• Well-known Wisconsin fishing guide Jim Hudson, 34, died when his snowmobile went through the ice on Lake Superior.
• The DNR confirmed zebra mussels were discovered in Lake Winnibigoshish, a popular north-central Minnesota fishing lake.

Jim Sable began the Minnesota Minnesota State High School Clay Target League after realizing and reacting to the average age of members at the Plymouth Gun Club.

Sherwood Schoch holds the Model "T" bow, which came on the market in 1975 and preceded the modern compound bow. Schoch was speaking at an induction ceremony of the Minnesota Archery Hall of Fame, held at the Pope & Young Club headquarters in Chatfield, Minn., on Saturday.

Photo courtesy of Pope & Young Club

MARCH

• The Minnesota State High School Clay Target League continued its rapid growth. In 2013, 3,352 kids participated in the league. Between 2001 and 2008, there were three schools and about 30 students involved.

• State officials announced that anglers at Lake Mille Lacs would have to abide by a two-inch harvest slot limit for walleyes – 18 to 20 inches. They also set the bag limit at two fish.

APRIL

• State, federal and tribal officials announced that Operation Squarehook, a three-year investigation into the illegal netting and selling of tens of thousands of walleyes, resulted in numerous charges. They called the case the largest case of illegal commercialization of fish in Minnesota in two decades.

MAY

• With the fishing opener looming, anglers waited anxiously to see if the ice would be off the lakes in the northern part of the state. Many were resigned to the fact that a cold spring would delay open-water fishing.

JUNE

• Fishing license sales were well off their normal pace, which DNR officials attributed to the colder-than-normal

Jerry Steinhoff, of Jordan, caught and released this 62-inch sturgeon while fishing Lake of the Woods on Dec. 26.

State conservation officers (l-r) Luke Belgard, Jayson Hansen, and Mike Fairbanks with Lake Winnie yellow perch seized from three Wisconsin anglers who had more fish than the legal limit.

DNR Photo

spring. As of June 1, anglers had bought 469,751 licenses, compared to 596,163 at the same time in 2012.

• A 72-year-old McGregor woman was attacked by a black bear near her home in Aitkin County. She received non-life-threatening injuries. The bear, a 190-pound female with three cubs, was shot and killed later that day.

Wisconsin guide remembered for love of family, friends, clients and the outdoors

By Dean Bortz
Wisconsin Outdoor News

Bayfield, Wis. — Lake Superior coldly claimed the life of one of her biggest fans and supporters on Saturday, Jan. 26, when Jimmy Hudson's snowmobile went through the ice on the South Channel.

Hudson, 34, a well-known – and well liked – Bayfield fishing guide succumbed to frigid waters despite determined rescue efforts by fishing partners and La Pointe ice rescue volunteers.

Jim Hudson

One of his fishing partners, John Esposito, of Ashland, saw Hudson go through the ice and quickly put himself in harm's way in an attempt to rescue Hudson. Esposito pulled Hudson to the edge of the broken ice, but the ice broke and he went in himself in trying to pull Hudson to safety.

Esposito, according to a number of sources, was wearing a float suit and was able to get back onto the ice. He pulled

(See **Jim Hudson** Page 6)

JULY

• The DNR pulled the permit of Ely bear researcher Lynn Rogers, and gave him about a month to remove collars from bears he observed in the Ely area. The revocation of the permit marked the latest in a long-running dispute between Rogers and the DNR.

• Jim Klatt, a founder and president of the Minnesota Outdoor Heritage Alliance, and one of the leaders in the passage of the 1998 right to hunt and fish, and the 2008 Legacy Amendment, passed away.

AUGUST

• The state added moose to its list of protected species. Given the species' decline in the state, the addition wasn't much of a surprise. The state had cancelled the fall moose season earlier in the year.

• A wolf bit a teenager camping on the shores of Lake Winnibigoshish. The attack occurred in the early morning hours. The teenager sought medical attention for his minor injuries. A wolf killed in the area was found to be the same one that perpetrated the attack, and officials said jaw abnormalities and other issues the animal had likely played a role.

MILLE LACS PIKE. Aaron Naugle, of Elk River, caught and released this 41-inch northern pike while fishing Lake Mille Lacs on Jan. 13. The fish had a 20-inch girth, and Naugle landed the fish on 4-pound-test line.

Northern Minnesotans charged for illegal fish selling, buying

Biggest Minnesota fish poaching case in decades

By Tim Spielman
Associate Editor

St. Paul — State, federal, and tribal officials announced this week that charges have been or will be filed against nearly 50 individuals in what law enforcement is calling the largest case of illegal commercialization of fish in Minnesota in two decades.

In all, "tens of thousands" of walleyes were netted and sold illegally during the course of a three-year investigation, according to the state DNR. The fish came from such premier lakes as Red,

(See **Charged** Page 12)

834,950 – was the highest in the state since 2003.

• The September 21 duck opener was the earliest in nearly 70 years.

• A hunter shot one of Lynn Roger's research bears near Ely. The 13-year-old bear was named Dot.

OCTOBER

• A shutdown of the federal government led to closures of national parks and refuges, and left some hunters confused about what federal land they could access.

• A Moorhead hunter killed an elk in Kittson County that had a net green score of 391 inches. The animal likely would become a state record.

• Hunters killed 1,856 bears in the state, the lowest total since the late 1980s. State officials had restricted the number of licenses available, and said they wanted a lower kill to help grow the state's bear population.

NOVEMBER

• Long-time DNR Fisheries staffer Don Pereira was named DNR Fisheries Section chief.

• Three years after a wild deer in the southeast tested positive for chronic wasting disease, the DNR still hadn't found another positive animal.

TWO TIMBER WOLVES. Mark LeDoux (l) and Barry Arnold, both of Detroit Lakes, shot these timber wolves within an hour of one another last December while hunting east of Detroit Lakes.

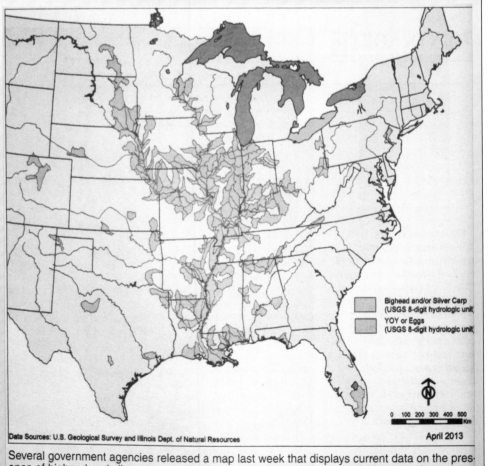

Bighead and/or Silver Carp (USGS 8-digit hydrologic unit)
YOY or Eggs (USGS 8-digit hydrologic unit)

Data Sources: U.S. Geological Survey and Illinois Dept. of Natural Resources

April 2013

Several government agencies released a map last week that displays current data on the presence of bighead and silver carp at all life stages (but not relative densities) across the country.

"*Dedicated to all of the Outdoor News employees who've made the business a success, past and present.*"
— *Glenn A. Meyer, publisher*

ACKNOWLEDGMENTS:

45 Years of Hunting and Fishing History
From the Pages of Minnesota Outdoor News

Many fine people contributed to "45 Years of Hunting and Fishing History From the Pages of Minnesota Outdoor News." Special thanks to Ron Nelson, Joe Albert, Rob Drieslein, Dianne Meyer, Jason Revermann, and Ken and Jan Sinclair.

Special thanks to all employees, past and present, who've contributed to building Outdoor News into a successful business.

— Glenn Meyer

In memory of Jim Peterson

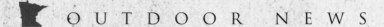

MILESTONES:

IMPORTANT MILESTONES FOR OUTDOOR NEWS SINCE 1967

Outdoor News has been around for more than 45 years and witnessed a lot of Minnesota history in that time. Here are a few significant dates in the history of the business and its content since 1967.

1967 — With an introductory edition, founder Jim Peterson begins publishing Outdoor News.

1968 — First full year of publication, Volume 1.

1972 — Normark began co-sponsoring the Rapala Fish Photo Contest.

1974 — Outdoor News started publishing Actiongraphs offering insight into peak fish and game activity periods. Outdoor News moved from Peterson's home to an office on Winnetka Avenue in New Hope.

1978 — Previously a mostly black-and-white newspaper, Outdoor News published its first four-color photo.

1987 — Lifelong Minnesotan Glenn A. Meyer purchased newspaper from Peterson.

1988 — Staff launched the first-ever annual Best Buck Contest. Weekly full-page Fishing Report begins.

1990 — Glenn Meyer announces Operation Stay In Touch to provide servicemen and women overseas with complementary subscriptions. To spark interest in waterfowling and nest-box building among youth, the publication begins the Wood Duck Challenge. The Minnesota Waterfowl Association co-sponsors the effort.

1993 — Joe Fellegy begins publishing the Mille Lacs Fishing Digest, which Outdoor News acquired in 2000 and continued publishing through 2006.

1994 — Outdoor News launches a newspaper very similar to its Minnesota edition, called Wisconsin Outdoor News.

1996 — The business hops on the Internet with www.outdoornews.com, which went live on July 31, 1996. Outdoor News published its first book, the Northern Ontario Outdoor Guide Book – a list of resort areas north of the Minnesota border.

1998 — Cuffs & Collars, a weekly run-down of reports from state conservation officers appears for the first time.

2000 — Seeing strong success with its Wisconsin title, the publisher announced the launch of Michigan Outdoor News. Editor Rob Drieslein began regular hosting duties on KFAN Radio's Saturday Morning FAN Outdoors program.

2002 — Popular contributor Gary Clancy published a collection of his past columns with Outdoor News entitled, "Strictly Whitetails – Tips, tales and techniques from a white-tailed deer hunting expert." Readers saw the first version of the Backyard and Beyond, or so-called "nature page," which has featured nongame and birding news and information ever since. Ron Nelson painted the first Outdoor News "Print of the Year." Entitled "Bite of the Century," it featured a large walleye and launch boat to commemorate the incredible bite on Mille Lacs that spring. Staff unveiled winners of the first-ever Outdoor News Youth Writing Contest. Many winners over the years have gone on to place or outright win a national youth writing contest sponsored by the Montana-based Outdoor Writers Association of America.

2004 — Business launches its exclusive Outdoor News calendar. Outgrowing its long-time rental space on Winnetka Avenue in New Hope, the Outdoor News staff moves to a new location in Plymouth near Highway 169. Glenn Meyer announces the inaugural issue of Pennsylvania Outdoor News.

2005 — Expanding further east, Outdoor News launches New York Outdoor News.

2006 — Ohio Outdoor News begins.

2008 — Illinois Outdoor News begins.

2010 — Staff began producing Outdoor News Radio, a one-hour radio program, plus five daily three-minute shorts, available around the state via the Minnesota News Network.

2011 — Editors add a revamped half-page recipe feature called Taste of the Wild that appears 26 times per year.

2012 — A compilation book, the Best of Minnesota Cuffs & Collars finds a receptive audience.

2013 — Outdoor News adds 2,000 square feet to its office space in Plymouth.

And Outdoor News continues to grow: Recently the staff doubled the size of the popular Fishing and Hunting Report section with new elements such as pro tips, bait shop and café profiles, and rut reports. The business's new book, "45 Years of Hunting and Fishing History from the Pages of Minnesota Outdoor News," celebrates four-and-a-half decades of Minnesota sporting history.